HILDA HOLLINGSWORTH was born in Portsmouth in 1929. She left school at fourteen to work as a junior clerk. She married at eighteen and had a son and two daughters. Now retired from her job as a telephonist supervisor at a large Midlands hospital, she lives in Redditch, Worcester. She and Winnie are still friends.

D1517970

They Tied a Label on My Coat

HILDA HOLLINGSWORTH

Published by VIRAGO PRESS Limited 1992
20–23 Mandela Street, Camden Town, London NW1 0HQ

First published by Virago Press in hardback, 1991

Copyright © Hilda Hollingsworth 1991

The right of Hilda Hollingsworth to be identified
as the author of this work has been asserted by her
in accordance with the Copyright, Designs
and Patents Act 1988.

All rights reserved

*A CIP catalogue record for this book is available
from the British Library*

Printed in Great Britain by
Cox & Wyman Ltd, Reading, Berkshire

FOR MY CHILDREN
VAL, GLENN, REVIS

and to the memory of
Ivy Callaway Hollingsworth

Thanks to –

My husband John for whom this book was written

Elizabeth Hubbard for her certainty that it would be published

Her mother Val Hubbard who persuaded me to approach Virago Press

Heartfelt thanks to Ruth and Gillian at Virago Press for lots of hard work and excellent guidance, I'd have been lost without them

Lola and Robin Vane for always being there

And to Dr Wychrij, Dr Franklin, Kevin Parsonage, Paul Holder and the choir, Alice Walker, Pat Harland, Joy Simmonds, Dave Hollingsworth, Ann Gee

And last but not least, thanks to Winnie Battlemaid Chitticks for being my friend

Chapter 1 ~~~

We'd marched in our careful twos across the grey gravelly playground. Our headmistress stood beside the open gate; she was smiling to us. *Her* girls, she'd called us, girls who would set a good example.

I gave myself a quick mental check. Gas mask, carrier bag, sandwiches . . . oh, and of course the all-important label that we mustn't touch and that didn't tell me anything at all.

A sudden surge of mothers as we stepped on to the pavement. Some children were crying, hugging at their mothers. A few were smiling just like Roberta, my elder sister, who was nearly twelve. A few minutes ago Mum had told her, as usual, to 'Look after Hilda'. Mum didn't know Roberta felt that a girl of ten was quite old enough to look after herself, sister or not.

The ladies in green appeared quite suddenly and one grasped me firmly by the shoulder just as I caught a glimpse of Mum, who was shouting something and pointing; I couldn't hear the words nor see what was being pointed at.

''Ild! 'Ild!' My little sister Pat, seven years old, seized my coat sleeve. ''Bert's gone! She's gone!'

The lady guided us firmly to the steps of the waiting bus. 'Three to a seat, children, three to a seat.'

We climbed reluctantly. A glance over my shoulder: 'Mum!' – the shout was out before I realised.

She heard, and now I could hear her: '*Look after Pat!*'

Roberta was waving from the open window of a bus in front.

The chattering inside our bus ceased abruptly as the engine shuddered: the few children who'd been standing in the gangway hastily moved to their seats. The clap of grown-up hands demanded – and got – our instant attention.

'*Now*, girls and boys. It is our duty to be Cheerful' (the backs of the seats were so high that we couldn't actually see anybody). We *did* wave, but it was to a blank space: the group of mums had already slid away from our patch of window. And after a bit the patch got filled with other things. Not the country yet, but we half-heartedly joined in the singing that was just starting:

'*One* man went to mow . . .'

*

1

'*Ten* green bottles . . .' We were going down a steep hill into what must be the High Street of this town. We slowed into a long line of traffic and saw people hurrying about; like us, they were all carrying gas masks. Some of them waved and smiled at us. The bus moved forward past the sandbags heaped outside an ARP post. I felt sad: the war was coming here too, then, it was just like home really. I looked up at the sky. Yes, there they were: big silvery cushiony balloons. Now we were on a bridge. And on its river were boats and barges and, to my surprise, aeroplanes!

'Cor! Lookit them seaplanes! Cor!'

'Flyin' boats!' yelled another boy – *all* the boys were jostling . . .

'Boys! Boys!' – the ladies were moving from their opposite ends of the bus. 'Now boys, do be quiet. That's Rochester Castle . . .' The bus lurched forward, her words floating past me, something about the Cathedral and a Norman castle right beside the river, and famous people: a King Charles – I forget which one – and Charles Dickens, who wrote books.

Our dad used to catch his ship on this river. But it was no use looking amongst all the other sailors to catch a glimpse of him, he was busy being a Chief Stoker Petty Officer on a big ship out in the oceans somewhere, no one knew where. I felt the tears overflow and did my best to stop them; it was Dad who'd wanted us safe.

I thought carefully. I'd heard Mum say something to the lady next door about it. Us girls and his pigeons, we had to be saved. Mum had sounded all proud about it, and then yesterday . . .

I felt my lip tremble, I didn't want to think about yesterday. But a picture of the pigeon loft swam before my eyes. The door hanging open, Mum and her friend shooing at the pigeons. They'd circled around and tried to get back inside, but the door was closed and at bedtime Pat and I nearly cried to see them huddled up on top of their home looking all sad and somehow helpless.

I suppose it was then that we knew it had happened. The war, I mean. First the pigeons and now us. I couldn't help crying a bit – they hadn't got a home any more because it was going to be pulled down today.

Today. The word sounded bleak and dreary. I had an awful feeling that we were having *our* turn, and that remembering the way home was one thing, but, I thought glumly, suppose we got there, would it be like that for us? No way in, 'cause we had to be safe.

★

2

''Ere, look – it's 'ops – it's the 'op fields . . .' Several girls seemed to be shouting at the same time.

Hops? They hadn't looked very interesting and I'd heard that anyone who came to pick them had to live in sheds.

Now we were slowing down outside a tiny little grey stone school; there was a house attached to it and a girl was swinging happily as high as the tiny bedroom window.

We stopped. The ladies were being jolly. It was time to get off.

The classroom we were taken to – well, it was two classrooms really – there was a sort of folding partition and they'd folded it back. It was sort of creepy in a way, as though we were in two rooms. And there was something different about the way the people stood waiting. You couldn't say they weren't together, but somehow you knew you were expected to look at each one separately. They reminded me of the Royal Family Coronation picture that Mum had cut out of a newspaper. Up at the front somewhere a man's voice sounded faintly; we didn't really hear what he said, though, till he started calling out our names:

'Sybil Adams, Cherrydene; Julia Andrews, The Gables; Peter and Frederick Chambers, Tyler's Croft . . .' I stood on tiptoe to see what was happening.

''Ere, you ain't leavin' me!' Pat dragged at my arm. 'You ain't . . .'

'Shush, 'course I'm not. I've got to find out what we have to do!'

Pat's voice sank to a whisper. 'I don't like it 'ere. Take me 'ome.' She was scrabbling for her carrier bag.

The man called, 'Roberta, Hilda and Patricia . . .'

''S us!' Pat was clawing at my arms again.

'Only two of you?' He looked kind but brisk.

I was about to stammer that we'd lost Roberta. One of the ladies said, 'Press on, Mr Stace, we've got the other one already' and beckoned us towards the doorway.

'You three are for Mayfield. Miss Armstrong isn't ready for you just yet, so sit quietly in this room till she comes.' She opened the door and there, sitting at a desk, was Roberta. As soon as the lady had gone she jumped up.

'Where've *you* been? Cor, it's not fair, me always having to go everywhere with you two. I could've got a place with me *friend*.'

We went across to the windows to watch the grown-ups coming up to the school. 'Ooh, jus' look at her.' Roberta sounded awed.

3

'*Her*' was striding across the playground. At first glance she looked like a well-stuffed, very neat rag doll. My next feeling was that she was knitted. Her stockings, jumper and skirt fitted snugly on her round arms and legs. She was wearing a battered-looking hat – all brown like the rest of her – and she carried a walking-stick.

'Coo, I bet she ain't half bossy,' declared Roberta as the knitted lady disappeared through the entrance.

'Hope she's not ours,' I murmured, feeling a bit uneasy. I stared out beyond the playground. Nothing but fields and trees. Not a sound. 'Here, listen!' I said. 'Must be something wrong. Nowhere's this quiet!'

'Is it Sunday?' asked Pat in a whisper.

'That was yesterday, you 'nana!' Roberta told her scornfully.

'Only where we comes from.' Pat sounded fearful. 'P'raps it's a diff'rent day 'ere.'

'It's the *country*. I expect it's always been like it,' I offered, still feeling a bit afraid of the absence of traffic noise, or any noise come to that. It was as if the place wanted to send everyone to sleep.

The door crashed open. Well, it didn't really, but the catch-thing being jerked open seemed to shriek into the soft downy silence. I turned, and there stood the rag-doll lady.

'Ha! – Three of you – all gels – must be our lot – this yer trappings?' She bore down on the carrier bags grouped around Roberta. She seemed to speak only in a shout.

'I'm Miss Armstrong,' she announced, looking at each one of us in turn. We said nothing. She tapped the stick on the floor. 'Nothin' to say for yerselves? Well, we'll be orf then.' She scooped up the bags and strode out.

Roberta stared with astonishment: 'Talks like a bloke.' We gathered up our remaining bits and followed the ringing footsteps.

'We ain't gonna have her for a muvver?' Pat's lip was quivering: I could see it.

The knitted lady was waiting beside a little black motorcar, holding the door open.

We hesitated. A motor: a real motorcar, surely she didn't expect *us* to ride in it?

'Stow yerselves away, gels.'

Roberta crept forward.

4

'Not on the fender, dash it, don't plant yer feet on the fender, blasted thing'll fall orf!' She was holding the front seat forward.

Pat went next and I squeezed in beside them. The seat dropped against my knees and we all shook with the motorcar as the door slammed.

'Wot's she doing?' Roberta was stretching herself as much as possible. Miss Armstrong was doing something at the front.

''S'orlright, she's winding it up,' explained Pat, having darted up and down again as quick as lightning.

The motor shook and coughed.

'Shush – 'ere she comes . . .' Roberta composed herself carefully into her elder-sister look.

The *brm brm brm* set the little motorcar rocking, and there was a very definite plunge on Roberta's side as the knitted lady heaved herself behind the steering wheel. 'All secure in the back? Right-oh, then . . .' She did something and the trembling grew more violent. Suddenly we shot backwards as the motor jerked forward; the carrier bags that had been stacked on the front seat flopped. 'I *say*. Steady on, old thing.' Miss Armstrong seemed to be enjoying herself.

'*Pardon?*' whispered Roberta.

'Eh? What, gel? Can't talk now.' She broke off as the motor swerved and leapt dangerously close to a hedge. 'Temp'rament of a mule!' The rest of the ride was something like a merry-go-round which had come loose somehow . . . sudden jerks and bursts of speed; the final halt pitched us forward like three dolls and Pat's head banged loudly against the back of the front seat. 'Ow!' – she started to wail; a look from Roberta silenced her.

'Well, that's that!' There was pride in Miss Armstrong's voice. She patted the steering wheel. 'Out we jump. Mind the fender, gels, mind the fender.' Miss Armstrong jerked open the door on Roberta's side. We scrambled on to the pavement.

The house was very large. 'This way, gels.' Miss Armstrong led us through a big shining front gate, across red polished tiles, up three pure white steps. And there we stood in the wide porch at the front door with its stained glass and satiny shine.

I swallowed hard. This must be the wrong place.

But our knitted lady was tugging at a shiny brass bell-pull.

★

5

'Oh, Margaret,' said Miss Armstrong. The door had opened ever so quietly and 'Margaret' stood there: black dress with a lace collar and cuffs and thin muslin apron and frilly matching cap. A maid. A real live maid. Roberta gulped aloud and Pat shrank back to hide behind me. I didn't know for the moment what scared us most, Miss Armstrong or the maid.

'*In*side. Wipe yer feet. Take these, gel.' The carrier bags crumpled against Margaret. We stepped carefully on to the polished woodblock floor.

'Yes, Miss Armstrong.' The maid had stepped aside with her burden.

'Go with Margaret, gels.' Miss Armstrong was already on her way back to the motor. From this distance it looked like a matchbox with buttons.

'This way,' said Margaret. 'Mind you keep quiet, too, or She'll hear you, and She's *restin*'.' Somehow this sounded more alarming than anything. We followed meekly.

'Open the door for me.' Her eyes rested on me because I was nearest. 'This is the kitchen. Are your slippers in those bags?' She dumped them on the floor.

'Slippers?' Roberta's whisper was for all of us.

'*Slippers*,' said Margaret, looking surprised.

'We ain't got none of them.' Roberta spoke as if she was in church.

'We've got plimsolls,' I managed to say through a thickness in my throat.

Margaret tutted and rummaged in the bags. 'And cut those silly labels off,' she said, handing Roberta some scissors. 'You look like walking parcels.'

The door swung open behind us, and there was Miss Armstrong again. 'Give 'em some tea, Margaret, and . . . oh . . . get them washed an' brushed up a bit.' A brisk friendly nod. 'Cheer *up*, gels.' The door closed.

Margaret put the plimsolls on to the tiled floor. 'Change into those, though what Madam will say . . .'

There was a sharp tinkle above our heads – the maid glanced upwards. 'It's Madam. Now, you lot, just behave yourselves or else.' She smoothed her apron and went away, leaving us to stare in wonder at the huge kitchen.

When Margaret returned she came towards us in a friendly way and told us to follow her. Taking Pat's hand in hers, she led us into *a glass room*. Well, it was nearly all glass. We'd never seen anything like it. 'This is the Conservatory.' She hung the coats. 'Madam says you'll be able to use it as a playroom when the weather changes.' We looked around. It felt a bit like a fish tank. 'You'd better get washed now. You'll find the bathroom with the door open, upstairs.' Roberta disappeared quickly upstairs. I came more slowly with Pat.

The hall was silent except for the ticking of a tall clock. The sun shone through the stained-glass panels at either side of the door, throwing pink and green patches of light on the pale walls. There were some nice little carpets on the floor, green-and-fawn flowery ones, and we carefully avoided treading on them. Mum had a little carpet in front of the fireplace in the parlour, so we knew what not to do. When I saw the staircase, though, my eyes nearly popped out of my head. Now what? A carpet stretched all the way up to the top! Pat backed away; her voice came out in a squeak. 'What we goin' to do *now*, 'Ild?' I tried to think. Somehow my thoughts kept getting lost in the beautiful soft bright green and orange leaves weaving their way right up to the very top.

I made my decision. 'Take our plimsolls off and walk on the sides! See, it's just wide enough.' I demonstrated with my stockinged foot on the white-painted tread nearest the banister.

Uneasily, we started our crabwise climb.

The bathroom was easily found. The door stood wide open, showing the huge white bath crouching on awful brown curly feet. As soon as we'd washed, Margaret called us to a bedroom. She and Roberta were sorting our clothes out on to the white counterpanes that covered the three black iron bedsteads. Each bed had a chair beside it, white with a cane seat, and there was a chest of drawers. A carpet lay rolled up under the window, from which hung dark-red velvet curtains.

'The youngest one in the corner bed, and Roberta has chosen this one.' Margaret was speaking from the far corner.

I stood by the bed nearest the door. A lonely feeling came and went rapidly away as a tall, elderly lady came into the room.

'Excuse me, Madam, these are the children. Sisters, Ma'am.' Margaret seemed a bit scared. 'They arrived late – er, later than . . .'

Madam held up her hand. 'Very well, that will do.' Margaret hung her head and put her hands behind her back.

'Your names, please?'

After we'd stammered out our full names we fell silent whilst Madam examined, without touching, the clothes that Margaret had taken from our bags and put on the beds. Madam then stood in the middle of the room and addressed herself to the three of us: 'I am Miss Peveril; you are guests in my house. I expect obedience, neatness and clean habits.' She paused. 'You will say Grace at meal times and prayers at night. You *do* attend church regularly?'

We nodded, and remembered our mum warning us about manners. I said, 'Yes, Madam.'

She smiled. 'You have the beginnings of good manners. But remember that I am Madam to Margaret, who is my maidservant. To you I am Miss Peveril. Now, Margaret' – she turned; the maidservant bobbed her head.

'Yes, Madam?'

'Make a list. These flimsy silk pyjamas will not do; most unseemly for little girls.'

'Yes, Madam.'

Miss Peveril walked towards the door. 'Bring me the list at tea time. Good afternoon, children' – as Margaret darted forward to open the door that was already open.

'Good afternoon, Miss Peveril,' we chanted, and she was gone.

'Whew – didn't expect her to come in 'ere yet: used to be 'er room.' Margaret stroked the red-and-gold-striped wallpaper and looked towards the roll of carpet. 'Lawks, I haven't even put the mats down; still, she would have said if she was annoyed, she's not bad – real gentry if you ask me, though that Miss Armstrong is said to be better born.'

Roberta giggled. 'What, 'er that talks like a bloke?'

Margaret tut-tutted. 'You mustn't say things like that. She's what's called eccentric; that's what they says in the village anyways.'

'What's that mean?' Roberta asked.

'The way she is, I expect, can't say I really know though. But come on, we've wasted enough time and I'm off at six. One of you could put these things away.' She indicated the drawers and went back down to the kitchen, taking Roberta with her.

'Yer won't leave me, will yer, 'Ild?' whispered Pat when we had finished. 'I mean, Bert's s'posed to look after us but she forgets, don't she?' We went towards the door.

'Only sometimes,' I said, more to cheer her up than anything else.

It wasn't till we got to the top of the stairs that I remembered about the stair carpet. Going down seemed somehow worse than coming up had been. Pat had begged to go first, and we'd managed only three stairs when she started to slip and slide a bit. I grabbed hold of the back of her frock and clung to the banister with my left hand.

'Orf! Orf! Get yer hulkin' great feet orf of that blasted paint!'

There was no mistaking the voice: we stood stock-still. We didn't need to look, there was only one voice like that. And now it seemed not only that you couldn't walk on the carpet, but the paint was just as valuable.

'Orf, I say!' The knitted lady glared up at us from the hall. '. . . the Devil d'yer think yer doin', gel – tryin' to break your blasted necks?' She was moving towards the stairs.

Pat started to cry. 'We ain't gotta jump right down there . . .?'

'What? What's that, gel? Jump?' The heavy feet pounded towards us; I watched with awe as they mashed down into the precious posh carpet.

Miss Armstrong had no doubt at all that our mum's little carpet was most expensive. 'And that', she supposed, 'was why it was put in a room no one ever heard of – er, used.'

'Fancy that, you not knowing and all . . .' smiled Margaret when Miss Armstrong had gone. She spread more gooseberry jam on her bread and passed the fruit cake.

Margaret washed Pat and me at bedtime. She heard our prayers, Pat's and mine. Roberta was last to wash because she was the eldest and didn't come to bed till seven o'clock.

When we were at last alone with the curtains tightly shut, I felt the coldness of the sheets all over me and longed for our big brass bedstead which the three of us shared at home. I moved my thoughts back to now and here, and felt the tears spilling. It was lonely and quiet, clean and silent. And in that moment I felt glad that we'd not been a part of this all our lives. It was, I thought, miserable and lonely to be posh.

''Ild! I'm frightened.' Pat's wavering whisper drifted over me:

the words held all the sadness, the most I'd ever felt. I lay there and cried, knowing that Pat was crying too. We didn't speak; there was no need. Words couldn't say what we were feeling, and to me it felt like the end of the world.

'Gas drill!' announced Miss Armstrong. 'Come along, gels, let's get this over with.' With shaking hands I took my gas mask out of its box, wondering if she was going to use real gas. The 'Gas Room', as Miss Armstrong called it, was at the back of the hall. Inside was a largish tin bath with a pile of blankets beside it, and there were several folded camp beds and folding chairs as well, and also a lot of tinned food on high shelves. There was also a covered bucket. Thick strips of brown tape criss-crossed the windows. Suddenly a terrible racket made us all jump: it was a wooden rattle. 'Gas masks on!' yelled Miss Armstrong as she lifted her own mask into position. We fumbled clumsily because of the scare until at last we all stood masked. 'Right! Orf they come!' said Miss Armstrong. 'Gels, that just wasn't good enough, we just have to do it again.' She handled the strange-looking rattle. 'Leave the masks alone for now, just get used to this sound' – she swung the noisy thing again with all her strength; the temptation to cover my ears was almost irresistible. The noise stopped. Miss Armstrong explained that this was the sound we'd hear if there was gas about, and that we must at once put on our gas masks in order to survive. 'Right-oh!' she said, turning to Margaret. 'This, gels, is what happens next.' Margaret put on her gas mask and lifted a blanket, unfolded it and dipped it down into the empty bath; she then hung it on several cup-hooks over the largest window, called a French window. She then repeated this with all the other blankets until the whole room was lined with them. 'Any questions?' Miss Armstrong seemed to expect at least one. I looked at Roberta and then at Margaret, who was taking off her gas mask. Nothing. Not a word. But Miss Armstrong was still waiting for a question.

I swallowed hard, remembering what the air raid warden had told us when we were getting Anderson shelters delivered. Suddenly I could ask a question: 'Shouldn't the blankets be wet, Miss?'

She was so pleased she positively beamed. 'Quite right, gel, quite right. The wet blankets will protect your bodies and the mask will keep the gas from being breathed in.' Then, to Roberta: 'It will be your job to help Margaret and myself with the wetting of the blankets. You little ones will be over there out of the way' – she indicated the bunks. 'Right, gels, let's go outside and start all over again; don't forget the sound and what it means.' We left the room and went back to the kitchen. Suddenly the rattle could be heard in the hall – and everywhere else, I supposed. Into our gas masks as quick as anything we went, then quickly hurried to the Gas Room. I hoped – oh, how I hoped that this practice would be all I'd ever have to do with gas. I didn't want to know what happened to people whose gas masks didn't fit.

Chapter 2 ~~~

The days at Miss Peveril's seemed ever so long, and the quiet seemed to become very much a part of us. We crept around our bit of the house and even whispered in the garden. We hadn't brought anything to play with, so Margaret handed out a slate each and Miss Armstrong gave us some chalk. She also gave us a ball, but we weren't allowed to have it in the garden, only on the village green where Margaret took us for an hour before dinner each day. She had to go there to see when a notice would be put up saying when and where we were to go to school.

Miss Peveril (I'd found out) was a 'Principal' and the brass notice on the front gate said that Mayfield was a private day school for young ladies. Roberta began talking posh when I told her about it, and one day she even pretended to another girl that she really lived in the big house. Pat and I were dismissed as billeted kids.

Miss Armstrong would pop in and out, and you noticed both times. Sometimes she'd give her brisk, friendly nod and scatter toffees on the kitchen table like birdseed. I never did find out what she had to do with anything.

When Roberta was asleep, Pat would creep her whisper over the dim space between our beds. ''Ild . . .?'

'What?'

'You keeps on goin' ter sleep quicker'n me an' you *promised*.'

'Shush!' I could see she was leaning over towards me. 'I can't help it' – trying not to feel rotten about all the times I had promised, like she said.

11

'Why d'yer go to sleep so *early*, eh?' She was creeping out of bed. I sat up.

'I 'ave ter stay awake 'cause you likes everythink better'n me,' she went on. She was fumbling under her pillow.

'Ooh, I don't! And if you say that again, I – well, I *will*, so there!' I whispered hoarsely.

She crept back towards me. 'Will yer stay awake wiv me?' she coaxed.

I nodded. 'All right. I promise. Now get back in bed. Bert'll be awake soon, and you know she'll tell on us.' But Pat was pulling back the bedclothes.

'What d'ye think you're doing?' I tried to drag them back.

'*This* – see – gonna tie it ter *mine* – see – an' if you don't answer me I can pull it an' wake you *up*.' She was busy with a reel of cotton; it tickled like anything where she'd been tying it round my toe!

I grinned at her in the twilight. 'Dopey thing! 'Night!' We settled back into our beds.

We weren't used to this big-house-and-maid life. Our mum didn't have a mulberry tree, nor an apple store where rows of apples and pears lay in wooden trays, each wrapped separate in its own wax paper.

Mum. Mum and the smell of carbolic soap. Corned beef and mash. Michaelmas daisies. And the pigeons. The tears were soft and quiet like the gentle country rain outside.

The sudden pain darted from the tip of my toe up to the top of my head. I smothered a yelp as it began again.

'Yer *asleep*, ain't yer?' Pat sounded as if she was talking from a very long way off.

'Ooh! Stoppit! Stoppit! I'm not . . . I'm not . . .'

The pain stopped. 'Talk to me. I kept yer *awake*, see . . .?' – giving another tug. The pain was unbearable – I'd have to stay awake, if only to stop her from tugging that cotton again.

It was worse than that, too, because she had the other end tied to *her* toe, and she wouldn't take it off. Every time one of us turned over in her sleep it woke both of us, and it hurt. One 'Ouch!' would follow the other, but still she wouldn't give up the idea. So that's how we slept – when we slept – all night, every night.

★

12

At first one of the grown-ups took us to church, but after a few weeks we were allowed to go alone. It was lovely to walk in the quiet lanes and hear the birds chirping in the hedges. Sometimes we even saw rabbits, and once they'd played around the bank so long that we'd been late for the service and all the brown knitted heads of the Brownies had turned to look at us.

Going home was best, though. The leaves were falling from the trees and they spread all over the place like a real carpet. It was a lovely carpet, too – red and gold, yellow and brown, just lying there in beautiful changing patterns. But the most delicious feeling of all was the crisp rustle as our shoes ruffled gently this way and that. Even in the rain, when the colours glowed and the raindrops sparkled, to me there was nothing more beautiful than the carpet of leaves; no wonder all these rich people had tried to copy it. But they'd forgotten the most important parts: the sounds and the smell.

School for us evacuees began in October when we attended the Church Hall three afternoons a week; we also got two mornings at the village school. It felt a bit strange to be taken and fetched by Margaret, but we soon got used to it, especially as the evenings grew darker. The blackness of the countryside, with its rustlings and strange animal sounds, could be very frightening.

At the Hall we sat around in little groups and the teachers gave us spelling bees, mental arithmetic and poetry. We also wrote letters home to our mothers, carefully copying what Teacher had written on the blackboard. But if you didn't have a mother – and some didn't – one of the teachers would spend a whole afternoon just helping you to write to whoever you had come from.

Our letters were easy enough:

Dear Mum (and Dad),
    Thank you for your lovely letter (and pocket money) which (I) (we) (was) (were) very pleased to receive. It is very nice living here in the countryside. (Miss) (Mrs) —— is a very kind lady and (I am) (we are) very happy with her. (I) (We) hope that you are all well and happy too. On Saturday ——

– here Teacher expected us to write about whatever we'd done last Saturday, and when we'd finished we had to go back and copy the end of the letter off the blackboard:

> With lots of love from your (daughter) (son)
> (Ann Best) (John Brown)

– at this point we had to write our own name – not like the girl near me, whose mother wrote and asked Teacher who Ann Best was.

Our mother received three almost identical letters every week, and although she didn't have time to write to us every week, when we did get a letter I knew that there would be one-and-sixpence in postal orders, and I knew too just what she'd say:

> My dear daughters,
>   Thank you for your lovely letters. Be good girls and here is sixpence each. I will be coming to see you soon. My respects to the lady.
>   I remain your everloving
>   Mother

She'd always finish it with a row of kisses, and although it was lovely to receive and to share, after a while I began to think that all mothers were being collected up on certain days to go somewhere and copy their letters off somebody's blackboard.

'*Nuts*, gels – *nuts*. Hedges are full of 'em.' Miss Armstrong's yell filled the little motorcar as we jerked, bumped and swerved round the twisty lanes. It was hot, and we were packed close together in the back seat. Miss Armstrong's large overflowing basket always stayed next to her, indoors or out, and that little front seat seemed to be its real home. Several different partly knitted garments nestled inside it among the pieces of coloured felt, embroidery silks, slippers and odd balls of tangled wool.

It was quite a surprising basket, really. Apples, sweets, sticking-plaster, bandages, iodine, Vaseline, scissors, ribbons and even dried-up strands of old-man's-beard and pine cones: I used to think that Miss Armstrong could have produced anything from that basket.

At first we'd been unable to see the hazelnuts: they were so pale in their green bell-like cups that it was hard to notice them among the leaves. But Miss Armstrong soon had us busy. 'Don't jest *look*, gel: *see*!' – pointing and tugging at the hedges with her stick. We obeyed instantly and suddenly the nuts were there in plain sight.

It didn't take long to fill the little sack, and we were all disappointed when she told us to stop. 'But there's plenty still left!' protested Roberta.

Miss Armstrong snorted. 'Hear this, gel. Never take more than you need. Leave some for others to enjoy, and never forget the creatures whose lives depend on 'em in winter.'

We followed her back to the motor and watched the sack being settled on the basket. 'See that oak tree?' She plodded towards it, chatting. 'They say King Charles hid in it. Wonder of it is that anyone ever saw the man. Must have spent all his time up a tree. Eh, what's that? Oh, acorns. No, don't take them, squirrels'd starve.'

She took us to a clump of trees in the far corner. 'Shy of humans, mind. But cheeky too if yer watch 'em long enough.' She stood still quite suddenly and motioned for us to be quiet. Our eyes followed the pointing walking-stick up to a sweep of dark branches, where to our delight sat a bushy-tailed squirrel holding a nut ever so neatly and delicately between his paws and staring down at us, cocking his head first this way, then that. A flash of rusty-red moving on the grass showed us yet another, by now peeping at us from behind a tree trunk. We smiled politely, hoping he'd come out. But the game of peek-a-boo went on.

'Shush! Jest *watch*!' He must have heard Miss Armstrong's whisper: his little pointed ears twitched and he flashed quick as lightning up the side of a tree trunk.

There were other nuts. A rough green case with big fat green spikes. And inside a rich brown conker! A different kind of prickly case: green, turning pinky-brown, with hundreds of thin spikes covering it, and inside something to roast and eat with salt.

It was time to go. I looked back at the clump of trees, their shapes almost black against the evening sky. I'd looked at trees before, of course, but this time it was different, I was really seeing. Leaves, fruit, colour, bark, they didn't matter, not the parts didn't. I just loved the whole tree – all the trees – for just being.

*

The young ladies, when they arrived at Mayfield, weren't exactly young ladies at all. They were, I saw, mostly girls of about the same ages as us. But there was a difference: they all looked out from under black felt hats with silver and orange bands, brown leather satchels hung from their backs and there were no wrinkles or holes in their neat black stockings.

'Oh, Nanny, Nanny, my hair ribbon!' A plait waved about with a loose bow, drooping, half untied. Nanny, wearing a grey Burberry and matching hat, tied the bow and departed, carrying the black coat and hat.

'Mummy and Daddy have landed at Dover, and Nanny says I'm to have dinner with them tonight.' Interrupted by someone else: 'Oh Clare – you don't mean . . . well . . . you can't still be having tea in the nursery. I've been joining Mummy at dinner for simply ages now.'

Another voice, exclaiming: 'Ooh, stocking-tops! Nanny! Nanny, it's happened again and just look at the mess, ink everywhere' – the fountain pen passed from ink-stained hands to the cleanest, shiniest hands I'd ever seen.

'Golly! I say, look!' A finger pointed itself up the staircase to Pat and me. 'Are they really motherless?' The voice had dropped.

'Stuff and nonsense, Miss Barbara, evacuees do have mothers.' The stern voice belonged to a brown Burberry and a glimpse of stiff white cuffs.

A bell rang softly from inside a room at the front. The young ladies showed themselves to be just that as they ceased to chatter and filed quietly through the doorway, neat and sure in their blouses and knife-edged pleats. Not one of them had had a hem let down either.

Pat screwed up her nose. ''Ere – big girls like that talkin' about Mummy and Daddy. Coo, it's like babies, innit.'

I agreed. 'Sounds daft somehow. And why couldn't that one tie up her own plait?'

'Yeah, an' fancy not eating wiv yer mum. What's *she* done?'

We crept down the stairs and let ourselves into the comfortably familiar kitchen. Roberta looked fed up. 'Margaret's joining the ATS.'

I stared at Roberta's unusually sad face. 'What? Leaving? Margaret?' I stammered, unable to believe it.

''S what I said – an' us an' all, see!'

★

16

On our last day, everything had been as usual. But at bedtime I saw that the chest of drawers was empty and there in the corner of the room stood three little cases. Not ours, of course; we'd come with carrier bags. But those cases were for someone. I tried to piece it all together. I lay awake a long time wondering who would be here instead of us, wondering too if Miss Peveril would allow us to keep the toothbrushes and face flannels. And what about the nighties she'd got for us? I didn't know which I liked best really, the pink rosy one or the blue with forget-me-nots. There were the felt slippers too that Miss Armstrong had made. Pat and I had gymslips too and thick black woollen stockings, but I was really the luckiest of all. Three pairs of shoes had come the day before, and each of us had had to try them on. Roberta's were the usual tie-up ones, but much softer than our own. Pat's had a bar-and-button fastening and they were just what she wanted, even if they were a bit too big till Margaret used some tissue paper.

The third pair had delighted me from the minute I saw them. They were just what I'd always longed for: shiny black patent ankle-straps! 'Oh yes – yes – they fit – really they do, they don't pinch, not even a tiny bit!' I was lying, lying on purpose; the pain from my cramped toes was swamped by my determination to have them. I walked around the kitchen turning the pain into laughter, begging myself not to limp until Margaret was satisfied that my white face must be due to excitement. And now, there on the chair beside me – yes, on top of my pile of clothes – lay the most beautiful shoes in the world. They'd come a bit late really, but I'd wear them and I'd smile. The punishment for the lies was mine every time I put them on, but that seemed fair enough to me because I knew that these lovely shoes would never come again.

By the next morning new labels had been tied on our coats and packets of egg sandwiches lay on the dresser. Margaret gave us a hankie each with a silver sixpence tied in the corner. She didn't say anything, though I think that was because her cousin Norah, whom she was training to take her place, was standing at the sink waiting impatiently for us to finish with the breakfast things.

Miss Peveril didn't come to say goodbye, she was with her young ladies. Miss Armstrong put her hand around the door and said, 'Well, cheerio, gels, and cheer up, it won't last for ever, yer know.'

17

'Goodbye, Miss Armstrong!' we chorused. But the door had already closed.

'Humph, I don't like 'er for a start!' snapped Norah as she scoured the frying-pan.

Three pairs of cold eyes fastened on her back, but it was Margaret who spoke: 'She's very nice. In fact she's the best lady I've ever served, see!'

Norah seemed about to say something when the doorbell rang.

'Ooh, it's him, I bet – the billeting officer chap. Get their coats and things, Nor'' – Margaret was gone. Norah stuffed us into our coats and crammed our hats down on our eyebrows.

'Ready?' Margaret called from the hall.

''Bye, kids.' Norah sounded as if she might be going to cry; I didn't know what about.

A man was waiting in the hall, bowler hat in one hand and umbrella in the other. He glanced at us and turned to Margaret. 'My respects to Miss Peveril.' He moved to the door. We followed him out over the white step and joined the little group of children who stood, labelled like us, waiting on the pavement. I looked back to see Margaret and caught a glimpse of her smile before she closed the door.

Chapter 3 ~~~

Seagulls swooped and shrieked in the grey sky; a damp salty breeze snatched at our hats; it was cold and everywhere seemed deserted. We were at the seaside. We'd been met at the station by another man, and after a cup of tea in a café we trudged along behind the two men until it seemed we'd been walking for ever. I'd lost interest in the rows of tall seaside houses, many of which had iron or wooden balconies high above the pavement. The man had knocked at some of them and turned away again because heads had been shaken and arms folded across flowery overalls in a way that plainly said 'No'.

At last someone said Yes and the two boys were left at a house called Sea View. The view must have been from the back, though, because the front faced other tall houses.

The lady who took us was Mrs Cobden, and as she let us in she told our man, 'Only a *week*, mind – got war workers comin' then, see. 'Sides, I didn't get none when it first started, did I? . . . One of the first ter put me name down, too. So I says to Mr Cobden, I says, war workers is what we want, an' war workers it's goin' ter be now.' She smiled her satisfaction as she showed him the bedroom.

'Yes, yes, very good of you. One week it is, then.' He turned and gave us a pretended smile. 'You'll be all right here. It's just for a week, mind.' The last part sounded like a promise. We nodded our understanding but didn't smile. A week could be ever such a long time.

The man went. Mrs Cobden read our labels and showed us where to hang our coats. Then she took us into the tiny living-room and told us to sit on the sofa.

A man wearing a cap was asleep in a chair by the fire. Mrs Cobden sat in the opposite chair and picked up her newspaper. We sat there a long time just listening to breathing sounds. A tiredness had overtaken us because of all the walking from house to house, the shaking heads, the aching arms, till at last we'd been let in – well, let in for a week anyway. I wondered what would happen to the two girls who'd still not been let in yet.

''Spect you'll want some tea.' Mrs Cobden rustled the paper and didn't see our answering nods. A few minutes later she rose and went out into a tiny kitchen. The man mumbled something, turned his head from his left shoulder to his right. His eyes stayed closed. I stared at the flypaper and counted only three unlucky ones . . . three of them and three of us. I looked away quickly. I had a feeling that being let out would seem a long time coming.

Tea was ready in the kitchen. Three cups of Oxo and three thick slices of bread stood in the very middle of the table. Mrs Cobden stood against the gas stove and folded her arms. We stood near the table waiting for her to say something.

At last Roberta said, 'Shall we say Grace?' Mrs Cobden leapt away from the wall, fingers to her lips.

'*Shush* – 'e can't *abide* bein' disturbed.' She glanced into the living-room and pulled the door closed.

We sat down and folded our hands.

'Nah. P'raps you'd better not. 'E can't abide that sort o' thing.'

She spoke in a whisper. I nodded, reaching for the cups. Roberta gave out the bread. We sipped and bit till there was nothing left.

'Please can we leave the table?' Roberta was already beginning to stand up.

'*Shush!* I told yer once. Sit on the sofa an' no talkin'. Mr Cobden can't *abide* it, 'specially while 'e's 'avin' 'is doze.'

We sat. The doze went on and on. The smell of frying kippers overflowed from the kitchen. I stared at the dozer with interest. Could he abide it?

Suddenly he came awake. Stretching and yawning, he stood up facing the mirror. Pat's startled gasp brought his mirrored eyes to rest on us with some surprise. I swallowed noisily, wondering if 'Good evening, Mr Cobden' was the right thing to say.

It wasn't. The kitchen door closed behind him.

'What'd you do *that* for, eh?' It was Mrs Cobden from the doorway. We fidgeted in confusion.

'Do what?' Roberta sounded amazed.

'*Stare* at 'im.'

'We didn't mean to,' I began.

'Can't *abide* it, 'e can't. *Out*, come on – *out*.' She led us into what she called the best room. 'Yer'll 'ave ter wait in 'ere now' – she pulled the blackout curtains and switched on the light.

We sat ourselves on the tall straight-back chairs; I shuddered with the cold.

'Takes a long time to eat kippers,' moaned Roberta after a while, wrapping her arms across her chest.

Pat slumped gloomily. 'Yeah – an' didya see wot I see'd . . .'

'*Saw!*' corrected Roberta.

Pat sighed. 'I sawed 'is gums an' 'e ain't got no teef.'

Roberta tittered. 'Then 'e'll jest 'ave ter suck 'em.' We giggled nervously at the rude remark.

Mrs Cobden was back. We sat once again on the sofa. Mr Cobden had had his tea and Mrs Cobden explained that he was now having forty winks.

We sat. And sat. Mrs Cobden darned some socks. Roberta moved her leg. Mrs Cobden looked up. There was nothing for us to do except breathe. Everybody was breathing. I listened carefully and decided that it was an untidy do-it-when-you-like sound. He – Mr Cobden – was loudest. His chest rose and fell as the air went in and out. After watching him for a little while I found myself keeping pace with him. In . . . out . . . In . . . out . . . Pat, sitting close to me, moved restlessly. My new deeper breathing became hers too. Soon the three of us sitting along the sofa were breathing in time with Mr Cobden. It sounded much nicer.

'Shush!' The darning-needle hovered. Our rhythmic combined breathing sounds scattered. The room was quiet again. We sat some more.

Bedtime came at six o'clock. Thankfully we followed Mrs Cobden up the steep lino-covered stairs. Roberta darted to be first.

'Not there . . . Not there . . .' Mrs Cobden held out a chamber pot; she didn't have to tell us why. 'You'll 'ave to empty it in the morning,' she said over her shoulder. We followed her along the narrow passage into a big gloomy bedroom full of old furniture and dark paint. Our three nightgowns hung over the bedrail. Roberta put her gymslip on the bed. Mrs Cobden seized it and put it over the bedrail. 'Mother made that quilt.' Our faces turned. She was nodding up towards a big brown photograph hanging over the bed. Obediently we followed her gaze. A severe face under piled-up hair stared back at us, the cold eyes following our every movement. I wished Mrs Cobden would take the quilt away.

After she'd gone we lay there trembling in the dark. 'I'm frightened.' Pat's whisper sent our heads darting under the bedclothes. Roberta giggled. I think I did too, but my heart was beating so loud that all I could be sure of was that I too was scared.

'Whooo . . . oo . . .' moaned Roberta eerily. Pat scrambled away from her and clutched hold of me; she knew this was only the *start*.

'Whooo . . . oo . . . ooo! I wants me *leg* . . .' Pat's shriek wasn't any louder than mine, and both were muffled by bedclothes. I felt all goose-pimply. Roberta was enjoying herself. She didn't have to repeat the tale any more, she knew only too well that by the time she'd finished her second moan both Pat and I would be closing our eyes tightly against the dark, trembling at the pale ghost of an old sea captain who came on his one sound leg to poke around with his crutch in search of the other. Pools of ghostly blood would for ever drip and drip and drip from the little stump, but pale and weak though he was, the search would go on . . . and on . . . and on . . . tip-tap . . . tip-tap . . . drip . . . drip . . . drip . . . Nobody breathed now, he was so close. We'd hear him groan softly as he lifted the crutch . . .

Then, in a paralysing panic, we'd *feel* him. Prodding it across the bed. *Counting the legs*. Then he'd wail his heart out at the even number; the wail was terrible to hear.

Twaannggg . . . Roberta's tapping finger had found the bed-spring. '*Whoo . . . whoo . . . whoo . . . oo . . .* who's got me leg . . .?' Stiff as thin pokers went our legs, proving we hadn't a spare one.

The door opened. Somehow I had time to notice that Roberta screamed loudest.

'Oh . . . didn't mean to frighten yer. Jest fetched yer this' – tucking the stone hot-water bottle just under the blankets.

''Ere, she didn't *do* nothing!' was my astonished comment when the receding footsteps ceased on the stair.

'She *did*. Frightened the *life* outer me.' Roberta's voice sounded thin and pale.

'Serves you right!' I told her.

'Yer've got yerself scared now, ain't yer?' whispered Pat.

'Shut up.' Roberta's voice was very big-sister.

We lay quiet for a while, then I remembered the woman with the sliding eyes hanging up there just above my head. I wriggled towards the edge. Pat's body hastily filled the space I'd left. 'Wot's up?'

'Nothing . . . Er – I was just . . .' My voice was a whisper. I wondered if the eyes had moved too – I was already on the bed-frame.

'Ooh, you 'narf *brave*, 'Ild. 'Ere, Bert – she's gettin' out ter say 'er prayers . . .' A feeling of dismay flooded through me. Until she'd spoken I'd been certain that nothing on earth could have persuaded me out of that bed.

'*What?*' Roberta's tone held awesome respect. Now I *had* to get out.

Hardly daring to breathe, I lifted the covers. Then, eyes tightly closed, I stepped down on to the very cold linoleum. Pat's murmured 'Ooh' helped me to kneel. Indeed, it frightened me so much that my knees just gave way. From above me I could feel the sliding eyes. 'Oh God' – the plea was out. To Pat it must have sounded like a prayer.

'Wait – wait – I gotta say *mine*' – suddenly she was beside me and everything was all right. As we began our prayer I had the distinct feeling that the lady of the quilt had closed her eyes and gone to sleep.

★

During the next few days we got used to the routine of the house. Mr Cobden always had his porridge before we got up, then he went out somewhere whilst we had ours. But he was always back by ten o'clock, and then it was time for his nap. He wore just the same hat for it as he had for his doze and his forty winks.

Mrs Cobden made beds and dusted the stairs, swept the kitchen and added things to what I came to think of as an everlasting dinner. On the stove stood a big, bulging iron pot. Bacon bones usually stuck out of its top. Inside went a daily stream of potatoes and carrots, and now and then an onion or Symington's soup powder. The special thing that happened each day was when she'd grate a lump of suet and make a big pudding dough, which was then pulled into two halves. Six pennyworth of bacon pieces went into one of the halves. Then she tied the whole lot up in a pudding-cloth and dumped it in the pot. Dinner never varied, but we didn't mind; to us it was the best meal of the day. Mrs Cobden would be standing over the pot, cup in one hand and soup plate in the other; the bacon end of the pudding had been cut up and she'd be pouring cupfuls of broth over it. We enjoyed every morsel, even to the bits of rubbery bacon rind.

We weren't so sure about tea time, though. That's when we'd each have a great slice of the plain end of the pudding smeared with jam. It wasn't *so* plain an end, though, not when you bit it. The sharp bacony taste stung right through the bright red jam, making your eyes blink a bit. And then there'd be the suet, big coarse lumps of it glinting in the slab like pearly transparent currants.

Sometimes we'd have to hurry a bit because as soon as Mr Cobden came in at the front door Mrs Cobden let us out at the back door, having already told us several times that he couldn't abide noisy games, kids getting into his shed or playing on the grass, climbing the fence or pulling the lavatory chain. So we would stand more or less in single file on the narrow path and wait to wave at the trains that roared by on the high bank at the end of the garden.

There was more waiting than waving. It was Roberta who picked the first rose hip. Pat and I stood wide-eyed making 'Ummm!!!' and 'Ah . . . you'll-cop-it-now . . .' sounds, but she took no notice and we watched enviously as she threw it up and down from one hand to the other, its lovely orange colour flashing faster and faster – till she dropped it, and to our dismay *stamped* on it. We were pleased to see her go. The rose hip had split and inside we saw that it was soft and furry, a perfect nest for its many tiny little seeds. Pat picked it up. ''Ere – you better put it somewheres or she'll kill it.' She sounded sad. I picked up a largish leaf and wrapped it gently about the wounded berry. Now what to do? In whispers we decided to put it under its bush.

'Come and see what *I've* found!' Roberta was calling quietly from the fence side of the shed. We tiptoed down the path and squeezed along the narrow gap behind her. 'See . . .' She was pointing to a pile of flowerpots lying on a soft muddy patch behind the shed.

'They ought to make some sort of game,' I whispered.

A little while later we'd got them all standing upside-down in a circle and we were stepping carefully round and round and round on top of them. It wasn't much of a game really, but we pretended it was dangerous.

The days slipped by. Mr Cobden napped, dozed and forty-winked under his cap. Mrs Cobden darned, made puddings and kept the pot boiling. Outside in the late November chill we walked the flowerpots and played rather cramped games of pig-in-the-middle with a pair of tightly rolled socks sneaked from Roberta's case. Nothing ever changed, and just as we began to think that it never would, 'the man' came.

Chapter 4 ~~~

'And how do you like living at the seaside?' The man was talking to Roberta, who shrugged.

'*Seaside!* All we seen is the railway bank.'

'Really? Well, bless my soul!' He sounded surprised.

'We even forgot we was *at* the seaside, din't we?' Roberta looked back; Pat and I nodded. It felt a bit strange to be out and walking around the streets again, and we had indeed forgotten the closeness of the sea.

We passed endless varnished gates guarding blank-faced houses; windows heavy with lace curtains sometimes parted sparingly at the bottom for an aspidistra or Alsatian dog ornament to display itself. Nearly every house seemed the same. *And* the next one.

Then suddenly it was a white gate wide open, and as we turned in a red-brick house with frilly net and flowery curtains, 'Here we are at last!' said the man. The plump fair-haired lady waiting on the step smiled back and said something nice. I knew it was nice even though I hadn't heard it.

Inside the little front room she poured tea from a round chromium ball teapot just like Mum's. 'Come on, my chicks, let's have a *proper* tea!' Her eyes were soft and so was her hand as she slipped it around mine.

She was called Auntie Vi.

The hot spicy smell of buttered teacake reminded me of hot cross buns on Good Friday morning, though this was tea time. And there was strawberry jam too. But best of all, Auntie Vi was there with us eating and sipping and talking. Inside I felt not only shy but happy too. It was such a lovely feeling to be sharing with a grown-up person. The row of black elephants on the mantelpiece seemed to grow bigger as their shadows danced higher up the wall in the firelight; logs hissed and spluttered, showing us pretty flaring greens and blues. Driftwood, Auntie had said. What, I wondered, was driftwood?

I roused myself out of the firelit pictures. Auntie Vi and Roberta were back with a big brightly coloured box. 'Ludo' it said on the front. Playing Ludo, we found that Auntie Vi had quite different rules from the ones we were used to. For one thing, the green counters had no special magic of their own, nor did they always go to the eldest person playing. Green counters could be sent back to the start just the same as the others, and a six *did* have to be thrown before they could come out again. But those other rules had been Roberta's and she'd always been the eldest person playing. We liked Auntie Vi's rules much better, and Pat's red counters won the very exciting game.

Bedtime too was fun. Pat and I had a little blue room with an eiderdown and a rug all of our own. Roberta was next door, being all grown-up because she now had a *my* room. The new auntie listened to our prayers and tucked us up in bed, and then came the story: 'The Twelve Dancing Princesses', just a little bit each night. I didn't know then that she did sewing for a dancing school, and sometimes she'd even go and play the piano for them too. When she'd finished the story bit she'd go away, after a kiss, leaving a nightlight burning in a saucer of water. Somehow right from the first night she didn't *seem* new at all, and I found that I had really kissed her just because I wanted to. This wasn't home and she wasn't Mum, but I felt as if I belonged.

As soon as we'd had breakfast on Saturday morning, Auntie Vi wrote out her shopping list. Roberta was all dressed up and being grown-up too, for she was going shopping with Auntie Vi. Pat and I were going to explore the big green stretch of grass behind the back gate. It was called the Links and it went right across to the beach. We wandered hand in hand past and over the ditches that threaded through the bright-green grass. Auntie Vi had promised frogs in the spring, and tadpoles too.

On the beach we collected seashells and pretty pebbles. Then we sat huddled against the wooden breakwater watching the lonely rolling sea. Our dad was out there somewhere . . .

Pat shifted herself on the grinding pebbles. 'There ain't no sand, is there?' she said with a big sigh. 'Paintin' books 'as *always* got sand. Yer paints it yeller . . .'

I didn't say anything.

'Is sand at the seaside *true*?' she wondered.

''Course it is! Crumbs, there must be miles and *miles* of it . . .'

'*Where?*' She'd got hold of my arm.

'Oh, somewhere . . .' I was becoming impatient.

She let go of my arm. 'Yer *say* there's miles . . .'

Suddenly the answer came – or at least something that would do: 'Pat . . . I know where the most sand is.'

Her face lost its disappointed look.

'Egypt!'

She smiled. She was happy again.

I smiled back at my little sister. At least I could still find *her* answers.

When we got back, the smell of frying sausages told us it was dinner time. But it wasn't polite just to open someone's door and walk in. Pat and I stood on the step hoping that Auntie Vi or Roberta had seen us coming, but they couldn't have done because inside sounded all busy, with rattling china and music from the gramophone.

'We'd better knock,' I whispered.

Pat nodded. "'Ope we ain't late.' She looked worried. Being late was far worse than just ordinary bad manners. I tapped the door with fast fingers, hoping somehow to make up for lost time. A voice on the other side said, 'I wonder who that can be?' and the door opened.

'Why, it's you two!' Auntie Vi gave us a surprised look. 'Have you been out there long?'

We followed her inside: she went to the stove and turned down the gas under the sizzling sausages.

'My, you *do* look worried! There's nothing to worry about, now is there?' She bent towards us, smiling. I shook my head.

'Didn't you like the beach?' she asked kindly.

It was Pat who answered. 'Ooh yes! It's *ever* so nice, innit 'Ild?' I nodded. 'It's lovely – and we got some shells.'

'We fought we'd get a 'iding for bein' late, din't we?' Pat's voice was light and happy with relief; we knew that punishment came first and questions after. And – these were questions.

'Late? Goodness me, I'd have popped your dinners in the oven. Hungry tummies soon come home. And that reminds me, this *is* home! – well, for a little while anyway – so there's no need to stand out there knocking on the door!' Auntie Vi tried to look serious; I felt myself wanting to laugh and cry at the same time. Suddenly she gave us both a big kiss each.

'*Shoo!* Off you go and warm yourselves by the fire.'

The first raindrops splattered against the windows as we finished dinner, but Auntie Vi didn't seem to mind and after we'd all helped with the wiping-up she let us play blind man's buff. The game got noisier by the minute and we were delighted when she joined in. A grown-up playing! It was something very new to us and for a time we played quietly, remembering the difference between us and them. But it was Auntie Vi who changed things. She squealed and laughed and crawled about in such a way that after it was all over I felt as if she'd really taught us *how* to play. We'd never enjoyed anything so much.

At tea time we toasted muffins in front of the fire and Auntie Vi told us about her husband, who was called Uncle Jack. He was away on a ship and so was the eldest of her two sons; the younger one was in the air force. I could see that she was really pleased when she knew about our dad. 'My, my – a Petty Officer!' she chuckled. 'You've got one and I've got one – Uncle Jack's a Petty Officer too!'

I smiled my surprise. Roberta said something and Auntie Vi laughed, but I was wondering just how many Petty Officers there were in the Royal Navy. It had never entered my silly head that there might be more than one, and now here suddenly between us we had two. Crumbs, there might even be dozens of them!

'Penny for your thoughts . . .?'

Auntie Vi had said it quite loudly; I felt my face go red as I cleared my throat ready to say something. But nothing came except a mixture of smile and yawn, which made me feel sillier still.

'Tired. It's the sea, I suppose. But you're a quiet little thing anyway. Not to worry, love.' She stood up, stretching and yawning. 'Well, I must get on with my sewing.'

'Mum says she's deep.'

Roberta's voice had spoken above the noise of the sewing-machine that Auntie Vi was pulling into the middle of the room.

'Deep?' Auntie Vi didn't even look round.

'Yeah. She thinks. An' when she ain't doin' that, she *looks*. Oughter 'ave bin a boy really, our dad wanted a boy. They used ter call 'er Billy once – didn't like it, did yer?' – she glanced at me; I felt dislike meeting in the middle of our looks – '. . . an' she gets called Mona. Or Driptin. An' Mum says she's Isaiah, 'cause of them glasses I s'pose . . .'

My face was burning red. I fully expected her to say all the other things Mum said, like me belonging to the coal man and how Mum laughed when her friend Peg had said no wonder he didn't come no more. It was some kind of grown-up joke really because the coal man had still come sometimes, and not always the same one either. But it had all been a long time ago now and anyway I'd stopped believing it on the day someone called Auntie Lou had come. She was Dad's sister and as soon as she saw me she'd said how I was the spitting image of him and I had his ways too, took after his side I did. I'd loved her for it. Dad *was* Dad, for me as well! I'd been about seven at that time and now my eyes filled with tears as I remembered even farther back – to the time when, whenever he'd come home on leave, I'd hidden. Or cried. Even though he brought me presents and spoke kindly, no, I'd never go near him.

'Don't cry, dear – oh, don't cry.' Auntie Vi was wiping my tears with a hankie; Roberta suddenly hurried from the room without a word.

'Now just don't you take notice. She doesn't mean to be unkind. She won't do it again.' I stared at Auntie Vi's crumpled hankie in my lap. Her hand patted my back and rocked me to and fro. What was she saying?

'Nasty things, nicknames.'

She was talking to herself really. I felt all lost and found and lost again because it wasn't the nicknames at all, it was Dad, that's who it was, it was my Dad, he'd been home on leave only twice since Auntie Lou had come and I'd tried to show him that I loved him and that I knew I was his. But there'd never been much time.

The first letter he'd written to me – how eagerly I'd read it over and over again! And then I'd written my first-ever letter to *him*. And signed it with love just the same as *he'd* done.

His last letter had said about coming home on leave: 'Soon, really soon . . .' But the war had come sooner.

Chapter 5 ~~~

The school playgrounds – there were two – were swarming with girls of all ages: running, hopping, skipping, jumping, and in a far corner thumping one another.

'Evacuees?' The monitor at the gate smiled sweetly at Auntie Vi and made a big show of the book and pencil she was holding. Auntie Vi smiled back as we followed her past the now rather startled girl, whose question was left unanswered.

'Evacuees don't come in this way . . .' Her call followed after us. Auntie Vi seemed not to hear it and continued to lead us through a loose crowd of interested girls who'd hesitated long enough to see us, the new arrivals.

We climbed some steps and entered through a stout wooden swung-back door. Auntie paused outside a door with 'Headmistress' on it. Her smile for us was comforting. My tight answering smile had plenty to do with the familiar smell of chalk and polish and the faraway sounds from the playground. Somehow Auntie

Vi's knock sounded too loud: we stood awkwardly facing the door, waiting.

'Come in!'

'Wish we wasn't 'ere,' muttered Roberta, moving herself farther away from the door.

Pat took a deep breath. 'Wish we was on the beach agin.'

So did I. I'd rather be anywhere than here. New girls had always been something special before the war: something to be examined and found out about. An end-in-view for the friendless or the lonely; a question mark for the venturesome girls who'd won friendships and popularity the hard way. I knew now what it felt like to be new: the linked arms ever drawing you into tight little groups who waited none too patiently with endless strings of questions . . .

'Miss Daley, you say . . . Well, goodbye, and thank you . . .' Auntie Vi sounded pleased as she came out and closed the door carefully behind her.

'We have to go round the other side. Miss Daley looks after evacuees.' Auntie Vi grinned. 'That's *us*!'

We found Miss Daley. She was all pale grey. Hair, eyes, costume and stockings echoed foggy days. Her gaze, however, reminded me of frosty windows.

'. . . so it's three days at school and two at the Church Hall the one week, and then they change over' – the moving parts of a little lost sum slid anxiously around in my head; the frosty gaze seemed to be watching it happen. 'We hope to get sorted out for January . . . staff shortages . . . overcrowding . . . really three classrooms is quite generous . . . but it's not enough.'

Auntie Vi smiled politely; Miss Daley continued to stare into me, where the sum had died with a hopeless sigh. I wanted to look away, but found to my surprise that perhaps I needn't, because the sum wasn't the only thing in me. There was yesterday's windy beach, for instance. And Auntie Vi and the borrowed pram. Gradually filling up with smooth sea-washed driftwood.

Nice thoughts about nice things.

'*Onward Chris*-chun *sol*-ul-jers, *march*ing as to *war* . . .'

Miss Daley motioned us to halt. Through the glass panes in the top half of the door I could see the girls singing over their hymn books. Somewhere out of sight a piano thumped and tinkled as only school pianos know how.

Suddenly there came the wail of a siren. Air raid! A hand grasped my shoulder. 'It's only a practice. Do as the others do.' Miss Daley pushed me into the stream of girls moving from the hall, down the corridor. There was no sign of either Pat or Roberta. Miss Daley must have pushed them first.

'Hurry along, girls, mind the steps,' said a teacher's voice by the cloakroom door. We crossed the playground in rather ragged order.

'Quick as you can, no talking, girls,' urged another teacher already waiting by the red-brick air raid shelter. Groping reluctantly in from the entrance, we were swallowed up in darkness.

'Move farther back, girls – farther back.' A torch beam flickered over us, lighting the way we were required to go. A buzz of whispers was quieted by Miss Daley's call for silence.

'Lights, please.' And there were lights, a dim bluish sort that flickered weakly behind thick ridged glass covers high up on the wall, just one in each corner. I peered hopefully into the hazy light. Surely now I'd see where my sisters had got to.

But Miss Daley hadn't finished yet. 'Any girl who causes a nuisance will be severely dealt with.' I, like all the rest, could really believe it, and I turned my head slowly round to face the entrance again. It wouldn't do to let her see it facing the wrong way.

Names were being called, and girls were answering 'Present, Miss'. My name wasn't called, nor was Pat's or Roberta's. I wondered if I ought to do something about it. But what? Boldly go out to a teacher and be a nuisance, or let a teacher find me later and still be a nuisance? It looked as if there was no way out of being severely dealt with.

'Eh! *Four-eyes!*' A finger prodded sharply along my rib. 'Put yer gas mask on or you'll cop out, see!' I caught only a glimpse of the face before it disappeared inside its mask, as others already had.

I had a bit of trouble with my mask: it never had been a proper fit and the webbing-straps kept slipping on my newly washed hair. Suddenly the window-piece slid down past my eyes, pulled by the weight of the snout. Up went my hand to grab the straps.

'That girl – yes, *that* one.' Heads turned their rubbery fronts towards me: a teacher half in and half out of her gas mask was pointing a long purposeful finger. '*Fifty lines,*' she ordered and snapped back inside her mask. A hand patted my arm sympathetically.

Fifty lines? What were fifty lines? I looked at the arm-patter beside me. She nodded back. The dim blue light didn't allow me to see her eyes behind the celluloid, but her hair was fair and soft-curling like a baby's. She was a friend, of that I was sure. Maybe she'd explain what I'd done wrong and, even more important, what I had yet to do.

At last – long, long last, it seemed – we were told to remove the masks. A sort of shuffling movement from somebody behind me was easing me forward and sideways. I glanced at my new friend and found my eyes level with her chest. 'I'm Joyce,' she whispered as I glanced up into her big round blue eyes. The pushing behind me was getting more insistent now; suddenly I'd lost my place and could only see my new friend's head from several places away – golly she was tall; she must have been bending when she patted me.

The teacher had come out of her mask altogether now. 'I gave someone fifty lines. Who was it?'

I went all hot. The teacher was peering around looking for *me*. She must be thinking I'd moved away on purpose. My unwilling hand started to raise itself.

'Git yer 'and down, muggins!' The poke was as harsh as the whisper. It came from behind. I began to turn my head.

'Wotsa*marrer*wivyer?' – another poke, harder. '*She* don't know 'oo it was.'

Unable to bear the suspense any longer I called out, 'Please Miss!' only to be told 'Not now, dear, not now.'

'All Clear! All Clear!' several voices called loudly.

A buzz of chatter filled the shelter. Miss Daley silenced it. She announced that we were going to do it all over again.

Outside again, blinking our eyes against the daylight, we lined up in twos and waited for the signal, which was to be a waving scarf. The girl called Joyce was only a little way in front of me, and she turned to smile. I couldn't see either of my sisters, but I didn't feel quite so lonely now. Somehow I'd get near Joyce when we were inside the shelter.

Back in the shelter, I held out to Joyce the posh coconut macaroons Auntie Vi had bought me. 'Ooh, ta!' Joyce's long thin fingers found their way into the rolled paper cone. She was nearly twelve and in the 'big girls' already, yet we were going to be friends. I felt very proud to have a 'big girl' asking me to be her friend, and hoped she wouldn't change her mind when she found out about me wearing glasses all the time, which she would when this gas-mask business was finished.

A sudden push sent both of us sprawling against the rough brick wall. 'Ooh! Ooh! You . . . you . . . rough thing!' squeaked Joyce at the brown-haired girl who'd suddenly stood herself in between us.

'Yerss, innit a shame, nearly choked yer bloomin' greedy self, din't yer? Cor, *some people*, chewin' an' swallerin' an' piggin' it *inside-of-their-gas-masks*, 'ow mean'n greedy can yer get, s'worse'n scoffin' in the bogs . . .' The stream of scorn seemed somehow to be edging Joyce slowly but surely away into the gloom. I wished she'd come back or, better still, not go away; my elbow hurt – that rough brick wall – I felt my eyes going all narrow, now all I could see was parts of things, I opened them quickly . . .

'Git yer gassy on, ducks.'

My eyes darted back to her face, but she'd already pulled on her mask and was making it snort rudely at me. Mine wouldn't snort, not even if I'd wanted it to. But I put it on anyway, it would help me to ignore her; she might snort but at least she couldn't talk now, that was something. I remembered the voice, though, it was the same voice – this was the one who'd jostled and pushed and poked with that nasty sharp finger, and I'd been silly enough to decide she must be meaning to help me. Well, if she had been I decided I didn't like her help much.

But what could I do? She had me in a corner. Overhead the pale light flickered and floated lazily along the flat roof. Presently I took a peep at her and saw she'd taken off her mask! I peered around the shelter. The other girls still had theirs on.

''S'orlright, chewers is let orf the inspection.' Her whisper was wrapped up in a wicked chuckle as her fingers prodded playfully into my ribs. She was testing me, trying to make me disobedient! I tossed my head slowly and carefully, just as I'd seen the posh kids do it at Miss Peveril's. *That* ought to show her, I thought hopefully.

She chuckled. 'One nosebag comin' *orf*, scaredy-guts.' The hands reached out to my snout and pulled at the stretching rubber; a deft twist, and cool air touched my hot shamed face. But I wouldn't cry, not for her I wouldn't. My trembling fingers fastened on my glasses and I turned away, not only to put them on but also in the hope that she would at last see I wasn't afraid and go away. But she didn't, and anyway I *was* afraid.

Suddenly she spoke. ''Ere – you ain't pretty, are yer!' She wasn't asking a question either, and both of us knew it.

I shrugged. 'No, I'm not,' I said truthfully, and reached out for my gas mask.

'An' I ain't no oil paintin' meself, am I?' She stuck her face nearer to mine. I looked at it. From what I could see she was speaking the truth.

'No, you're not,' I told her.

She giggled. 'Wot's me face remind yer of?'

'Nothing!'

The giggling stopped. I tensed ready for the blow, feeling the unfairness of it.

'*Nuffin'* . . .?' She repeated the word several times. 'D'yer *mean* it? I looks like *nuffin'*?'

I shook my head. 'I didn't say that. I said you don't *remind* me of anything.'

She was silent.

'. . . You did ask,' I added, hoping the last bit would lighten her hand before it struck. But it wasn't her hand that moved. Instead, to my astonishment, she imitated my head-tossing bit!

'You know wot . . .' Something seemed to be stirring in her. 'You're honest an' yer tells the truth.' She sounded all grown-up.

'Well, so are *you* honest too!'

She was silent for a moment. 'Yerss . . . that's right, innit? Me an' all . . .'Ere!' she said with sudden discovery. 'I'm *honest! Me!*' She sounded all pleased; I smiled my relief, trying not to feel the strong hands clasping mine.

'An' you – *you* got *brains* . . .' My head shook itself, but she plunged on. 'I'm Winnie. Got a "fred" stuck on the end of it, though.' It sounded as if she was saying sorry for it.

'All Clear! All Clear!' The general movement inside the shelter sounded like a sea of rubber being folded up.

'Wot's *your* name?' Winnie seemed to be trying to read it straight off my brain.

'Hilda,' I mumbled, stupidly hoping that somehow she would be satisfied not to hear.

''Ilda?'

I nodded. The name I hated swung between us like a grandfather-

34

clock pendulum: I waited for the bellow of mirth or the 'Erk' of derision. I'd always disliked my name, but here was Winnie practically adoring it. 'Ooh! Yer don't really mean it? 'Ilda's me second name, see. Means "Battlemaid". An' jest fancy, 'Ild, you an' me is both *Battlemaids*. Friends!' went on Winnie encouragingly. 'That's what we are, 'Ild. Cobbers. Oppos.'

I shuddered just a little. 'I've got a friend already.' I tried to make it sound as though I was a bit sorry about it.

'Yerss, you gotta *friend*, 'Ild, an' I'm *it*, see. Cor, *two* of us. Both *Battlemaids* . . .'

'Ah, Hilda. You'll be in Class Two.'

Winnie pressed herself eagerly forward. '*I'm* in Class Two, Miss.' Miss Daley's glance seemed to turn her into clear glass: 'Ah, Beryl . . .'

'Are you in Class Two?' I asked Beryl as we mounted the steps.

'Miss Daley seems nice,' I offered as we rounded the fire buckets.

'Have you been here *long*?' I was almost trotting to keep up with her long legs. I hadn't had an answer yet.

The hurry turned out to be about a Test I was to start on at once in the empty classroom. The classroom began to fill up after a bit. I didn't look up. I was too worried about a seemingly endless long division that kept gulping noughts and growing. It looked like knitting that had gone on too long.

There was more than that one Test for me, though, and more than one lesson going on too, because there were two classes in the one room. Sometimes half the wrong class would obey the voice of the other one of the two right teachers. I just ploughed on with 'A Day at the Seaside' that kept trying to turn into a homecoming because it had Auntie Vi in it. By the time I'd arrived at the baked potatoes in the tin can under the driftwood fire, the school handbell was being rung for dinner time. Everyone stood up. Miss Kenny must have said they could. And now she was waiting for something.

Oh crumbs – *me*!

The nicest part of every day was going home to Auntie Vi with dinner or tea ready and waiting. We'd got used to going home and hanging around in the back garden because Mum would be out at one of her friends' houses. One dinner time Pat had arrived home to see the fearful gypsies with their baskets going from door to door, and, finding the back door locked as usual and Mum nowhere to be seen, she'd smashed a pane of glass with her hand and run inside the house to hide under the little table that had a red chenille cloth which hung to the floor. I'd been the next one to arrive home, and both of us had crouched under the table crying, Pat because of the gypsies and what they might be exchanging their pegs and paper flowers for, and me because Pat's hand was cut and bleeding and all I could do was wrap it up in the skirt part of my frock so that neither of us had to see it all the time.

When Mum did come home she'd been cross about the bloodstains.

But Auntie Vi didn't seem to get cross. When we did something naughty, a few words quietly spoken in the privacy of the front room soon taught us that there were different kinds of pain and remorse. I began to realise that at home I'd cried after a beating simply because of the beating, and this was wrong. At Auntie Vi's I cried because I was really sorry for whatever it was I'd done to make this kind auntie unhappy. But Auntie Vi was never unhappy for long. As soon as we left the front room she'd act as if we'd never been in there.

It wasn't *fair*. After all, Miss Daley had only asked her to take me to Class Two, and that had been *three days* ago: three days of saying 'Yes, Beryl', 'Sorry, Beryl', 'Please, Beryl . . .' whilst skipping-ropes spun and balls bounced and juggled.

But today I felt quite pleased with myself. I'd got my sweets safely hidden away in a place where they'd never be found. And when Beryl had to go and get the playground teacher a cup of tea, I'd sneak one out of hiding for Joyce – my friend Joyce – who thought Beryl was awful and gave me aniseed balls when she wasn't looking.

Pat had a friend too. Her name was Mary. They played games of make-believe in a corner of the playground and shared their secrets as easily as they shared a bag of sweets.

Roberta had several friends. They wandered about the play-ground with linked arms talking about what they'd do when they were fourteen, grown-up and left school. Roberta wanted to go on the stage, but I never found out about the others.

Winnie seemed to be back to being a Battlemaid all on her own. She'd been shocked at the sight of me in my uniform coat and my felt hat with the silver-and-orange ribbon that Margaret forgot to take off. I'd nearly cried when she stood there laughing and jeering at me with a group of her so-called friends. But later she'd followed me into the lavs and said, 'Eh, 'Ild, I didn't mean it, yer know, but it's that Jane Offam – finks yer clo'es is cissy, see. An' – well – I s'pose I do an' all really . . .' She wasn't looking at me when she said it, and I felt that there wasn't anything I could say.

But Winnie liked things sorted out. So after a bit she said, 'Didyer go ter one o' them cissy schools, 'Ild? Or are yer an Ah Sea?'

'What's an Ah Sea?' I asked, full of suspicion because she'd made it sound like something frightening.

'You ain't one, then?' asked Winnie.

I shook my head. She sighed and tried to pretend she wasn't examining my clothes any more. I decided to tell her where I'd got them. By the time I'd finished she was grinning from ear to ear. 'Cor, charity clo'es. An' me thinkin' you was a snotty got lorst. 'Ere – wait a mo',' she said suddenly. 'You 'ave got other clo'es? I mean, our sorta things' – she waved an arm towards the playground.

'Of course I have!' Crumbs, she ought to have known that.

'That's orlright, then, yer can still be me friend,' she said airily.

'Thanks very much!' I snapped and walked away from her. Hadn't I told her that Joyce was my friend?

I pretended not to hear when she called out 'Got any sweets?' One sweet was never enough for her. Two were a start. Three were better. And so it went on till you realised with dismay that she wanted them all. The last time we'd got to five. She'd then got her cronies to hold me whilst she went through all my pockets and gas-mask box till she found and triumphantly carried off the rest of my sweets. 'Cor, silk sherbet cushions up 'er drors': some of the girls stopped to stare. I hid in the lavs till I heard the bell, vowing that I'd never be friends with such a girl as Winnie, never-never-never.

Miss Kenny didn't know about Battlemaids. To her we looked like girls. She'd even sat me next to Winnie. So Winnie, in spite of all I could do, had made me her friend. It felt more like a capture.

37

Joyce sighed at the impossibility of any Joyce becoming a Battlemaid. But nobody else was sighing. Words like 'rough' and 'rude' were used instead, especially by a stuck-up girl called Jessica, whose mother was a milliner. A posh milliner, at that – so Jessica said. We didn't let on that we were ignorant enough not to know what she was talking about. That would have made her swankier than ever. But Auntie Vi came to the rescue when she told me that it meant a lady who made hats. When I told this to Winnie she laughed and went straight up to Jessica and said "Ow's yer muvver gettin' on wiv the titfers, eh?'

Jessica obviously knew that 'titfers' was a Cockney word for hats. Her face went all mean and white. 'I hate you, so there!' she said angrily, and hurried away.

'I 'ates you an' all!' Winnie yelled. And then, turning to me: 'Copped 'er luvverly, ain't I? She on'y pretends to be stuck-up, else she wouldn't know words like that, would she?'

Chapter 6 ~~~

The shoe shop was big and Auntie was served by a lady who'd started off by saying, 'Wood Moddom k'are to teak a sate?'

Auntie, noticing our astonishment, gave us a broad grin and we nearly giggled when she answered, 'Whey thenk yew, ay don't maind if ay doo!'

The lady raised her thin eyebrows and hurried off muttering, ''Oo's she fink she is then?'

Auntie chuckled. 'You sit here, Hilda. And Pat, you come round this side.' We took our seats and sat swinging our legs, wondering what was going to happen next.

The lady came back with two boxes. 'These is red an' them's blue,' she said carelessly.

'Will you try the red ones on this little girl . . .?' Auntie's request was all wrapped up in a smile.

The lady smiled back. 'It's the job . . .' she whispered

Auntie Vi nodded. 'Yes, I know dear – done it myself once!'

The first box was opened amid quiet giggles and a pair of the prettiest red slippers were placed on the astonished Pat's feet. I stared and stared. 'Are they fer a princess?' asked Pat. But I didn't hear the answer; my eyes were staring now at the beautiful blue softness that was being fitted on to my own feet.

Auntie and the lady seemed to be sharing something, but I don't know what unless it was a smile.

On Christmas Eve there were other children at the railway station. Roberta bought our penny platform tickets and promised the man who clipped them that she'd take us straight into the waiting-room. She didn't, though, because there were others there – others like us – waiting for the all-important two o'clock train from London.

I looked up at the big clock. Ten to two. Not long. The feeling inside me said laugh, run, jump, you're happy. But best Sunday clothes dictated otherwise. Although this wasn't Sunday, it was a wonderful day, the *best* day: Christmas Eve, and Mum was coming . . . Another look at the clock. Five minutes. Just five little minutes . . . Pat's face glowed red with cold and pleasure, her long curls trembled playfully over her shoulders. We exchanged warm happy smiles of love and joy. Three minutes . . . One minute left! Grown-ups and children left the warm waiting-room and spread themselves thinly along the platform. Looking up at the clock, I *saw* the big hand leap! A far-off whistle-cry was snatched away by the hurrying wind. Heads turned. Excited eyes saw tiny mashed-potato puffs of steam riding an iron marble that grew to a cauldron, became instantly a boiler, was suddenly *it*: the train, the train that shook the rails and became the large black clanking engine that slipped slowly by. Doors opened in its trailing carriages. People on the platform moved back and then forward again. Came the first *slam*: a man tripping to slow his pace. The train halted.

Eagerly I scanned faces. Mum? Where is Mum? 'Quick! Run! One to the far end! She's small, she's small.' I ran. Roberta waited by the ticket man.

I listened to the laughing happy chatter and footsteps on stone stairs. The platform is empty. No it's not, the lonely guard is waving a green flag. The doors, each with its big golden 3, slip by faster and faster.

But it's gone now, leaving only a cokey smell and wet marks on the wooden sleepers.

★

Three hours later the five o'clock train came and went. Shadowy figures stumbled down the stone stairs to the street: none was the right shape, not the shape of Mum. We'd somehow missed Mum altogether. She'd be with Auntie Vi, waiting? Yes, we decided, that's what'd happened and that's how it would be. We left the desolate platform with its dim lights and set off on our first journey through the blackout, stumbling along the dark street, tripping painfully off kerbs.

It was time to knock. But it was Auntie Vi's expectant face that looked beyond over our shoulders, her kind face that quickly made an our-sort smile at us. And it was Auntie Vi who quietly cleared away the extra place at the table.

Things happened in grown-up lives, things that couldn't always be explained to children. We listened to the warm kind feeling in Auntie's voice, wishing guiltily that we could make it be enough. Auntie was busying herself with the gramophone handle. 'Perhaps tomorrow . . .? Surely tomorrow . . .' We didn't seem to want to look anywhere special, not even at each other, just listening and feeling the hope of a promise ebbing away as the kind voice went on being kind with its few things-to-say. 'The Laughing Policeman' filled the room with his cheer. But it seemed to stay his. We pulled the crackers. Wore the hats. Laughed as Auntie Vi wanted us to laugh.

But I couldn't understand, not really I couldn't.

''Ild! 'Ild! Wake up! 'E's *bin*! Santa's *bin*! Come an' feel . . .'

Auntie had said we could switch on the light. Our woolly stockings bulged temptingly. Sticking out of the top of each was a celluloid doll with feathers stuck around waist and head. I delved inside. A rolled sheet of transfers. Picture colouring book. Paints with names like Vermilion, Indigo and Yellow Ochre. A round wooden pillbox full of hundreds-and-thousands. A whip and top. Chocolate medal. A bright new penny. Then the apple and orange that today were just usual, and right deep inside the toe the three nuts which Mum always called Faith, 'Ope and Charity, I never knew why.

I picked up the metal canister. It was disappointing; there was nothing inside it. I turned it upside down. 'Gas Mask Container' said the label. I laid it beside the woolly stocking. The real treasure was the *other* one: the coarse white-net stocking edged with frilly crepe paper. Its wonders had delighted us year after year. Rolled cardboard games of Ludo and Snakes-and-Ladders. A kazoo. A feathered streamer that squeaked and tickled. A cardboard trumpet and a tin frog clicker. A tin whistle. A big coloured picture of Father Christmas. A game of five-stones that we never played because it hurt our hands. A net-covered silver-paper ball on thin elastic. I really liked that. Tiny tin scales with two miniature sweet jars full of tiny sweets to weigh on them. A box of coloured chalks. Another delight: Japanese water-flowers. I think these were always my favourite because I never did get over the wonder of the little round wood shavings that opened and bloomed instantly in a glass of water. The fat little flicker-book. I flicked the pages and saw matchstick men running, jumping, swinging whilst matchstick ladies pushed prams, danced and skipped. It was marvellous: a sort of moving story that you could only see, never hear. Next came a paper fan and then a peashooter, the dried peas in a twist of paper. Mum had always taken this delight away; I wondered if Auntie would.

We were near the end now. A card of coloured Plasticene. And – deep in the toe – a little sorbo ball. It was the same every year. Nothing ever changed. We didn't know it ever would. So we now sat facing one another wondering what to do next. The transfers. We each made a careful wet-spit patch on our forearm and applied the picture – mine was a galleon, Pat's a stagecoach – face down. Then, with much licking, we managed to wet it into position. Now we had to count to fifty. Pat waited to see me peel back the first corner. I held my breath, slowly peeling . . . peeling plain paper . . . watching the bright damp shiny colours miraculously choosing to stay with my waiting arm. It wasn't just a corner now. I peeled carefully on, knowing about the flaw in the spell, the sudden ragged empty gash – right across the galleon maybe – when some of the colour remembered common sense and stayed with its paper. Clean and bright, the last of the galleon sailed smoothly upon my arm from out of the magic nothing beneath the peeling paper. Just a last corner of sky now . . . yippee! I'd got the whole picture first time! I was holding my breath for Pat's stagecoach – she'd only lost a little piece of highwayman – when Roberta poked her head round the door: 'I'm givin' Auntie a present!' The transfer jerked and a piece of wheel absented itself from the stagecoach: Pat sighed.

'Pardon?' I asked.

'I said I'm givin' Auntie a present. A bottle of scent. It's a sittin'-up dog wiv an 'at on. The 'at's the lid, see, an' it's got a tassel.'

I wondered why she was giving a present. She'd given one to Mum only last year. I'd thought it beautiful: a silky lavender heart with pink rosebuds, paid for each week from her pocket money. But Mum hadn't liked it nor even kept it: 'Rubbish'. And what did she want with things like handkerchief sachets? Roberta was to take it back to the shop and get the money back. Mum hated us to waste money.

The little bespectacled man had handed over the one-shilling-and-sixpence as if he was glad to get his heart back. But whenever I passed the shop and saw the heart back in the window, I couldn't help remembering Roberta's pleading its loveliness.

On other Sundays at church we children always had to sit in front. The grown-ups at the back could watch to see that we listened and learned – at least, that's what it felt like. But this Sunday we couldn't get anywhere near the seats we sat in all the rest of the year. They were full of familiar faces all crowded as near the front as they could get. Farther back were more grown-ups – sort of visiting ones – who tutted us away from their nearly-full rows. There was a place left for us, and Roberta led us back up the aisle and over to the far side where two or three empty rows remained. We couldn't see anything because of the big stone pillar, nor could we hear the vicar very well. But the grown-ups would know that today there would be no hard things to watch us learn, because *this* Sunday was Christmas Day. It was lovely to join in. The organ could be heard everywhere: 'Hark! The Herald Angels sing . . .' And the story we all loved to listen to every year, all about no room at an inn.

The front room was there for 'best days'; even our mum used hers at Christmas – I think everyone did before the war came, because lights used to shine through the windows all the way along our street. It was the only time in the year that they did, and it looked all friendly, as if people wanted you to know they were there.

Roast pork and plum pudding. Auntie's house was full of lovely smells – smells of a new part of Christmas that Auntie knew about. Our own Christmas smell was . . . well, I hadn't really realised we had one just like Auntie's, till I was helping arrange her bowls of nuts and fruit and crystallised figs. A smell from the fruit bowl had a Christmas smell, a smell to make me feel that my feelings had grown from other feelings and that they all belonged together. Oranges! Soon all three of us were sniffing at them. Auntie laughed. 'Oh, *have* one! But don't spoil your dinners.' That's what was worrying me too, and I don't suppose Auntie ever knew we *really* peeled our oranges just to get the smell.

But the home smell didn't bring Mum. I stood at Auntie Vi's window taking my turn to stare out through the net curtains. It was beginning to get dark. Not a light showed anywhere. I wondered if anyone else missed the friendly lights. The street was silent and deserted; no one either came or went. No lamplighter nowadays.

Roberta sighed loudly. 'She ain't comin', then.' I shook my head and moved so that she could take my place. 'Won't be able ter see soon.' Roberta's head was pressed tight against the curtains.

Auntie Vi came into the room with a tea tray – Pat stopped cuddling her new doll. 'Tea time! Now let's see . . . better do the blackout first.'

Auntie Vi set the tray down on the little table and crossed to the window. Roberta turned a white-looking face towards her. 'It's not *really* dark yet . . .' Her voice sounded thin and wavery. Pat and I stared at each other. 'Not yet, please not yet.'

'Oh, perhaps not; another few minutes to go yet,' agreed Auntie Vi as she turned her bright smile towards us.

Our long sigh of relief ended in offers to help, efforts to smile and please this dear kind lady who didn't mind that we loved our mum best, who would let us eat the salmon sandwiches and mince pies in the dying firelight and pretend with us that it wasn't quite dark enough to close the curtains yet.

Chapter 7 ~~~

Winter's ice and snow had melted away. The hardly remembered icy winds had abated to become today's almost-warm playful breeze that blew the newly washed curtains and bedspreads high and low on the squeaking clothesline. Ladies everywhere seemed to be washing everything they could lay their hands on. 'Spring cleaning!' Auntie Vi had told us, and somehow it seemed to be all to do with birdsong and little lambs as she rubbed the living-room chair-covers up and down on the zinc rubbing-board, sending soapy spring clouds to splash damply all around her.

Springtime was everywhere. We'd gathered the pretty budding twigs, seen the first primroses flowering in the hedgerows, and stood in wonder around the beautiful white starry blossoms of the blackthorn. The tadpoles had come, just as Auntie Vi said they would, and beyond them the beach too had a spring crop of rusty iron poles that pointed this way and that, but never at the sun.

The familiar title 'Evacuee' had by now become part of us. A number of children had returned to their homes, but most of us remaining took a rough sort of pride in being 'Evacuees'. Our lives were becoming settled and happy, and if we had no visits from our mums, well, there'd still be a letter sometime. And we'd all got borrowed sort of mums now anyway.

Then one day Miss Daley gave each of us a sealed letter to take home. Auntie Vi sighed a bit as she read the notes it contained, and looked, I thought, a little sad as she slipped them into her apron pocket. 'Shepherd's pie for dinner! And guess what! A holiday from school tomorrow *and* Friday. Maybe we could see that Shirley Temple film or have a picnic if the weather's nice.' Her hands were busy with a serving-spoon, her eyes bright and sparkling. 'Phew! These blessed onions!' – blinking and dabbing at her eyes with the corner of her pinny.

We chattered happily through dinner, surprised at the unexpected holiday and wondering aloud if perhaps Winnie and Pat's friend Mary could come and play in the garden. But Auntie Vi had an even better idea. Of course they could come, and we'd have a tea party too! There'd be games and the paper hats and balloons left over from Christmas that she'd been *wondering* all this time what to do with. We were almost dancing with joy and nearly forgot to ask which day it was to be! 'Friday at half-past four!' called Auntie as we scrambled out through the front gate.

Friday came at last, and upstairs we found the freshly ironed cotton dresses and starched petticoats laid out on the beds, with matching smooth satin ribbons on the chest of drawers. Winnie had brought her party things in a paper carrier bag and Auntie Vi had carefully ironed out all the creases for her. A little while later, and with a lot of help from Roberta, we surveyed ourselves in the full-length mirror of Auntie's wardrobe. Pat was without doubt the prettiest: her long blonde ringlets topped with a wide blue satin bow to match not only her frock but her eyes. Winnie, in contrast, with glossy shoulder-length brown hair, wore pink, whilst I, with stubby dark-brown plaits and glasses, did my best in pale green.

The party was lovely. It was the very first one we'd ever had. There was a real party cake with pink icing, jelly and custard and sandwiches with *salmon* in them.

After tea we played games until, tired out at last, we said goodnight to our friends before it got too dark for them to go home alone.

That night, as we were getting ready for bed, Auntie Vi told us that what we'd just had was called a Farewell Party. Which, she went on hurriedly, was the nicest, happiest way she could think of to say Thank you. Thank you for all the happy times we'd shared with her. But inside of me was trembling. 'Farewell' meant 'Goodbye', even Pat would know that: Pat who was wriggling into her nightie and quavering, 'We ain't goin' a-*way* again . . .' into a tangle of hair and winceyette.

Auntie Vi smoothed the nightie. 'Now, now, dear, don't let's spoil it all with tears, it'll be just like a holiday, you see if I'm not right, why, you'll forget all about me in no time at all.' I could hardly believe she was really saying it – the bit about forgetting her, I mean.

Kneeling was automatic, but instead of praying all sorts of other thoughts came. It *couldn't* be us – no, it just *couldn't* be us – not *again*! First Mum – then Miss Armstrong, Margaret, Miss Peveril – the Cobdens – people slipping by like telegraph poles . . . and now . . .

There was little time for tears the next morning. Auntie Vi bustled about doing the last-minute packing whilst we sat around the breakfast table trying to eat the suddenly very properly named cereal, 'Force'.

Auntie Vi was being very jolly and very busy. The packing seemed to be finished. 'Come on, slowcoaches, we'll all be late' – her face bobbed around the living-room door. 'Now mustn't forget those ration books' – her footsteps hurried into the front room. Then back she came again. 'I'll put these inside your gas-mask tins with your identity cards. And for heaven's sake don't go and *lose* them.' She glanced around the room, not needing to tell us it was time to go. But time it was all the same, and the little white gate that had once waited wide specially just for us clicked shut behind us at Auntie's touch.

The school hall next, to be checked and labelled.

'Gas mask. Ration book. Identity card. Hand luggage. Sandwiches. All correct.' The WVS ladies reeled off the words to heads that seemed permanently bent over list-strewn tables. Behind these tables waited our teachers. And the labels. Labels with string. String that tied on to us as easily as anything.

And now we were ready. Ready to join the long two-by-two crocodile that was already moving slowly but surely to the station, where a long empty train seemed to have nothing to do but wait.

'Oi! Battlemaid! Quick – in 'ere!' – the thud of a swung-open door and there they all were: the Gang. Barring the way of unwanted fellow-travellers. Saving Places, Places for Pat and me. We scrambled through the crowd and each into her precious Place. 'Cor, fought you two was never comin'' – Winnie's perspiring face looked as if she'd been in a *real* battle. 'Reckon they tried ter shove dozens in 'ere. *Sardines*.'

Jessica laughed. 'Yeah, Winnie told 'em she'd got six brothers and sisters to come. *Rough* brothers . . .'

Winnie chuckled. 'Crumbs, look at 'em pilin' on *now*.' The corridor was full of moving children. WVS ladies shepherded them into compartments yet still more seemed to come, some pushing, losing brothers and sisters.

'My auntie's out there!' My thought was words and movement at the same time, checked by Winnie's rough tug at my skirt.

'Too late now – an' we'll never get near the winders.' I sank back on to my seat. Too late! Too late, and the train hadn't even started yet. I felt tears smarting; we hadn't even said goodbye.

Joyce put her arm round Pat, who was crying. 'But she's there!' cried Pat. 'She's there! She wants us!' Winnie shrugged.

Joyce made soothing noises. 'We've got to be saved, see. They *always* saves the women and children first, don't they?' – the big blue eyes were serious. I nodded, suddenly remembering the pigeons. They'd had wings, but they still hadn't wanted to be saved away. The scrummy corridor and the crying where nobody else wanted to be saved away either . . .

The train gave a sudden squeak that became a shrill whistle sound. The familiar jerk told me we were moving. Out in the corridor tears and arms, yells and promises to write spilled out of open windows. Some children were squeezing at the back, hoping to find a piece of window to cry at too. Auntie Vi would be looking. A last look? She'd know what'd happened. But would she know . . . would she really know . . . that we loved her? The clicks were coming faster, we were saved away . . .

To where the Places waited. The ones our headmistress had spoken about. Places of Greater Safety.

Chapter 8 ~~~

We were tired, hungry and thirsty. The journey had been long and wearisome, with offhand absent-minded sort of halts in the middle of nowhere, where we'd just sit waiting and waiting and more waiting, a bit nervous about the impatient jerk and the weary bored hiss that had stranded us there. Twice we'd even travelled backwards for quite long distances. There was no way of knowing where we were, and we'd lost all interest in trying to guess. One place was as good as another to this train; all the station name-boards were completely blank.

At long last, though, on the outskirts of a big town, we slowed down properly and stopped. ''Ere Mister, Mister, where are we?' A boy's voice from somewhere up the corridor.

'Newport, boyo! Newport, Wales!' The man's reply held a note of Arrival; his singsong voice was so full of pride you'd have thought we'd arrived at Buckingham Palace.

More children were yelling from the windows; the train lurched and we were moving on again. 'We're in Welshland, then,' Jessica sighed.

'Where's the mountains if this is supposed to be Wales?' I asked, looking at the countryside now flashing past.

'S'right! Wales is *all* mountins.' Winnie peered out of the window. 'Can't *see* no mountins.'

Teachers and helpers began hurrying along the corridors, telling us to get our things together. Roberta had been a helper and we hadn't seen much of her during the journey. But she was here now, buttoning on the smaller children's coats, hanging gas masks round their necks and smiling like sunshine all the time. *She* wasn't afraid of anything new. I wished I was twelve, then I wouldn't be either.

The train had stopped. Out on the platform we were grouped in batches of twenty, and somehow the Gang seemed to flow like one drop of water into the very beginnings of such a batch. Then we were hurried down the stone steps. There were some people about, smiling and waving, and a man was handing out long green-and-white onion things. We stared. 'Our National Emblem. Wel-come to Wales.' There it was again, that curious rise-and-fall in each word: a speaking full of ups-and-downs as if it had itself travelled over invisible mountains.

We didn't quite know what to do about this emblem thing. If it had been a flag we'd have waved it. If it had been a flower we'd have worn it. Well, it couldn't be waved or worn so we just sort of held it; it looked like a giant exclamation mark being clammy-handedly minded till somebody could think what to say. Nobody could, though, and we clambered on to the waiting buses wondering whether we dared put the walking-stick onion under the seat; it'd be bound to be trodden on and the whole bus would reek with the smell of trodden emblem.

''Ere, they do'narf tork funny,' was the comment around the onion maces as we sat close together within our own piece of travelling world.

Roberta wasn't with us. As before, she'd got on to one of the leading buses so as to be with her friend Queenie. She didn't look round when it turned off to the left, but I was looking and so was Pat. Our bus began to slow for the traffic lights. We waited a few moments. The lights changed, the engine thrummed, the singing faltered . . . *our* bus was going straight on! And now we were turning *right*! ''Ild! 'Ild! Ooh 'Ild, we're goin' off on our ownses!' Pat's white face stared into mine.

Voices . . . still singing. Roberta, like us, had not known that it was time to say goodbye.

We were passing through countryside with fields and hills. The hill got steeper, the road narrower and darker, because wooded slopes rose steeply either side of us. Then, quite unexpectedly, we turned a corner and there below us lay a small town: a town that seemed to have grown upward on to the hill as if it was making its own way out of the deep valley of its beginnings.

We went, of course, to the school. It was no surprise any more; school had become a sort of starting and finishing point from which everything began or ended. This one had dirty sandy-yellow bricks making patterns around the doors and windows. Its playground, steep-sloping, shot sideways and upwards away from the far side of the big iron gates. Railed-in yet unbelonging-looking, its emptiness was for us. Winnie decided on a corner at the highest point. Whatever was going to happen here could be safely watched from this distance, and we at least would not be first. Now we could quench our thirst, each one carefully wiping the rim of the heavy iron cup, thickly-chained from its rounded base to the iron basin. 'Reminds me of a horse-trough,' I murmured.

'Rotters!' laughed Jessica, whose turn it was, but all the same her wipe seemed extra careful and Joyce too showed enough distaste to sip carefully from the hiccup side.

Winnie just grinned. ''Orses big as rats!' Joyce paled and looked back at the iron cup; Winnie's eyes rolled heavenwards. We sat down against the low wall supporting the railings, idly wondering why the buses hadn't gone away and why nobody had led us inside the school where our teachers already were and called our names in the usual sharing-out way.

The first of the ladies to arrive at the railings was old. She even had a thick fringed shawl wrapped round her stout shoulders. Heedless of the warm sunshine she stood rather like an inquisitive bird, head jerking this way and that; it was hard to know whether she was looking or listening. Then other ladies came. The birdlike movements were part of them, too. Curiosity began to draw some of us nearer to the railings. They stared at us – and we at them – for a long moment. Then it began: 'How far is it you've come, bach? Kent, you say – Dew, Dew, there's a long way off that is. No mothers with you? But there's mothers you do have, surely? And your fathers? They'll be fighting in the ar-my?' The voice rose like the playground's steep slope. 'Brothers and sisters you do say, sep-arated you've become is it, bach? Whole families . . . there's heartbreak to leave behind' – a suggestion of sorrow as the voice sank; the ladies were passing and re-passing the answers among themselves as if learning some new lesson set by a difficult teacher. 'There's funny they do talk' – a light ripple along the railings. 'Indeed yes, I was only just thinking to it myself. Cottage Homes?

Is it an orphan you are, bach?' The voice held shocked excitement; the ladies twittered quietly; several children in Cottage Homes frocks moved back amongst us; but we'd started to move back too, back and away as far as we dared when grown-ups were speaking – unusually – to *us*. 'What was it Da Da did before the war? War work was it that Mam did now? Oh, somewhere else we'd already been to, why was it we'd had to come here . . .?'

Miss Daley had stepped into the playground. I watched interestedly as the bus drivers stood by the passenger doors of their buses instead of climbing inside the driving cabin. The twittering outside the railings was stopping. Miss Daley was speaking: '. . . brothers and sisters will make every effort to keep together on the same bus. These buses will be taking us to several different villages. So remember what I have told you: brothers and sisters – families as such – *must* stay together.' A general hubbub of excitement broke out; some – like Pat and me – had already lost a sister or brother. But Miss Daley was telling which teachers were to go to which buses.

'Come on.' Winnie's gruff order as she tried to drag us and our cases all at once was quickly acted upon. With much pushing and shoving, the Gang presented itself in neat pairs at the iron gate: Winnie and me. Joyce and Jessica. Pat and . . .? Winnie's gaze darted not to the milling playground but along the railings . . . this side of the bars a girl, small, thin and fair, stood before the shawl-clad lady, the long green emblem still clutched tightly in her hand; the paper parcel and carrier bag told us she was a real brand-new evacuee. ''Ere, quick, grab *'er*.' Winnie and I darted off – and slowed to a reluctant walk: it was the old lady speaking loudest, the others who 'ya ya'd' and nodded.

'Londoners. Ah yes, indeed yes, all explained it is now, public houses and fish and chips in paper, late nights and picture shows, used to it they'll be' – the darting eyes seemed to hold the small girl in place as though she were a lantern slide required for a lecture.

'But – but – I come from *Tankerton*.' The thin little voice was sure about where it had come from. Nobody was listening to it, though; it hadn't been asked a question.

'Come on, yer little . . . er . . . er . . . bin lookin' fer yer ev'rywheres.' Winnie's grasp on the thin arm was firm – it needed to be; the Tankerton girl looked alarmed. Winnie marched the stolen girl to where the rest of the Gang waited, leaving me to pick up her fallen parcel and carrier bag.

'Rough and ready, just like I was saying; there's a difference they'll be finding' – I ran pell-mell and reached the gate just as the Gang were being counted through first out to the first bus.

Pat, Joyce and Jessica climbed aboard. Winnie and I stood aside for the Tankerton girl, remembering her still-startled eyes as she ran with us. But she'd turned away and was holding out the clammy green stick to a rather surprised lady who seemed to just happen to be passing. The lady was already holding the emblem and saying, 'But look you, there's . . .'

The little girl grew taller as she stepped on to the first step. 'Thank you, but it's not mine. I don't want it, you see.' Then she sort of half-smiled – a shy smile – and disappeared inside the bus.

'*Blimey!!!*' gulped Winnie.

There seemed nothing else to say. Not daring to look at the lady, we scuttled aboard.

It turned out that her name was Connie. And she'd been twins once, but that had been ever such a long time ago. Right now she was Connie-all-alone, and had been ever since we'd got off the train. A forgotten carrier bag had caused her to be separated from her school party. Then, to make matters worse, someone – a grown-up, of course – had just told her the usual 'Not now, dear – not now . . .' and pushed her on to the nearest bus. And that was it, here she was where she didn't ought to be.

'You ain't by yerself no more, mate!' Winnie told her proudly. The rest of us nodded, knowing what was coming next.

'I gotta Gang, see. An' after wot you done back there, well, if yer wants t'be in it . . .'

Connie nodded; gulped a bit. 'You really mean it? Oh, I in't never bin in a Gang before' – her eyes were shining.

'S'orlright . . . yer can be one of us.'

But more had to be known about the newcomer. The bus was jolting and swaying around the narrow twisty lanes, up sudden steep hills and down into deep unexpected hollows. There wasn't much to see on the high grey-green slopes apart from grazing sheep and odd little stone walls over which sometimes tumbled tiny waterfalls.

'Wot 'appened to yer twin?' Winnie asked carefully.

51

Connie looked out of the window. 'She's with the angels, that's what my mum says. But . . .' she faltered.

'Wot's up? You ain't gonna cry, are you?'

'Oh no, it's not that. It's jus' that since I bin living with my auntie at Tankerton . . . well, I heard her say something about she'd bin took off with . . . with . . .' she seemed to be finding it hard to get the words out.

'Oh, go *on*!' It was Jessica who was impatient now.

Connie took a deep breath. 'You'd better hold your collars first.' We did so, rather worriedly, Winnie even moved slightly away from the closeness. 'Gallopin' Consumption!' – the words shot through us like pins and needles, visions of fever hospitals and ambulances jerked in time to the jerky ride: 'hold yer collar, never swaller, never ketch the fe-ver . . .'

''Ow long ago?' Winnie spoke hoarsely, her hand over her mouth.

Connie looked puzzled. 'When we were four. I told you. It's *ever* so . . .'

Winnie sighed loudly. 'Couldn't'ya 'ave said that at first?' Our hands left our collars; Connie nodded meekly. 'Well? Wotcha worried about then? Wiv wot she got she prob'ly got there a lot quicker'n *most*. It's a long *way*, yer know.'

'Is it really a village?' wondered Connie.

We wondered too. Miss Daley had *said* 'villages'. Trees and cottages grouped around a green. Maybe a duckpond to one side or a trough for horses on their way home from ploughing fields or doing whatever horses did in a village. Miss Daley hadn't said that such things made a village, but neither had she said that it would be entirely surrounded by high flat-topped mountains like these. Nor had she mentioned coal mines: two of them breathing like monsters and surrounded by their ugly black slag heaps. It was true there were sheep – wandering boldly about the streets – but all the same it wasn't, we thought, anything like a village.

The bus halted and we had to get off and climb the two steep steps up into the 'Workmen's Hall'. Winnie looked a bit glum as she came puffing up behind me. 'Cor, I don't like this place. Fancy 'aving rotten ole sheep wand'rin' all over the streets.'

'Over by there, bach.' A man waved us towards a corner of the long, cheerless hall.

Winnie dumped her case and sat on it, scowling at the chairs stacked on tables at intervals around the bare plaster walls. "'Ere, you ain't saying much, 'Ild.' I sucked at the choking lump in my throat. "Omesick already, ain'tcha?'

I nodded. 'Win . . . how did we get in here? I mean – well, from the top of the steps I looked for the road, but it wasn't there!' I started to explain to her how I'd felt those mountains *snap together*, but Winnie just grinned.

'I ain't int'rested in 'ow we got in, mate, all I wanter know is 'ow we get out!'

"'S'orrible,' muttered Joyce.

'P'raps we're jus' restin' a bit.' Jessica tried to sound hopeful; nobody bothered to answer, the silence between us filled with our own thoughts, barely conscious of the light footsteps of other children arriving and a gentle hushed whispering as they, like us, sat on their cases or crouched on the floor.

Then grown-ups started coming into the hall. We watched as they wandered about, now and then pausing to ask a question or in some cases *to feel the thickness of an arm*. One of these arms belonged to a big boy near us. We watched as his face reddened. His friends were nudging and grinning. 'Is it strong you are, boyo? Strong as you do look?' And at his nod: 'Not a bedwetter you are, is it?' – the friends stopped grinning and looked away. But the boy must have given the right answers because he was led firmly out, head held stiff like the rest of his body. There was no backward glance.

Winnie forced a grin. "Ope nobody chooses *me*. I don't wannem to, see. Then I'll 'ave t'be sent 'ome agin.'

We began to take an interest in what was going on around the hall. It seemed that when someone had selected you, they took you to a table by the doorway where some old men sat writing on pieces of paper. We noted how the bigger boys and girls had been taken either by men or elderly shawl-clad ladies, whilst there was a great deal of cooing and clucking over the smaller children, especially the little girls. But us sort of middle-aged children seemed to be getting left behind. The hall was gradually losing its thick crop; our corner had so far escaped the seeking eyes. I didn't know whether to be glad or sorry; what would they do with leftovers? I felt suddenly very homesick.

Then there was a voice: a man with a walking stick. 'Two sisters is it you are, bach?' He was talking to me but seeing the matching blue coats – our Sunday coats – that made me the sister of the little girl with the fair ringlets. I stood up, nodding; but he'd turned away to a big white-haired lady who stood smiling and nodding as he spoke to her in his foreign language. She reached for Pat's case and hand, the man took me and mine. We'd been chosen.

Chapter 9 ~~~

We turned with our grown-ups up the narrow climbing street. It was only then I thought about Winnie and the Gang. I wondered no more about those others who'd been chosen already. Now I knew what it felt like. Here outside the hall were familiar faces, following or hanging on to New Ladies. No smiles or waves. We'd become strangers among strangers. Here and there between the steep rows of grim-looking terrace houses were the messy grubby sheep that bleated stupidly and for ever seemed to be going together nowhere special. There were questions as we walked up that hill, gentle questions that soaked up our answers like a soft towel.

The house had a quiet sort of difference about its outside. The varnish was darker; it shone around the fawn curtains. No lace there, just a peep of flowery-covered armchairs. We passed through the open door on to a thick woollen rug that ran the length of the little passage, and to my surprise all the way up the stairs too! Bright blue and red mixed with fawn, it was. It was like nothing I'd ever seen before. The dining-room glittered with dark polished wood; there too the floor was soft with rugs. The kitchen had two big cane armchairs with flowery cushions, a table and two small round stools with fitted flowery cushions and frilly skirts that touched the floor. There was warmth from the kitchen range, black and shiny with a glowing red fire and a singing kettle.

I cried, the lady soothed. The man made tea in a flowery china teapot and spread a pretty check cloth on the table. My tears were dried up – on the outside. Our coats were off. We were going up the soft, soft stairs to a little room. More softness. Green this time. And a bed that wore a huge frill right to the floor, all soft green. And on it two little dolls. The lady stood quiet behind us. We stared and waited. She sighed and went to the high soft bed, holding out the dolls now, holding them for Pat to choose. My eyes were fastened on the blue dress and bonnet with pink cross-stitch round the hem, but now she rested in Pat's hands. I smiled at the green-and-yellow twin and wished that there hadn't had to be a choice for me not to have.

The teacups were pretty with roses that matched the plates but they felt fairy-like, too thin to be handled, like the bread-and-butter, brown and white and sagging soon under the weight of our first-ever home-made blackberry jam.

The new auntie was soft and quiet. The uncle had a gentleness too, sort of inside himself – I saw it when he sat in the cane chair to smoke his pipe.

Pat and I sat stiff and erect on the little stools, just as the dolls sat on our laps. At bedtime we washed upstairs at the washstand, where next to the big flowered jug-and-basin set soap and towel lay ready, and ready too to disappear again afterwards, because they really lived under the frilled flounce so as to leave the marble top with its tiny swing mirror and embroidered mats quite free of their heavy interference with the soft quiet amongstness of the room.

We said our prayers and climbed into the high bed. And sank and sank right deep down into the feathers.

Sunday morning. The wash-things there waiting. Our green silky crepe frocks with the shirred waists and white collars waiting too. I'd lain awake in the darkness waiting for now. Growing more and more sure that I wanted to go home.

We washed carefully – not a single sound of splashing water, not a drop spilled on the marble top, just the smell of lemony soap filling the room.

We waited in silence after we'd dressed and brushed our hair, waited to see what would happen next.

The soft opening of the door, and the lady beckoned. A new smell now, of fried tomatoes. We said our Grace, they said theirs; the quiet singsong matched them to what was all around us. I didn't want to eat the tomatoes on toast, but the words wouldn't come. Nor would the breakfast go down inside me. I hung my head and felt tears splash on to my arm. The man said something and led me from the table. I sat alone in the shiny dining-room feeling nothing but the ache that wouldn't get out of me. No tears came, just deep shudders as silent as the place I was in.

The lady came. 'Homesick you are, see. Everything passes . . . with time.' She went away again.

Pat came, wearing a pink slipover pinafore with bows at the sides. 'There's one for you, 'Ild. 'S'nice, innit . . .?' I took the pinny and put it on. Together we went into the kitchen and carefully washed the fragile china, dried it and found out where it all went. But there was no sound in all that softness, just the man puffing slowly on his pipe and the lady putting salt and pepper on the big joint of meat that was soon hissing gently in the fire-hugging-oven-part of the coal range.

We waited on the stools.

The man stood up, sighed and tapped his pipe into the waiting bowl on the floor beside him. 'There's time it is to be ready for going.'

It wasn't a church, but it had the look of nearly being one. There was a funny unpronounceable word over the doorway and the windows were just frosted glass.

Inside there were sort of pens, polished wooden rows of them, with divisions at odd intervals and little gates to close when you'd taken your place. We entered one at the front. Five hymn books lay on the ledge in front of us. Five kneeling-cushions hung on hooks. Five round clips stuck out waiting to hold something. People whispered – not very many of them, mostly men. Music from an organ. Not like the church organ; this one was behind us right in the middle of the rows. There was a railed platform in front of us; a man sitting to the side, waiting. More men in a gallery above to start a sort of creeping blending getting-nearer-and-nearer chant. The people joined in. I tried to understand the words. They weren't ours, not Pat's or mine. I picked up the book in front of me and stared at the print. A knowing came now of what it must feel like to be unable to read. The voice above us spoke the words of the people who belonged there, the people who understood and nodded or whispered a loudish 'Yeh!' 'Yeh!' sound. The voice carried on getting louder. An arm raised high slapped down to clutch the rail. The 'sloy', 'slan', 'eins' and 'oys' meant something. Everyone knelt. 'Ein tard . . .' For a moment I thought it sounded like 'I'm tired', but no, it was a prayer. Then came a hymn, a tune we knew. But the words cut it away from us. We stared blankly ahead. When would it finish?

At long last we were passing through the little gates, our heads being patted under Sunday smiles and words we still didn't understand. Why didn't the man tell them? Why didn't he tell *us*? I wondered more and more as we followed him down the hill. He'd given us a mint each. 'It's a little late you'll be . . .' He'd stopped opposite the grey stone church. A proper church. He was sending us in. 'You know the way home, do you, bach?' I nodded, and led Pat towards the porch.

'All people that on earth do dwell, sing to the Lord with cheereful voice . . .' We'd have to wait. No, Miss Daley had seen us, was beckoning. We crept eagerly forward and joined those we knew in what we knew: 'Come ye before Him and rejoice.'

We crept along the soft rug, past the table already laid with glasses and cutlery, rolled-up cloths stuffed through bracelet-like rings, and a bowl of roses. In the kitchen we put on the pinnies and watched the joint being lifted on to an oval dish; vegetables put into china dishes with lids. All was ready. We took our places behind the high-backed chairs and at the lady's nod mumbled our Grace. But nobody moved to sit down. The man raised his hands and clasped them together. The man and the lady knew the sounds. A warm blue plate was handed to me, its slice of meat looking somehow lost, all alone like that. Vegetable dish covers came off. Spoonfuls of potatoes, cabbage, now the pale gravy. The language was their own as they pulled out the rolled-up material and left the bracelets on the little side plates. Soon soft pieces of potato lay inside my mouth. Other mouths were being wiped on the white squares. Sips of water. Another wipe. Now it was time to take the plates away: only one at a time, no collecting-pile like at Auntie Vi's. In and out of the kitchen went Pat and I, scraping the plates into a bucket. Now there could be a pile. The lady smiled and led us back to the table. Gooseberries tumbled out of pie-crust, thick custard from a jug of shining glass. The plates were passed again, the talking-sounds went on, Pat and I there yet not there, both wondering how long a lunch lasted, it had seemed so long since the beginning.

★

The lady was by the kitchen door. 'It's the glasses you do wash first, then the spoons and forks, separately, mind, careful of scratches, knife handles must not go into the water . . .' on and on went the soft voice and again on, over the little silver tray with two tiny doll-like cups and saucers being brought from the pantry. The lady put thick milk and brown sugar into the matching but rather larger jug and basin. 'You may go into the garden later.' The door clicked gently behind her.

Pat was already washing the glasses. It took a long time to wash everything and put it away. Then we opened the back door. Steep steps led sideways down on to a brick path. A door at the bottom with a padlock: we crept down to see. A patch of green smooth grass. High bushes down each side. One of the bushes was prickly; I rubbed the scratch on my arm: 'Ooh, look Pat! It's gooseberries!' There they were: roundish, greeny-pink and hairy, growing among the many stiff spikes and pretty soft frilly-edged leaves.

There was a tall back gate. We inched it open. A wide paved alleyway. Empty. More tall gates.

We closed the gate. Climbed the steps. Sat on the stools to wait for whatever came next.

Powder-blue coats, over the lady's arm. '. . . to the church Sunday school *after* chapel.' It was to chapel we'd be going now. 'Not the front doors, mind . . .' Down the side entry we'd find the other boys and girls.

We trudged the long hill, hoping it would be the last time for today anyway.

A shyness held us for a moment at the long sloping-down passageway beside the chapel. But it was no use putting it off. And anyway, some of the others might be in there. Too much to hope for one of the Gang, though, but anyone would do. Please God – up there – put someone else like us inside this place?

But there was no one we knew. A few boys and girls sat on the little chairs watching the fat man who spoke in front of a large pot-bellied stove. He smiled and beckoned us to seats right in front. The stares were *direct*, nothing like the peeping we would have done, not even Winnie and the whole Gang would show such open interest as that, not in church they wouldn't. But this wasn't church – was it? The man had started to speak. We didn't understand, but the other children sometimes said something to him in English and he would rock backwards and forwards, hands deep in the pockets of his trousers, which were grey and all wrinkled where they buttoned up the front. I stopped my moving fingers, folded my arms and thought about what I'd say to the lady. She'd really *do* something when she found out we didn't even understand what any of them said to each other.

The long, only-half-understood Sunday worshipping was over. Pat and I lay crying softly into the feathers. The faint lemony smell clung to our skin, as foreign to us as anything about this house with its softness: the frills, cushions, rugs and gentle sounds that covered sharp edges, hard floors, and even us. We lay there knowing that we must become part of it. There'd never be anything for us to whisper about – no asking, no explaining, no anything that would ease our tears, make us happy and laughing again. The words and kindness in the shapes of the lady and the man had told us how they already knew we didn't understand. Sometimes they'd spoken so that we could understand. That was the kindness. We'd waited for the good night that must come. 'Gwelly, bach, gwelly . . .' The man had smiled as he'd said it. I'd seen the slight wave of his hand and the way the flounce round his chair had swayed when he'd sat down. Now why did I keep mixing up the frills with 'Gwelly' and everything else we hadn't understood?

Suddenly there was a tap at the door. Mr Sleweslin popped his head into the room. 'Would you like to hear a little music?' Pat and I nodded, lifting our heads from the pillows. 'Good, good, it'll be just a few minutes, mind . . .' He left the door open. We waited, not daring to speak, and then a little while later we heard it, lovely pieces of music played by a band. I lay wondering about the anthem-like sounds. Last of all came our own sound: 'God Save Our Gracious King' . . . followed by the chimes of Big Ben. We counted to eight and were starting on nine when the sound was cut off by the closing of the door downstairs. Mr Sleweslin explained to us next morning that each Sunday before the nine o'clock news all the Anthems of all the Allies were played. We were to enjoy this music every week. 'Now won't that be nice, bach?'

*

Mrs Sleweslin . . . Sleweslin . . . I wasn't saying it right, but that's what it had sounded like and that's what I kept on repeating to myself over and over again as we joined the stream of school-going children. It was easy to pick out the evacuees; we all carried our gas masks slung over our shoulders by a length of string. The school, like the chapel, was high on a hill. We couldn't help but stand by the gate and look – not down into the village but up and up and all around at the huge circling mountains.

I wondered what had become of our sister Roberta; she certainly wasn't here. One or two other girls had lost a brother or sister and, like Pat and myself, were left to wonder about where they all went to. Nobody but us seemed to think it was in any way important; they were *somewhere else*, and that was all we could find out.

The morning began with us singing 'There is a green hill far a-a-a-way . . .' Winnie nudged me slightly. She wouldn't be able to do much of that sort of thing now; no whispering or note-passing would ever get past Miss Morton, who was really strict.

Playtimes was our getting-together bit of the day: moans and grumbles, giggles and tears, the fearful and the fearless, were today equalled out. There wasn't time to say or hear everything, but tonight after school . . . well, we'd all meet outside that Workmen's place and up them mountains we'd go. Just to see . . . or maybe to . . . It was left unsaid.

Mrs Sleweslin never became Auntie. Aunties were, she'd explained, true family relations. Besides, Mr Sleweslin was retired long ago, respected in the valley as a member of the Secondary School's Board of Governors. No, not here . . . somewhere else it was. Out to play? Why, of course! Mrs Sleweslin held the back door open and gave us a red ball to play with on the lawn. We wondered how much playing we could do with those pink pinnies on. It was only to school and chapel we went without them.

The ball rolled in under the gooseberry bush.

'It's lost,' Pat said. I nodded willingly. Let the ball stay there, there wasn't anywhere else much to send it.

The lady called us in: 'Chilly it was getting out there.' We sat on the stools and looked into the red glow of the fire through the black iron bars. 'Was it knitting or sewing we'd like to amuse ourselves with?' The sewing was coloured silks and pretty scraps of material. We chose. 'It was something for our dolls we'd be making?'

The milk and biscuit came at last. Now the soft climb to bed. Another day was ended. I thought about Winnie and the Gang waiting for us. Somehow I felt that the lady would never let us go playing in the street. Or anywhere else. After all, there was the garden.

Chapter 10 ~~~

The swish of stiff cardboard lids being raised passed around the classroom like a giant sigh. Celluloid eye-pieces stared blankly at the ceiling as the air raid warden, with his tin hat and whistle, strode up and down the narrow gangways. He'd stop, plunge his greyish hand into a box and wave a mask from the tips of his fingers – fingers edged and rimmed, like his eyes, with black coal dust. Dust that lay deep in the tiny creases that criss-crossed his face and neck. A miner taking his turn at being warden.

And the slips of paper, what were they for? None of us dared look, not whilst he was near. It might seem as if we dared think a question.

'Wossi*say*?' Winnie's growl slid sideways towards me, along with the slight nudge. I groaned. '*Well?*' – and her sudden hacking cough bent her forward far enough to hide me and my answer. I opened the slip: '"Turn left. First right. No. 6."' My whisper contained all the surprise I'd ever felt.

'Eh?' Winnie peered for herself.

'What's yours . . .?' I began, but she was already telling me. '"Turn left. First left. No. 21."' She stared. 'Someone's 'aving a game 'ere, mate.'

But teachers don't play that sort of game. Nor do tired-looking warden coal miners, I thought carefully.

Miss Daley was calling for order. The warden stood wearily by the piano, on top of which was the new plain edge of some sort of wooden thing. Miss Daley was explaining about new air raid precautions. No shelters in the village. I watched the warden's arm straighten, saw the fingers grasp. Miss Daley's explanations were

61

becoming instructions, as usual: 'Now, girls. This is most important. Listen to this sound. And then I want you to do what it tells you to do.' The sudden whirling clatter held us stunned. Then there was a dive into boxes, and on went the masks – some right first time; a few others, unnerved by the noise, struggled with tangles of hair ribbon caught up in webbing, whilst their pink chins hung below or beside the all-important snout. But everyone had tried. And when the din ended, only the air raid warden was without a gas mask. After two more tries everyone had it right and the warden was transformed into a monkey-faced creature with a sort of pleated elephant-nose snout.

Then the teachers came round again and each girl had to read her slip of paper. These were, it seemed, directions to our shelters. Shelters that were really just ordinary houses with people living in them, all within three minutes' *run* from the school gate. In two minutes the warning would be given. We'd file quickly out of school, not forgetting our masks. And remembering to set a good example to the people who were bound to be watching because this was the first such drill ever held in the village. And we were not – absolutely *not*, reminded Miss Daley – to start running until we'd passed through the gate.

The two minutes seemed to take for ever. Then the loud wailing rising and falling, echoing round the valley like an infuriated devil's howl. We moved with speed, careful to obey and not run. But then a warden pushed me through the gate: 'Run, girl. Come *on*, there! Run. Run . . .' More wardens stood on corners, rattles in hand, whistles at the ready; girls wafted and fled like scraps from a clothesline . . .

I sped across to the first right-hand turn, and looked for No. 6. And there it was, large and bold, like the lady who overflowed from a stool beside the door.

'Inside now, bach – inside – there's tea brewing on the stove.' I crept gasping up the dark passageway, feeling the big lady shuffling behind me making wheezing noises and giving me gentle pushes. We entered a small, heavily curtained room, its dimness lit not from the sunshine but from the smoky wood fire in the coal range. 'Sit by there, bach, and old Carrie will take care of you.' I was thrust on to a box-stool right beside the fire end of the range. Potato peelings littered the hearth and a strong smell of onion stew came from a bubbling pot. Old Carrie, as she called herself, lifted a soot-blackened kettle and carried it to the table. And what a table!

Dirty cracked cups. Jam in various jars. Cheese, shiny, sweating and hard, lay on the greyish hardened cloth. Several tins encrusted with sugary milk stood around a huge pale smoky-gold glass sugar bowl that had lost one of its four legs. On a sheet of newspaper lay a big cake with a knife beside it. 'Tea, bach' – my astonished eyes saw the kettle pour tea, already milked and sugared, into one of the cups. 'No sense wasting money on having a pot when this does the work of two, now is it.' It wasn't a question. I took the scalding tan-coloured tea. There was no handle to the cup, so I set it down on the floor and licked quickly at my burnt fingers. 'Seedcake. Fill the stomach to make good humour, as my Dai used to say.' A huge lump of cake came to rest on my gymslip skirt; there was no plate. The kettle spluttered back on to the hob. Carrie lowered herself into a huge, much-worn armchair. Out in the street girls could be heard still running about. Carrie sighed as the hand-rattles started. I grabbed at my box, but she reached out a massive hand. 'Eat your cake, bach. It's games; all games.'

The seedcake was heavy and rather doughy in the middle, but as I'd never had it before I thought this was how it was anyway. I ate every last crumb and swallowed the hot tea. A cat hair clung to the side of my cup but it wouldn't pull off, so I just let the drips of tea run down it, hoping it would soak off. Another lump of seedcake. More tea. And the cat hair still clinging – but big Carrie, gazing mostly at the mantelpiece, was just being comfortable. To be polite I told her my name and who I was living with. 'Grand folks, the Sleweslins, they tell me . . . But old Carrie wouldn't know. Can't be told about people, see, bach. Know them first, know them last. But if they don't want to know *you*, how grand are they?' She shifted in her chair. 'It's too much talking I'm doing, child, but set out there all day, who's to care, that's what I'm looking for, bach – who's to care?' I followed her gaze up to the ceiling. Flies flew gloriously free around a crowded flypaper. I lowered my eyes to the gilded mirror that had a lot of spotted patches all over its surface. The bright-blue china vases before it seemed the cleanest, brightest things in the room, yet crowded around them were faded postcards, birthday cards and misty-looking photographs, some in rusty-looking frames. 'My Dai, that is.' Her eyes lay on the centre photo: a soldier standing by a table, one arm seeming to hug the huge potted plant it held.

I stood up. 'Is he your son?'

She sighed. 'No, bach, that's my hubby before the Armistice.

There's Evan, see, to the left by the seashell.' Evan was a soldier too, and very much like his father.

'Flanders it was. Going, we were. Away. Away from here. The pits were too dangerous for our Evan, see. A proper life we was going to 'ave. Come!' She heaved herself up and shuffled out along the passage. A pause at the door to the front parlour. 'See! It's real wallpaper we do have' – she suddenly sounded young as the door swung open and I glanced up at the big smiling wobbly face. The door crashed against a huge bed piled high with pillows and blankets. A stale mouldy smell lingered around a big stuffed settee squatted under its two matching armchairs. Splits and tears showed springs and stuffing. 'Never been used really. See! Look at the wallpaper, new still, just like the day he brought it home.' I let my gaze travel around the leafy walls, seeing the paper sagging limply from its drawing-pins. *Drawing-pins?* I stared at Carrie, waiting to know why. But there were other things to occupy her. She was tightening the strap around a wicker basket. Now she fiddled with a large box of paper-wrapped ornaments. She seemed excited. *Happy.* 'Must keep everything ready. Yes, everything ready. Only the bed and the wallpaper to take down. Moving away from the pits, see. Dai was a bright one . . .' She stopped talking and it was the old Carrie who straightened up the feather-strewn eiderdown. Outside the wardens were shouting. Carrie sighed loudly as if waking from sleep. 'Flanders it was, bach. In the trenches. Mud . . . instead of coal.'

The *thump-thump* of the door-knocker made me jump. ''S'open,' muttered Carrie as a warden clumped up the passage and poked his head into the room.

'There you are. Two of you, is it? That's right. Under the bed with you if Jerry comes, safest place, see.' He was going away, marking something on a paper.

At that moment the wail of the All Clear sped around the valley. The street became full of the sounds of children and women calling to each other; wardens tapping on doors. 'All Clear! All Clear!' they called.

''Bye, lovey – see you next time. And bring a friend or two if you like.' She went outside and flopped on to her stool. Her great hand reached out and gave mine a squeeze. 'That's if they let you come to old Carrie again.'

I was filled with sadness. ''Course they will. It's my *shelter*' – the words hardly hid the dismay that was moving me towards tears.

'There's faith you do have in youth. Now be off with you.'
Carrie pushed gently and I was moving slowly along among other
children back to school and my friends, away from Carrie who, as
I glanced back from the corner, was overflowing her stool and
staring up at the sheep-strewn mountains.

Lots of us were looking forward to the next weekly air raid drill,
but Winnie wasn't one of them. 'Cor! "Shoes orf!" she says as soon
as I gets ter the bloomin' doorstep. Blimey, she even looks t'see if
me *socks* is clean enough. So there I sits under 'er stairs wiv 'er
brushes an' brooms, 'olding me shoes an' sweatin' inside this ruddy
thing' – the gas mask swung in a wide arc . . .
  Jessica laughed. 'I had lemonade and a swing in the garden.'
  Connie looked surprised. '*I* read from the Bible.'
  Winnie chuckled as we turned out of the school gate. 'Go
somewheres else next time.'
  That afternoon we did country dancing in the playground. A lot
of the village ladies gathered around the high roadside to watch. It
made us extra careful to dance well. Legs kicked high, skirts spun
wide, and we smiled our widest smiles. If only every day could be
like this, I thought wistfully as we walked, Pat and I, carefully
separate from the Gang, towards home.

We had expected to be asked about the air raid drill, but no
questions came. Tea was a dainty sandwich-and-cake business, but
both the lady and the man were dressed for going out. And out we
went with them after the washing-up was done.
  A steep stone-strewn alley led us to the first slope of the chosen
mountainside. A sheep-trodden pathway took us up the first gentle
slope. We felt rather like bridesmaids as we walked behind the lady
and the man, and at first this was enough of a pretend game to
keep us happy. But then it was soon time to rest. A large, smooth,
flat rock served our elders as a seat. We stood uncomfortably beside
them, wondering what to do now. Behind us the mountain rose
steep and tempting. A scrambled climb right to the top . . .? I
looked at the man. He was sucking his pipe. The lady produced
Imperial mints and indicated a rest on the grass. We sank down
obediently, looking with longing eyes at the lovely roly-poly
slope. Oh, the fun it would have been! I glanced at the lady. Maybe

if I asked. But her eyes were roaming the village. A sort of pride came out of her sigh. The man echoed it, his eyes fastened mainly on the distant school building, then shifting with vague interest to the collieries that thumped, pumped and clanked day and night. Now he was looking at the chapel; looking at it as if it was home.

The Imperial mint was finished, and so was the rest. We sauntered a little higher up the mountain. Our legs began to ache a bit. 'See the glorious sunset,' the man invited, sweeping off his Panama hat. Pat and I stared at the red-and-yellow ball; saw the silvery-pink tint of the clouds; watched the dark grey creeping ever nearer. I glanced down at the village. It was filled not with the rays from the setting sun but with an eerie grey that had crept in unnoticed. Night was coming early. The grey, we soon learned, was *rain*. And the rain came often, bringing a mist that blotted out the mountains and left only the gloomy grime of the valley to run fast down the hills into gushing drains, whilst the little river rose higher and eagerly hurried its wending way under the iron bridges, past the stacks of pit-props, to twist suddenly away behind the waiting coal trucks. *It* knew the way and nothing stopped it, rushing and racing to the open sea.

Chapter 11 ~~~

Carrie looked around at the new faces. '*Friends* you are, is it?'

The sooty kettle spluttered its tea into the waiting array of odd cups. Winnie nodded, staring past Joyce. Joyce tried a smile that could avoid Winnie's stare. 'I see, I see.' Carrie put the kettle back on the hob and looked again at Winnie and Joyce. I felt myself reddening up. It was awful really. Anyone could see they weren't the least bit friendly at the moment. I'd explained to Joyce that I'd invited Winnie because of the broom cupboard, but she'd followed us anyway.

'This is my sister,' I announced ever so bright and loud, pushing Pat roughly forward so that she bounced off Carrie's huge stomach.

'Ooh, gracious. Well, well, bless my soul, there's not *sisters* you really are, is it?' Carrie's hands were fondling the ringlets, upturning the pretty little face and pretending – yes, really pretending she didn't believe it!

'But we are! We are! And everyone always says what you've said! Only they usually *mean* it!' I told her earnestly.

Carrie smiled and the large head nodded. 'They don't really *look*, bach. Why, anyone can tell who's sisters and who's brothers, just as easy as they can see what's what about *friends*' – she was looking at Joyce again.

'We *are* friends really – well, nearly all the time,' I said, hoping Joyce would ignore Winnie's glare.

'So this is Winnie. This is the friend you were thinking about last week. And Joyce is your friend too. Not wanting to be left behind, is it, bach?' The fair head hung and nodded itself with a mutter of "Ild was my friend *first*.'

Another glare from Winnie. 'That don't make you 'er *best* First. An' yer gotta 'ave a best friend, ain't yer, Mrs . . . er . . . er . . . well, ain'tcha?'

Carrie looked at Winnie's face. 'Yes, we all need a best friend – and there are plenty while we're young. It's old friends that are best friends, as time will prove. So don't go fighting time, lovey. Leave it to the test. Cake . . .?' The big knife with a burnt handle had now sawn its way through the yellow seed-scattered lump on the table.

'Cor, ta! Er, I mean: thanks.' Winnie hardly winced at all at the unfamiliar taste. Only Joyce hung back, but a sharp dig in the ribs from Winnie had her groping eagerly for cake and tea.

Carrie was back in her chair. 'Sorry I am about the cups and that. All the best things are packed, you see. Ready. Ready this long time. Just waiting for Dai and Evan to come home. It's a proper home we're going to have. Away from here, see. Away from the pits. I'll show you . . .'

The door-knocker rattled. Carrie, interrupted, sighed herself out of wherever it was she went in that dreamy chair. 'Who . . . who is it?' she called.

'S'me, please. Jess. And I've got Connie. We've come 'cause 'Ilda said . . .'

A huge grin creased Carrie's face. 'Come in, come in!' – heaving herself up out of the chair.

I stood dumb with shock. Fancy Jessica saying that I'd invited her. And Connie too. I avoided Carrie's face. It was spoilt. All spoilt. The whole Gang was here, and all because of me.

Carrie was chatting and sawing at cake. Tea slopped into empty milk tins. There *were* no more cups, not even cat-hairy ones. Outside the rattles were sounding; inside I was saying, 'I'm sorry. I'm sorry. It's all gone wrong, there were only meant to be two . . .'

Carrie was chuckling. 'It's a party now,' she said gaily.

Just wait till we got back to school, I thought. I wouldn't be in that silly Gang any more. As for Jessica, sipping from a tin and nudging Winnie about the flies . . . And that sulky Joyce. How *dare* they come to my shelter and do this in front of Carrie?

A large fat arm grasped me tightly. 'Roll out the barrel, we'll have a barrel of fun . . .' Carrie, booming away, and all the rest were singing too and marching round the floor laughing and holding one another's waists. I stood staring stupidly. They hadn't spoilt it – *I* had. 'Oh, Carrie, Carrie, I'm sorry, I'm sorry . . .' Her kiss fell on my head like a huge raindrop. 'Best time I've had in years, bach' came the big whisper as the warden's crunching knock sounded on the door.

The singing stopped. Carrie pointed under the table. Winnie dived. Jessica was waved to the back door. Connie and Joyce darted after her. Pat allowed Winnie to coax her in under the long cloth. Carrie waddled off up the passage. 'Just the two of us,' she called, and slammed the door shut.

But the party was finished. Only Winnie, Pat and I were left now. The others had gone far away down the back alleyways. Carrie shrugged her big shoulders. 'Trust Dandy Goss to have his big ears glued to the wall.'

The All Clear shrilled, and I was first out of the front door. Carrie overflowed on to her stool. 'Next time, lovey. See you next time. We'll have another party, shall we?'

'Bring all the others!' she might just as well have said! I smiled, kissed her cheek and ran with Pat and Winnie the three minutes to school.

Jessica's dress hung limp and long. Its pretty violet colour was as vivid as ever, but the crispness was gone. And so was the wide hem, which had been unpicked and now drooped sadly well below her slender knees. I glanced at the tear-reddened eyes, wondering what to say – even whether to ask why – but a glance from Winnie warned me to look around somewhere behind me. Yes, there was

Connie and another unpicked hem. Only Connie hadn't been crying and her busy fingers were trying to smooth away the telltale line that had stayed about three inches above where the hem now finished. Winnie drew me closer. 'There's lots of 'em, 'Ild' – her voice held a note of warning. I glanced around the playground, seeing limp long frocks and glum-faced girls nearly everywhere.

'Why?' The question slipped out before I could stop it. This was Wednesday, our favourite day: air raid drill and country dancing. This was Smiling Day; crisp best showing-off-frocks day. If you had the right sort of lady, that is. Or the right sort of frocks.

'It was the dancin', see . . . Showin' orf our bloomers. 'Eard Rose Middleton tellin' 'er mates. 'Course, I din't 'spect it ter be *true*.' Winnie sounded and looked bewildered.

Pat stared wide-eyed first at Jessica, then at Connie. I glanced down at our hems. Still there where they ought to be. But then our frocks had always been rather long to allow for the growing that somehow never seemed to happen.

'Wait'll yer see Joyce, then! She's locked 'erself in the lavs. 'Er 'ems wasn't long enough, see . . .' Winnie sounded as if she was having a rather bad dream.

'Can't be true,' I muttered stupidly.

''Tis, though – you'll see, mate. 'Ere goes the bell – an' Joyce'll 'ave ter come out now.'

I didn't look for her. But nearly beside me in the next line I caught a glimpse of bright-blue check: Joyce! I turned my gladdened eyes, only to see her sad, forward-looking face. My eyes slipped down her dress and rested with shock on the broad band of black overall print material that had been *sewn on to the bottom*. It looked awful. My eyes filled with tears. I wanted to call my friend, tell her not to mind. Tell her I cared. Tell her anything.

But she wouldn't look.

'There's gloomy you do look today,' Carrie said as she sawed away at the seedcake. 'Lost a shilling and found sixpence, is that the way of it?' Her glance rested on me, and her question hung like a big dark cloud over the table. Winnie swallowed a noisy swallow of scalding tea. Pat stared blankly at the rusty coal range.

'I'll be putting cups ready for the others.' Carrie pretended not to notice the awkward silence.

'Oh . . . you mean Jessica and the rest; well . . . they won't be coming any more . . .'

But the sharp rap at the back door gave the lie to my words. There they were, all three of them, long frocks hitched up with bits of string, and *grinning*.

'Well, there's nice of you to come. It's cups I've got for you this week, see.' Carrie splashed the strong hot tea into and around the cups and beamed her great big smile down upon us.

'I didn't think they were coming,' I explained. 'Miss Daley's getting stricter about us going to the Proper Places, you see.'

'Yeah, but I ain't never goin' ter where I got sent afore, so there!' declared Winnie. She took a big bite of cake.

Carrie looked surprised. 'It's here you'll be coming then, bach?'

'Mmm . . .' Winnie nodded and hastily finished her huge mouthful of cake. 'Yeah. Up the back alleys, see. We all will. We're a Gang, see. 'Sides, we like it 'ere, don't we, 'Ild?'

'Ooh, yes! I'm glad it's *my* Proper Place, though!' I said proudly, and saw Carrie's grin as she lowered herself into the big torn chair.

'Your Proper Place is it, bach . . .? Is that how you feel? Or what you've been told?' Her eyes were searching my face; I felt her searching go deeper and touch something inside me.

'It's my Place of Safety.' The words came, but wrapped up in them somewhere I could hear myself saying something else; I tried to find out what it was, but the words had been said. Carrie had heard them, though; there was a sort of soft special look in her eyes – eyes that somehow seemed to belong to me too. Could I ask her what I'd meant? Yes! Her face was sort of cocked, waiting. Wanting.

'Yeah, an' she's the on'y lucky one. An' 'cause we're a Gang, we shares everythink – er, well, if anyone'll *let* us. An' we won't be no trouble, honest.' Winnie had spoken for all the nodding heads. Carrie was big comfy Carrie again, giving her big smile and promise of eternal shelter to all comers. The special moment still there in me was covered safely over as we began our party. 'Knees up, Mother Brown . . .' Feet stamped, voice-pipes shrilled, the table became a trembling slopping mess as the floorboards shook beneath our carefree dancing.

Then we were all sitting down again and Carrie was listening intently to our misery of the let-down hems, the vanished crispness of starch, the rumours that our dancing was the cause of it all. Surely that couldn't be true, could it?

70

Carrie shook her big head sadly. 'There's much that's strange in the valleys. Children not being children. It's anything new, see, bach. There's time it does take, see. Time . . .' – the word came out like a big long sigh. We all sighed and somehow managed to turn it into a big all-round-the-room yawn. Carrie chuckled. 'There's tired you are, see! That's time passing, if you like!'

That afternoon's country dancing was moved to the school basement.

'But it ain't rainin', Miss!'

But down the gloomy stairs we had to go and into the damp cellar, where most of us started to rub at the sudden crops of goose-pimples on our bare arms and legs, and we began to hear less about 'More Enthusiasm!' and more about 'Grace!'. We found to our dismay that the minuet was thoroughly ladylike – except for the angry scuffles about which ones were ladies. From there on, country dancing was just another lesson. We no longer enjoyed the twirling-galloping-swinging-weaving sort of dances. They just didn't happen any more.

And besides, we were out of the sun.

Chapter 12 ~~~

'Carrie Thomas!' The name seemed to have a nasty taste, for Mrs Sleweslin had spoken it quickly and with a secret sort of hush, as though the very walls of her spotless kitchen would tumble down if the sound of it ever touched them. Mr Sleweslin sat silent by the gently hissing frying-pan. I didn't know if it was breakfast or something else he was watching and waiting for. The silence was waiting for me to say something, but I couldn't because nobody asked me anything. I felt myself beginning to tremble. Pat looked ready to cry, but that might have been because the lady was tying on the huge ribbon bow that always made her head ache. 'It's Pat who's going to Mrs Griffiths, only Pat.' Mrs Sleweslin was talking still, soft and quiet like the fruit of the plum, but inside I knew there was a hard, hard stone. 'It's such girls as Hilda that do lay the shame on someone's doorstep. And to think . . .' I glanced up. She was talking to the man, who was turning the fried bread and shaking his head with solemn sadness – '. . . to think that never a word passed her lips . . . all these weeks and never a word. There's where I find myself feeling that it's a wanton deception, Da Da. Hold still, Pat. Now Da Da, there's a note you'll have to be writing to that woman – that headmistress of theirs. Carrie Thomas's is no fit place for animals, and Hilda must go elsewhere, maybe to Mrs Griffiths's with Pat.'

I looked back at the blank plates. Not to go to Carrie's again. Carrie not fit . . . A slice of fried bread slipped on to my plate; the two halves of tomato stared up at me like two red weepy eyes. I stumbled through the Grace, hearing Pat's voice that was only the echoing whisper of my own. She hadn't said anything about Carrie's. And who was Mrs Griffiths? The woman Pat had been to once? The tomatoes got even more swimmy-looking. I hadn't chosen Carrie, she'd been chosen for me, the piece of paper had taken me to her and I'd had to obey the piece of paper. But if I *could* have chosen – later on, when the others did – I too would have gone to Carrie's. The awfulness of this choice would have been unbearable to Mrs Sleweslin. So unbearable, I guessed, she might even have spoken to me about it, instead of to it about me.

Dear Mum,
    Thank you for the Postal Order and the lovely blue
cardigans. Our lady was very pleased that you sent them and
says that we shall be needing another one each and please
could they be green.

Here I paused, wondering what to say next. The cardigans were beautiful, the first we'd ever owned: powder-blue with embroidered flowers on the pocket. I wondered how Mum had been able to afford them and was a bit worried that the lady wanted more. The lady moved behind my chair; she was reading the little bit I'd managed to write. I sighed inwardly. What else could I say? The pencil moved towards the paper again: 'It's very nice weather here and the school holidays will be starting next week.'

The pencil stopped; the lady was leaning over Pat. Now she sat down beside her. Should I write what I wanted to say now? Quickly, before she looked? Sometimes she peeped only once. But even if she did, what was there really to want to say? Mum had never even heard of Carrie, and I hadn't seen her for nearly three weeks. And Winnie, who still went there, brought me lumps of seedcake that didn't taste at all the same without that hot tan-coloured tea.

The lady was folding Pat's letter. My pencil moved quickly over the paper:

> I hope you are well and happy as we are, Mum, and I almost forgot to tell you that our lady's son is coming home in ten days' time. His name is Bryn and he is a grown-up. Well, I'll have to close now as it's time to get ready for bed.
> Goodnight, Mum, and God bless you and Dad.
> Your loving daughter,
> Hilda

The letter was finished, read by the lady and folded up into the same envelope as Pat's. Somehow I felt guilty about that letter, as if everything in it was a lie. Yet it was mostly true; only the part about being happy was a lie really, but I'd had to write it, somehow the lady had made sure of that. And Mum would really like it, too. Perhaps that's why she never came. Perhaps she even thought we were happier here than at home with her . . . a feeling of panic raced through me: *maybe she'd leave us here for always and always.* Suddenly the letter was in my hand; the lady was leading me up the soft passageway – opening the front door – and then I was out walking to the red pillar box to take my turn at posting. How I wished she didn't stand there watching like that all the time! My hand shook as it hovered in front of the dark slit. It's lies – all lies. I can't post it. I want to go home. Don't watch me. Go inside. Leave me alone. Please, please, leave me alone.

But the letter dropped down into the inside darkness. Taking a smile to Mum. Making her glad that everything was all right.

Carrie's back gate didn't have any hinges. It just rested tall and free against an old rusty iron bed-frame that had been placed across the opening. So all it needed was a slight lift, and then I could climb into the back yard that was like a waist-high jungle of grass, growing around all sorts of surprises. Rusty iron springs. A rotting basketwork pram with big iron wheels. Broken china. Old boots.

A broken umbrella, or at least the spikes of what had been one. I crept up nearer the back door, peeping into the dark coal hole: only another pile of rotting rags and shoes. Now past the smelly old toilet with its deep bottomless hole that led straight to hell and the Devil. Carrie didn't seem to mind about it, though we were all much too frightened to go inside there and sit on that rotten ledge where bits of crumbly wood fell without needing even a puff of wind to move them.

'Carrie? Carrie?' I tapped timidly at the back door.

Heavy footsteps thumped across the floor. 'Who is it?' Carrie's question was underlined by the sliding of a heavy bolt.

'It's me, Carrie. Me, 'Ilda. I've come to see you.' The door swung wide and big Carrie clutched me to her massive body.

The letter was crumpled, as if it had been handled a great deal; grubby finger-marks showed that it had been folded and unfolded along its tired creases. I supposed it had once had an envelope, but now it came out of Carrie's pocket.

'It's the real writing, see . . .' Carrie was explaining as she pressed it into my hand. 'Never a scholar really – just simple words you understand.' I nodded at the sounds, unable really to believe that Carrie didn't know how to do something. The writing on the paper wasn't the clear 'Come to me' or other such messages that we sometimes found in our exercise books, but grown-up-to-grown-up writing. No wonder Carrie had found it difficult to understand: the quick squiggles had sped across the paper as if Miss Daley had been trying to get rid of them in a hurry.

'Can you read it, bach?' The voice had lost some of its worry-sound. I bowed my head, glancing first to try and make out what it was all about:

Dear Mrs Thomas,
    Something something something-or-other wish to inform you that squiggle squiggle squiggle is no longer required. [More squiggles.] As you are on the fringe of the safety area it has been decided . . . [More squiggles.] . . . to remove your name from the Warden's Roll. The child Hilda Hollingsworth has already been squiggle squiggle squiggle.

A full stop, large and heavy, as if Miss Daley had waited there for ages before going on with 'My grateful thanks for past co-operation in this matter'.

I'd been rather a long time puzzling at the letter. 'It *is* about you coming here, bach?'

I swallowed noisily, blinking away the sting of tears, grateful for the dim light of the front room. I spread a smile over my face. 'It's to say . . .' I began in a trembly sort of voice, '. . . er . . . well, it's to say thank you, see.' My voice brightened. 'Thank you about the air raid drill.'

Carrie looked uncertain. 'That's a lot of words just to say that, bach.'

I felt myself going pinky-red. 'Oh, grown-ups, 'specially teachers, always use a lot of words, there's some here even I don't know. But that's what it says, see: you look . . . I waved the letter, pointing to the words 'my thanks'. But I couldn't say them again, my throat was too tight with the pain of unshed tears.

Carrie was staring at the words. Slowly she nodded and let out a big sigh. Then she took the letter and crushed it into a tight ball. A tear-drop rolled down my face; I turned away so she wouldn't see. But I was only leaving her to see that a thank you was always for that which had been given. Been given already. And did she know, too, that often it came at the end of something? She did. Her great face was looking down into mine, waiting. I didn't know what to say, and the brightness inside me was battling to keep its hold over the awfulness of what the letter had really said.

Then words tumbled a quick way out: 'It's finished, see. No more drills 'cause it's the holidays!'

The inspiration won. Carrie smiled her biggest smile. 'Ah, I'd forgotten the holidays. Yes of course, the holidays. Six weeks, isn't it?' I nodded eagerly. 'And things can change a lot in six weeks isn't it, bach?' She was thinking her thoughts aloud. I watched helpless; they'd be taking her nearer ever nearer to what I didn't ever want to tell her.

And when they got to where they were going they sounded quiet and . . . weary?

'*So they send their thanks now, eh?*'

It wasn't my question, but I was the only one there to answer it. I flung my arm across the big waist. 'Oh Carrie, Carrie, I *will* come and see you. And there's *such* a lot to say thank you for.

You're the nicest, kindest person in all the world. And *I* say thank you, Carrie. Thank you, thank you, Carrie. Just from me.'

Chapter 13 ~~~

Saturday afternoon. The coming of Bryn. Not *now*, though. *Now* it was just the two of us, all alone, Pat and I in our freshly whitened shoes walking up the cobbly mountainside pathway hand in hand. 'Out to play.' That's what the lady had said. How strange it felt. How quiet, too. So far we hadn't dared to even speak. The newly given freedom – ours till four o'clock – felt somehow unreal and not really ours at all. Yet here we were turning on to that slopy pathway, and no one to make us stay on it. Yet we stayed, and hurried up towards the flat rock. The morning rain had been blown away. The higher grassy slopes looked dry; the lower ones were still holding raindrops that glinted like fairy jewels as they trembled gently at the edge of the wind's touch. We sat on the flat rock and gazed down at the gloomy grime of the village, the blackness of the wet slag heaps, the billowing clouds of smoke that struggled to rise up higher than the mountains, only to fail and fall back in thin wispy streaks of brittle dust to settle for ever inside the ring of mountains. A stone ring. A ring around people who dug – and not many of them in the strangely quiet streets. Both the morning and the afternoon buses had left crammed with Saturday-shopping housewives – some with children, but mostly the children were left behind the high fences of back gardens or the luckier ones let out to play. Like us. But somehow I didn't feel ready to play; I'd got used to small movements.

'D'yer think 'e'll talk to us?'

I shrugged. 'P'raps!' We were guessing about Bryn – or Mr Bryn, or whatever we were expected to call him. She'd called him a son, so perhaps he was really a boy. Somehow he was the reason for the unexpected freedom, even though he hadn't even arrived yet.

The flat rock became cold and hard. I stood up. 'Come on, Pat, let's climb. I ran and jumped forward and upward, feeling the rubber soles of my shoes slip but managing to clutch the tufty grass with both hands. A feeling of surprise mingled with my excitement as I struggled up. The coarse tufty stuff had a frosty look in some places. But it wasn't frost. Nor was it wet. Just horribly slippery, especially where the taller reedy clumps were, because they seemed to hide patches of crumbly moss that covered unsuspected patches of hidden rock.

We rested in a little hollow. My thoughts had gone far away from the tufty stuff under us and I was seeing real grass, green and springy, grass with daisies and clover and hidden cat's-eyes . . . The mountains were getting that grey misty look. Soon the rain would roll down and drench the gloomy valley. My heart sank. Pink pinafores and stools, a whole long evening of them. And this Bryn, who'd be a stranger to us. No, that wasn't right; it was us who'd be the strangers.

The first light drops of rain touched my leg. We scrambled back to the narrow path and walked slowly towards home. Heedless of the steady downpour, we felt only the loneliness of our first coming-in-from-play.

The back garden was empty, flowers drooping with heavy raindrops. Fallen gooseberries lay under the prickly bush and on the path. Together we climbed the rough wet steps that led up to the back door, the glossy shiny door that held out the cold. I tapped gently, knowing that soon it would open and then we'd be inside, strangers with strangers.

The door swung open. A tall, fair-haired man in a grey suit held it wide. 'What have we here, then, orphans of the storm? Now let me guess which one is which.' We were inside now, and the door was closed.

'There's wet you are.' The lady smothered our heads with towels, saying something about had we been paddling? The big fair man rubbed Pat's hair. He was talking and smiling to his mam and da. All the grown-ups were friendly, happy and dry. The tea table was ready, pink pinnies folded over the backs of our chairs. But first we'd better get out of our damp clothes. Nighties, the lady thought . . . yes, nighties . . . it's tired we'd be after all that lovely mountain air.

Mr Bryn – as we were to call him – was hearing about smoky old London and how we'd come here to be safe and happy. There's white we'd been. But see, red roses now – roses in our cheeks – and there's brown as berries we'd be by the end of summer.

We said the two kinds of Grace. Thin cress sandwiches and

home-made ginger cake, Mr Bryn's favourite it was. Rain spattered against the window. Mr Bryn ate a tiny piece of his favourite cake and said, 'There's good it is to be home again.'

It was because of Mr Bryn that we'd been allowed into the front parlour. We'd stood wonderingly just inside the door, our feet sinking into the deep woolly rugs, looking at the wide deep armchairs and their matching settee, all wearing what I'd come to think of as furniture pinnies. Mr Bryn had squeezed us both into one of the big armchairs where soft velvety cushions filled the corners behind our backs; where we sat rigid, not daring to lean on anything but each other. The lady seated herself on the settee and the man took the big chair like ours that faced the window. But Mr Bryn, all smiles, went to the big shiny piano. I felt a tingle of excitement, remembering briefly the gramophone at Auntie Vi's and the barrel organ that had come round the streets on Friday nights. But that was a long time ago now, like the steam organ at the fairground where the horses went up and down on their twisty brass poles, and wisps of steam escaped from copper pipes, and there'd be a man all dark and greasy doing things with rags but I never really saw what because there were the mirrors and coloured lights and the lovely up-and-down round-and-round ride.

The rustle of papers dragged my mind back from the trip to Hampstead Heath, back along the time to the present. Mr Bryn, seated now, studied the sheets of music and placed them on the little folding frame shelf that hung from the piano lid. The lady smiled at us and leant back into her cushion – the music had started. Soft and sweet, not at all like anything I'd been thinking of, it flowed and trickled all over the room and when there were no spaces left for it to go I felt it come inside me and fill me right up with strange new wonder; it was like nothing I'd ever felt or heard before. I could have sat there for ever but quite suddenly it was gone. Mr Bryn's hands had stopped playing and the music had fled back inside the piano.

'And now something for the little girls, I think . . . Come on, bach – what would you like me to play?' The question was meant for Pat. Pat's head hung shyly. Everyone waited. 'Well, Pat?' The silence stretched on. It wasn't a bit like the silence when we'd hidden with Auntie Vi behind the trees at a Teddy Bears' Picnic. Mr Bryn sighed and gave the top of Pat's head a big smile. 'Come on, bach – let's hear what they sing back in London.' But Pat's head went lower. Mr Bryn looked at me. I couldn't look at him and he knew it. He turned back to the piano and played 'Run, rabbit, run, rabbit, run, run, run . . .' Pat raised her face with a shy smile. "S'nice, but we dunno all of it, do we 'Ild?" The tune faded.

'What about this one, then?' He began to sing 'Roll out the barrel . . .'

'Hush, Bryn.' The lady's voice seemed somehow to be telling him something else. The piano tinkled on back to the first lovely tune he'd played.

But the lady had stood up. 'There's enough excitement for one day. Say good night now.' She was at the door; the music stopped and Mr Bryn stooped to kiss first Pat and then me before we climbed the stairs for a lemony wash.

Downstairs the piano played softly; grown-ups talked and outside it got darker and darker. I'd been awake like this before. Trying to remember . . . *really* remember Mum's face. The sound of her voice. The smell of 'Evening in Paris' that she sometimes put on her wrists. And Dad in his uniform smiling from a photo on the wall in the front room. Why didn't he write? Where was he? Where was Mum? Why had there had to be a war? I was still thinking about these things when the door opened quietly. From the faint glow of light on the landing I saw that it was Mr Bryn, and he was coming in. It was too late to close my eyes and pretend to be asleep, but I had a feeling that he felt I ought to be. But I needn't have worried. He just crept over to the bed and kissed Pat gently on the head before creeping away again. I wondered why he hadn't kissed me too, then I realised that he'd have to lean right over Pat because I slept near the wall and he wouldn't have wanted to wake her up. But all the same, I did wish he'd given me a kiss too.

We set off for the mountain, wandering slowly up the street that smelled of Monday morning soapsuds. From the lower slopes we could hear the heavy iron mangles groaning as sheets and things tortured their way through the big wooden rollers, shuddering their water in splashing cascades into the heavy iron buckets or baths that stopped the busy overalled ladies from getting their feet and legs wet.

A little higher up we could look down into the yards and see the scullery chimneys smoking as coppers boiled and bubbled the second or even the third load, whilst water-taps gushed rinsing water and Reckitt's Blue lay waiting in the wooden tubs next to the big enamel bowls of thick white starch.

But already the washing-lines were filling fast. Many were already full, with clothes props holding the lines taut so that the wind set the glad white sheets billowing with a gleeful sort of freedom.

Yet the ladies toiled on, staggering up the steep sloping gardens with more lines and more washing. And all because it was Monday. Monday, when nearly everyone had bubble-and-squeak for dinner so that the great Wash Day could go on from early morning till late afternoon. And everything would be ready for the big Tuesday Ironing and Airing Day.

We'd never actually seen our lady doing any of this washing and ironing. Hers was always magically done and blowing busily on the line before we'd even got up. But I knew what washing was all about. Winnie had to turn the big iron handle of her lady's mangle, and Connie knew all about feeding cardboard and wood into the fire-hole of the great stone copper. Joyce was the expert on starch. Jessica always came to school on Mondays with faintly blue hands.

We were far up the mountain now, the sun warm on our backs, the wind cool on our faces. Here was the rock and down there among all that waving whiteness stood 'our house', its windows glinting up at us like eyes – yes, that's how it felt, we could see it and it could see us. I wondered if the lady was watching from behind the glinting panes . . .

But the watchful feeling was turning into a stare – it at me and me at it. I jerked myself off the rocky platform.

''Ere . . . where we goin'?'

'Further up. Come on . . .' I grasped Pat's hand. Why were we whispering, I wondered?

We set off up the path, which got narrower and narrower till at last we had to walk in single file. But although Pat couldn't make up her mind about whether she wanted to be in front or behind, *I* had a sense of freedom. The house was slipping by; its eyes no longer glinted at us.

But we had to go farther yet – not much farther, just a little way. I looked back. No house. It had gone. Vanished behind the sharp roof of the Co-op. And we were high. High above the village. Breathless and hot but free. Free of that watchful feeling. Free of the smoking copper boilers. The washing and the village too, if we could only keep on going. But we couldn't. We sank gratefully down on to the tufty grass and puffed big smiles at each other.

After a while we found that we were really enjoying the mountain. We decided to brush the few dried sheep's droppings off our frocks and go right to the very top. But the higher we climbed, the farther away the top seemed to get; in fact the grey-green grass just seemed to go on walling itself up all the way to the clear blue sky. Impatient to solve this mystery, we left the path and began a tough scramble with the help of reedy clumps and jutting rocks. But we soon found ourselves so worn out that we had to give up and sink once again on to the steep slopy mountain-flank. 'There ain't no top!' puffed Pat, careful not to let go of her tufts of grass.

''Course there is! We just haven't got there yet' – hanging on to my bits of reedy stuff.

'Cor, look . . . Just look down . . .' Pat had somehow twisted round and sat herself up.

'*Whoo Whoo Whooo!*' The shrill of the twelve o'clock hooter filled me with dismay. 'Oh, crumbs . . . we're late home . . .' I glanced at Pat impatiently. Bits of grass and sheep's mess clung to the once white shoes, but too late to do anything about it now.

It was a funny thing, we both soon agreed, how everybody kept on about climbing mountains, whilst to us it was the *coming down* that turned out to be the hard part. But we finally scurried down the alleyway to let ourselves in by the back gate.

'Goodness gracious . . . what happened to your shoes . . . there's a mess you're in, to be sure . . .' The eyes left mine; the face turned to smile at Bryn, smiled and nodded. 'Leave them outside, we don't want them smelling up the house. Now Bryn, if David is . . .'

We didn't hear the rest, she'd gone back inside. We removed the dirty shoes, crept up the steps and slipped quickly into the pinnies. The smell of Fairy soap mingled with baked leeks and cheese sauce. When we turned to dry our hands, Mr Bryn gave us a wink. *He* knew what 'out to play' meant!

*

I looked up at the brown notice board that had gold letters telling the times of each service. The name of the village had been carefully painted out, but that didn't stop notices being put up, and what it was noticing this time was the *Picnic*. Tuesday at 1.30 p.m. All evacuee children cordially invited.

There'd be no need to tell our lady She knew already, even though I'd never known her to even glance at the church or to walk on its side of the road. But of course she was a grown-up, and they all seemed to wake up knowing already and not in the least surprised.

Picnic Day was bright, fine and warm. Each of us had a paper bag and each bag had a sandwich, a cake, a bun, an apple, and *a whole fourpenny bar of chocolate*. We passed with our bag to the vicar and his helpers for fizzy lemonade and a small cone of jelly sweets.

The eating part of this Picnic was soon over, except that most of us girls had saved our bars of chocolate for Last. It was so wonderful to see and touch that we couldn't just *eat* it. Not yet, we told ourselves, and tucked it away inside our gas-mask boxes or tins. Not the boys, though. They were gobbling theirs *now*; leaving the screwed-up paper all over the grass, wherever they happened to be. Two boys were ordered to clear it all up, given a sack. We girls helped, feeling the sun growing hotter and hotter on our backs. The ladies smiled approvingly. They must have been nice ladies, nicer than we were, for as far as we were concerned it was just a way of moving up the mountain, and that's what we wanted to do. We'd walked so far to get to this Picnic, it seemed a pity not to get to the top and see what was on the other side. But the ladies had other ideas: it was O'Grady and Statues for us and Tug-o'-War for the boys. The ladies were dealing with sick children and grazed elbows and knees; nobody had yet noticed the bright blue of the sky turning to steely grey. The first breezes blew warmly about us as we ran and stumbled after each other, panting and gasping, getting hotter and hotter till we fell to the ground for a much-needed rest. 'I'm gonna eat me choc'lit . . .' Winnie plunged her hand into her gas-mask box; her groan of dismay and the floppy melted bar sent us all delving – and there we sat, miserably holding the runny bars. The boys seemed to think it was funny. None of us felt like *throwing it away*, we just silently peeled off splongy suddenly-heavy lumps of silver paper and started to lick . . .

'Whatever are you doing? There's bad manners you do have!' A grown-up voice, a shocked-looking lady, and us licking faster and faster and faster before it was too late.

'Stop it at once, I say! Stop it!'

We stopped licking.

'Whatever are you thinking of . . .?' We sat there miserably watching the limp chocolate remains running to waste from the ends of the paper.

A chill breeze blew around us. The lady glanced anxiously up at the sky. Dark clouds were settling lower and lower. She clapped her hands, turned to gather the rest of her charges; we licked furiously . . .

And won! The papers could be screwed up now. We stood up and ran towards the paper-sack, feeling the first drops of rain warm and large on our arms. The ladies were jostling us into order. 'Is everyone here?' Their voices sounded worried. 'Yes, Miss!' The cry was echoing all over the place; the rain was coming faster. A hustling line of children trotted down the sloping pathway, some draping cardigans or jumpers over their heads, but most of us were without these things. Soon the unpleasant wetness made itself felt. There was nowhere to shelter so we just had to keep going, the ladies hurrying us through the pouring misery – a misery that changed all of a sudden into something else. We were *laughing*, spreading our arms and lifting our faces so that the friendly rain could pour itself even more over us; never before had we felt this freedom and joy. Rain had always been shut out by someone's sou'wester, someone's mack, someone's wellingtons, or just someone's borrowed bit of roof. The little bits of you touched by it shrank from it. But here, now, on this mountainside, with only our cotton frocks, we came to know the warm rain's pouring joyful friendliness. It sleeked through our mermaid hair, it danced on our faces, we reached upward and outward for more, laughing at its closeness, glad to meet the freedom that poured so plentifully upon us – oh the lovely, lovely summer rain.

Chapter 14 ~~~

'This', said the vicar, pointing to the picture his wife had flashed on to the screen; 'is how the natives walked about before . . .'

He paused. We stared at the huge African dressed in nothing but feathers. The picture slid away and was replaced by the back view of a native wearing nothing at all.

Winnie giggled. 'You can see 'is bum,' she whispered. The vicar glared and motioned his wife to remove the picture. Now we saw round grass huts.

'Hmm . . . to continue' – he began pacing up and down – 'Ah yes! That was how they went about before they heard the Word of God. Now in the next picture you'll see something very different.' He motioned his wife again: the grass huts vanished and an upside-down picture was quickly removed, turned round and flashed into view. We stared. The huge native was back again, wearing a shirt and short trousers.

'There!' said the vicar's satisfied voice. 'This man has accepted that he lives in the sight of God.'

The picture was replaced by one of a native woman, wearing a dress much too large for her.

'This woman too! In fact the whole tribe of savages covered their nakedness because they had learnt that they lived in the sight of God.'

The grass huts came back into view. This time lots of natives – all wearing clothes, of course – stood in a group in front of the huts.

'And so,' the vicar concluded, 'having accepted the sight of God – and, more important, the Word of God – they threw aside their weapons and lived peaceably together.'

He paused. 'Let us pray and thank God for the great courage and patience He gave the missionaries.'

As though on cue, another picture immediately flashed on to the bedsheet; Winnie dug me in the ribs: 'It's 'im an' 'er.' I looked up and saw the vicar and his wife, pale and nearly-smiling under their safari helmets. They both looked ever so white. The group of natives with them, however, looked very happy indeed. I supposed from the way they were dressed that they had all been very successful at some jumble sale or other.

The vicar coughed. With a guilty start, I bowed my head in time to join in on the Amen.

'Do sit up nicely, girls,' said the vicar's wife.

Legs sat-upon as a cushion from the hard floor were quickly recrossed.

'Are there any questions?' she asked, hopefully.

A hand went up: ''Im wiv the fevvers, Miss – wot's 'e tryin' t'do – fly?'

'Er . . . no, dear . . .'

Winnie chortled. 'Nah, it's springtime an' 'e's buildin' a nest!'

The lady looked a little flurried; her hand hovered over the box of slides. 'I think . . . well . . . perhaps it might be as well . . . would some of you like to see a particular picture again?'

Winnie's enthusiastic voice could be heard above all others: 'Ooh yeah – please, Miss – I mean Missus – could we see that . . .?'

'I think not,' said the vicar, quickly anticipating the request. 'Open the curtains, please.'

We groaned. Winnie said, 'It ain't fair – she *arsked* us . . .'

'Now girls – *girls* . . .' said the vicar's wife.

We stopped muttering.

'That's better,' she said gratefully. 'Now let us not forget that we too have work to do.'

We started muttering again, 'Blinkin' ole knittin'' being the most popular phrase. However, the ways of grown-ups are determined, to say the least, and soon we were all doing something with the hairy brown or grey wool. We were supposed to be casting on thirty-six stitches and then knitting thirty-six rows to form a square. 'Comforts for the Troops' the vicar's wife had called them. The sounds of the whispered guesses following this remark sounded rather like a swarm of bees:

''S easy, they're kettle-'olders,' Connie whispered, ignoring Jessica's '. . . little bedside mats', whilst Joyce seemed certain that they were for '. . .'ot-water-bottle covers so they won't burn their feet.'

'Wot a load of ole codswallop!' groaned Winnie as yet another suggestion reached her suffering ears. '. . . patchin' 'oles in their socks wiv!' she mimicked under her breath.

My wool had tangled, so I just nodded and carried on trying to sort it out.

Winnie moved a bit closer. 'Don't bother wiv that ole mess, 'Ild – jest break it orf an' chuck it away.'

I sighed, thinking that she might well be right. 'Perhaps nobody knows what they're really for,' I suggested. 'Perhaps they're hankies for the winter . . .'

But Winnie didn't seem to be listening. She frowned, knitting clumsily away with great concentration on the bright-red bendy needles.

'What's up?' I asked vaguely, now intent on the slippery green of my own needles.

'Dropped a bloomin' stitch, ain't I? . . .' She fiddled with the knitting, sighing loudly.

'Can I help?' The vicar's wife bent over Winnie. 'Are you having a little bother with it, dear?'

Winnie scowled at the stout brown shoes and lisle-stockinged legs, which were all she could see without losing her precarious stitches. 'I ain't 'aving any bother, thanks,' she said tartly.

'Oh . . .' The vicar's wife sounded uncertain. 'But I thought . . .'

Winnie, leaving her stitches to their fate, smiled a savage smile right up into her unexpecting face: ''S orlright, see . . .' – waving the knitting dangerously. The lady moved away and knocked into the industrious Joyce, whose knitting was the envy of all us less gifted girls.

'Clumsy thing – clear off!' said the angry Joyce without bothering to look.

Winnie and I made great efforts to control our giggles.

'Oh, I *am* sorry' – the refined tones acted like an electric shock; the precious envied knitting fell from Joyce's startled fingers; she was very red.

'Allow me . . .' The good lady was rather red in the face herself as she stooped to recover the knitting; unfortunately Joyce swooped forward at the same time and to our immense amazement and delight, the two heads clumped together. Shaking with mirth, Winnie and I bent our heads over our squares, but the mingled cries of a ladylike 'Good gracious' and the strident Cockney 'Christ orlmighty' snapped the last threads of self-control, and our hearty laughter burst forth on the startled assembly as together we rolled on the floor, laughing till our bellies ached.

'Ooh crumbs . . .' puffed the hysterical Winnie, trying in vain to struggle into an upright position.

'Ooh stoppit – stoppit . . .' I gasped, turning away from the threat of even more laughter.

Two large black shoes planted themselves beside my head. The laughter faltered.

'That', thundered the vicar, 'will be quite enough!'

We stopped laughing and sat up on the thin grey carpet. The stillness was quite sobering. I looked at the floor and wondered if the vicar had moved away yet so it wouldn't just be me that was wrong. Winnie, head bowed, was searching her pockets for a hankie to dry her laughter-wet eyes. I made a slight move to offer her mine, but she waved it away; her hand disappeared up her skirt and reappeared brandishing a rather grubby hankie. The vicar snorted behind me; I choked on fresh laughter and managed to turn it into a cough.

I picked up my knitting and counted the stitches. Thirty-five! I looked carefully to see where the lost stitch had gone. There was no sign of a hole, so I just made another stich on the end of the needle.

I jerked my head up at the sound of clinking glasses. The vicar's wife was pulling a trolley into the middle of the room. On it stood rows of tumblers with bright-yellow lemonade in them.

'Some's got *more in than others*,' said Winnie darkly. I looked and saw that she was right.

'Lemonade!' The vicar thrust two tumblers at me.

'Ta,' said Winnie, earnestly. ''Old still, let's measure 'em,' she whispered, peering to compare the levels. ''S orlright . . .' She sounded satisfied.

'Biscuit?' offered the vicar's wife.

Some were wrapped in coloured silver paper. My fingers hovered longingly, but I resisted the temptation and took a plain 'morning coffee'. Winnie differed by taking a 'rich tea', and we both said polite 'Thank yous'.

I bit into my biscuit and sighed, remembering the old Sunday school teacher in the days before the war who'd explained to us that Selfishness and Greed were weapons of the Devil, and therefore we must always be on guard and never ever take the creamiest cake or the largest piece of apple. Nor were we to give someone else something that we didn't like; we must give to others only the things that we *ourselves* liked.

There was a lot more, all about Truth and Honesty.

Winnie poked me with her knitting-needle. 'Cor, them ones wot's wrapped up must've bin choc'lit ones,' she declared wistfully. She sipped the lemonade. ''Ere – taste it,' she urged.

I sipped and swallowed and sipped again. 'Can't taste anything,' I whispered back.

'No, an' you're *supposed* to, see!' said Winnie. 'Cheats. 'Aven't used enough sherbet.'

I didn't say anything.

'It's wot we *come* 'ere for, ain't it?' she persisted.

I nudged her. Everybody was standing up. 'All Things Bright and Beautiful . . .' announced the piano. Winnie's voice rose with mine. There weren't any verses about lemonade or silver paper, but somehow she didn't seem to mind.

Chapter 15 ~~~

The day had been hot. Some said it was the warmest day in living memory. We'd left the house that morning and pleased Mrs Sleweslin by playing around the slopy path where the flat rocky seat could be seen from the bedroom windows. Playing at playing. Winnie's name had never been mentioned, but Gangs had. And Gangs were for the boys. *Boys*, who thought and behaved very differently from girls. No . . . little girls did *nice* things. They behaved quietly and played softly without quarrelsome fuss and rowdy noises.

Then Mr Bryn would remark on how brown we were getting; how very much happier we looked. It was true, too. Since he'd been here – well, he only had to say something like that and somehow everything would be all right. But this particular afternoon had proved hotter than most; a sickly sort of headache shared itself among us as we tried to play in the sticky heat. But we'd stayed there, not wanting to break up our new-found freedom. We remembered, Pat and I, how it had been only two weeks ago, before Mr Bryn had come. Those stools. Those walks. That awful separateness from anything around us. We didn't want to bring that back again. So we'd laid ourselves down and waited for the afternoon to pass, thankful for the first time when it was getting near four o'clock and time to go home for tea.

Tea . . . I shuddered. I didn't want any tea, just to get out of this sticky, dusty heat. Seeking the shady side of the alleyway, we walked softly and carefully home.

The cool inside of the dining-room made it the most welcome place on earth. We took our time laying the table, not wanting to sit too long in the warm kitchen. The grown-ups seemed to be out, but we knew they wouldn't have left the door unlocked, so we were quiet and spoke only in whispers.

Then the dining-room door opened and Mrs Sleweslin came to see if we'd laid the table yet. Somehow we managed not to feel the headaches so much now, but neither of us ate more than one slice of bread and butter and both of us said polite No Thank yous to the cups of tea.

Washing up was sheer misery; the kitchen range seemed to glow with extra-special heat.

But afterwards our stools were taken into the now-shady back garden, where deck chairs had sprouted on the yellowing grass. A jug of lemonade and glasses were taken from the cellar. The grown-ups sat quiet whilst Pat and I fiddled with the dolls' clothes and sipped carefully at the cool liquid.

The smell of the man's pipe lingered over the garden. I really felt quite sick now. And Mr Bryn had noticed. 'There's pale the girls do look, Mam!' He sounded concerned.

Mrs Sleweslin glanced. 'Indeed yes. Come, it's bed for you. An Aspro would help, I suppose. Dew, Dew, there's hot it is . . .' – we were following her up the steps, dreading the kitchen's heat. But she took us into the dining-room and brought us each a glass of water and first-ever Aspro tablet. 'Swallow it down. Quick now.' The bitter tablet stuck itself tight in my throat. I retched. She rushed me to the lavatory but nothing happened, though I wished and wished it would. I drank more water, feeling the tablet still there, dreading to taste its bitter sweetness again. Now the lady was back – a spoonful of jam – the tablet was gone. I drank some more water and waited. The sick feeling had gone. I crept quickly through the hot kitchen. Pat and the lady were upstairs; a clean soapy smell drifted down. I hurried to our darkened bedroom. It was cool. Behind the drawn blackout curtains the windows were wide open. Pat was already washed, her nightie'd shape sat on the bed waiting for me. Mrs Sleweslin waited while I washed. Then, taking the used water, she told us to sleep well and left, closing the door with a quiet click.

We lay together under the crisp sheet. All the blankets had been folded back to the end of the bed. The pillows were soft and soothing. A sleepy feeling had been with us all afternoon and now, fresh and clean, we soon drifted into dreamland.

Suddenly awake, I stared fearfully about the darkened room, noticing that the blackout curtains were drawn back. But the usual ones were still tightly closed, moving gently with a swishing sound as they brushed against the windowsill. A faint shiver reminded me that I was cold. Yes, that's what had awakened me in the first place: the cold. I reached down for the blankets and dragged them towards my chest as the great flash of brilliant bluish light lit up the room. Pat stirred and turned her face away from the window . . .

The huge crash of rolling thunder sent me darting down under the covers, heart beating nineteen to the dozen. Another flash of lightning and Pat was clutching hold of me whilst we waited fearfully for the horrible sound that must follow. It came, growling and roaring . . . rolling around the mountains like a huge trapped animal. Fearfully I listened for the sound of rain. Storms were dangerous without rain. I didn't know why, but that's what Mum always said as she covered mirrors and put all the knives and forks away under thick paper.

The room was suddenly as bright as day – Pat was so startled that she let go of me with sheer wonder. The terrible rolling thunder came immediately and seemed to last for ever and ever. We lay together trying not to see, not to hear, not to believe that thunder was said to be the angry voice of God.

The sound rolled away at last, leaving the panting breathings of the pit-pumps. Another blinding flash of light – the door opening and Mr Bryn standing in his pyjamas. 'There, there, bach.' He was bending over Pat, lifting her up into his arms. She hid her face against his neck as the thunder rolled on and on around the valley. I sat up in bed. But what was happening? Mr Bryn was *going*. Taking Pat with him. 'Don't be afraid, bach,' he was telling her. And they were gone; the door closed quietly. I waited fearfully for him to come back for me in the flashing lightning and rolling thunder that seemed to go on and on until my terror drove me under the blankets. Sobs of fear shook me awake even when sleep tried to claim me. Mr Bryn – please come. Please . . . please . . . I'm frightened too . . .

The sudden downpour of rain brought a wind that drove the curtains flying like the wings of some huge bird. Still the thunder and lightning came. But not Mr Bryn. Not anyone. I was afraid and I was alone.

Then it was morning and Pat was standing just inside the door.

'An' a colleague's a dog, see . . .'

I sighed. It might as well be. *I* didn't know what it was. But I knew that it was coming to tea and staying the night and that tomorrow Mr Bryn and whatever this colleague thing was were going away together, back to Devon perhaps. Mrs Sleweslin had come in, her best brown flowery frock no longer hidden by the big wraparound overall. 'There's ready we are, then' – her eyes took in every item on the carefully laid table. 'Now hurry to and wash your hands; it's clean frocks I've laid out upstairs for you and mind you don't soil them: there's to chapel you'll be wearing them on Sunday . . .' Her voice floated tired-sounding behind us and was lost in the whoosh of running water as I turned the kitchen tap. Crisp and clean, heads still tingling from the brisk firm brushing, we were taken into the best room, where we squeezed into our usual chair and sat in silence to await whatever was coming next. Grown-up voices in the passage. Pat stiffening beside me. The door opening. Mr Bryn and another man, his mam and da following closely behind: 'So nice to meet a colleague of Bryn's; we've heard such a lot about you.' I stared at the colleague. White flannels. A white pullover. Bright blue eyes and brown wavy hair. Just a man. A man with a quick smile. His handshake was for the grown-ups only; he didn't ask about us. Or rather me – Pat had somehow managed to hide herself almost completely behind me. We followed the chatting grown-ups out into the passage. I saw the colleague's tennis racquet strapped to a big brown case. We had tea in Welsh, Pat and I sitting mute.

At last it was over. We had a little while alone to do the washing-up. Mr Bryn came into the kitchen. 'There's a shilling each.' He laid the coins on the table. Pat hung her head lower over the sink. 'I'll be gone when you get up tomorrow, so it's cheerio' – he wasn't looking at either of us. 'Er, you could keep these a secret' – his head nodded at the money. I stared blankly into his reddening face. A secret? From his mam? I reached for the next cup on the draining-board. There wasn't one. Pat seemed to be huddled and frozen over the bowl, staring into the soapy water. What . . .? My question didn't get asked – Mr Bryn quickly swept the shillings off the table and into my pinny pocket, then before I could say anything he'd gone.

Pat gave a deep shuddering sigh and wiped a soapy hand across her face. 'We'll chuck 'em away, 'Ild' – her voice was a harsh little whisper, but the cups had started getting washed at such a speed I could hardly keep up; my busy hands worked, but something of a puzzle was trying to sort itself out in my head. Pat and the shillings. Mr Bryn and the shillings. Secret unwanted shillings that lay now in my pocket.

Later we sat on the stools and sewed the pieces of cloth. The grown-ups were moving about upstairs; the new voice laughed now and then. I took out the shiny coins. 'I don't *wannit* . . .' Pat was up off her stool and looking angry. Suddenly she snatched the coins and threw them both into the fire. I stared unbelieving. Two whole shillings. Burning money. But that was for rich people, wasn't it? Rich people had money to burn. Pat sat down again. We sewed and sewed together as the secret shillings sank deeper and deeper into the red-hot ashes.

Chapter 16 ~~~

'A feet? Twelve inches,' guessed Jessica.

'Ends of yer legs,' offered Joyce.

Connie tossed her head. 'All right. *You* have the fun an' *I'll* go to the garden feet all on my own.'

Our eyes widened and we sat up respectfully. Connie really did know something we didn't.

Jessica seemed to be puzzling. 'Oh, *now* I know what it is! It's a sorta garden party, see. Ladies wear big hats an' long gowns. An' there's food an' lemonade an' all sorts of things. Ever so posh it is. The King an' Queen 'ave one ev'ry year. Me mum took me once to see all the posh people goin' in – ooh, it was ever so lovely . . .' Jessica was back in London outside the railings of Buckingham Palace . . .

'But they're 'aving it '*ere*' this year, o' course.' Winnie waved a scornful arm towards the pitheads and slag heaps; we giggled politely; Connie looked worried . . .

'Oh, that's on'y the poshest one, see!' explained Jessica. 'Other people have 'em too – Mayors an' that – cor, talk about thick, you lot musta lived in a banana-box afore the war.'

'You ever been to one, Jess?' I asked hopefully.

She shook her head.

'Well, we're goin', ain't we?' demanded Winnie.

We all nodded, knowing that our ladies would decide *that*, but each trying to pretend otherwise. ''Course we are,' I said boldly.

And now the talk turned to the gowns and hats worn by the grand ladies as seen by Jessica. Nearly everyone had something to say. Only Joyce seemed to be keeping quiet, listening and taking it all in. But there were plans to make. Oh, these ladies were a setback. Always there and always watching. But we'd find a way. Maybe some of the ladies wouldn't be going. Wash Day had passed. Maybe they couldn't get those long gowns and big hats ready in time.

My dream of a long sky-blue gown and white daisy-covered hat disappeared; the silky green crepe slid down over my head. So much for the Beautiful Lady. Not for me the long silk gloves or the flowing-satin sash of ribbon drifting delicately behind me. Mrs Sleweslin fastened the neck of my dress. It settled its white collar far down my neck, to rest widely on my too-narrow shoulders. The stubby plaits were already done, tied with sickly faded greenish ribbon. I sighed and put on my spectacles. 'There's nice you do look.' Pat smiled under her wide green bow, her trembling ringlets glinting like spun glass. The lady had got us ready for The Fête. She herself had been busy there all the morning and felt the need to rest this afternoon. I joined in Pat's smile. The lady seemed pleased. We followed her downstairs and along the passage. 'Now here's the entrance money.'

I took the four bright cool pennies. 'Oh, thank you,' we chorused, eager to be gone.

But the lady wasn't finished yet. Out of her pocket came another two pennies. 'This is for you to go to the tent with. It's the Male Voice Choir that's singing there at four o'clock.'

'Oh, thank you,' we chanted again, delighted to see her hand turning the front-door latch.

The door swung wide. Brilliant sunshine flooded over us. About to step out, we were thrust back by her thick cool freckled arm.

An awful sighing gasp was the only sound she made. Pat and I were dumbfounded. For there, coming down the pathway of a house opposite, was a figure in stiff pink taffeta to which had been sewn dozens of blue-and-yellow paper bows and rosettes. The frock finished just above floppy white ankle socks and thick black tie-up shoes. '*Good Heavens!* It's that *silly* girl . . .' The figure had descended the steps and was opening the gate. The huge floppy paper hat lifted in a slight breeze, revealing the pink, happy face of Joyce. Joyce the Beautiful Lady. Gowned and ready for the wonderful Garden Party. No wonder we hadn't seen her yesterday. And from the looks of her, her lady hadn't seen her today either. Not in a too-small bridesmaid's frock. And crumbs – all those *paper bows*!

The door in front of us closed abruptly. Mrs Sleweslin leant against it. 'You *did* see her?'

Pat and I were nodding, backing away.

'It's *the whole village* will be laughing at her.'

We nodded obediently.

'You'll both keep away from her, you hear me?'

Another nod and me mumbling a small frightened 'Yes'.

The lady opened the door and leant out to look down the hill. 'Very well. My goodness gracious, never in all my life . . .'

We waved hasty goodbyes as the door closed. Of the beautiful Paper Lady there was no sign.

Winnie's voice could be heard before we'd even turned the corner. 'Not like *that* you ain't, mate . . . Now come on, them bows 'as gotter come orf.' Jessica and Connie stood giggling, hands clutched tightly over their mouths.

'Hey, you lot!'

They spun round, Joyce running towards me. ''Ild! Oh 'Ild! They've spoilt it – they've gorn an' pulled me all ter bits an' me 'at ter bits an' . . .' Her choking sobs rained wetly on my shoulder, the flowing ends of torn paper bows hung limply from the great black cotton stitches that had once held them tightly in place.

'Garn, it was 'orrible. '*Orrible*. You oughter *sin* it, mate, talk about a show-up' – Winnie was still holding bits of hat; Jessica and Connie were tearing up the crepe paper, letting it flutter along the roadway . . .

'Come on, let's play brides.' Jessica threw a handful over me and the weeping Joyce.

'Stoppit . . . *stoppit!*' I was angry. Angry that they'd been so mean. That they meant to go *on* being mean.

'Well . . . she looked *daft*.' Jessica was at least showing some shame. Connie screwed up her bits of paper and stuffed them down a drain. Winnie stuck the torn hat on her own head and laughed.

''Ere, look, Joyce, I'm Lady Muck, see, jest arrivin' at the Palace' – one hand held the hat, the other an invisible parasol; Winnie, up on tiptoe, minced along the pavement, swaying and giggling . . .

Joyce watched. No smile touched her face, yet the rest of us were in fits of giggles in spite of ourselves. Suddenly Joyce spoke: 'It don't look *too* bad, does it?' She indicated the awful frock that was too tight across her chest and the wrong length, even if you ignored the black cotton and bits of bright blue-and-yellow paper that still clung to it.

Winnie walked around her, considering. 'Can't yer go 'ome? In the woodshed or somethin'? No, I mean can't yer get changed?'

A tear trickled down Joyce's cheek. 'Me lady's gone shoppin', see.'

More sobs to come, but Winnie was making signs to me. 'Oh come on, Joyce, it's not that bad, let's try to get some more paper off. Anyone got a belt?' Jessica handed over a long piece of cat's-cradle string. Winnie and I pulled up the almost-skin-tight dress and tied the string round Joyce's waist. Then we eased the tight wrinkles down over the string.

I stood back to see the result. Sighed. 'Well, it's a proper length now, anyway. And . . . well . . .'

'Yeah, it looks ever such a bit better.' Connie was willing to agree. Winnie nodded. Jessica said nothing, but at least she didn't laugh either. Connie spoke wistfully. 'Hopes yer enjoys it. Can't go, see. And I had to leave me pocket money indoors. It's a chapel do, see. The *wrong* chapel,' she finished lamely.

Winnie kicked at the kerbstone. ''Ave yer sin it? There's swingin'-boats an' cakes an' tents wiv hooplas . . .' – the picture grew and coloured itself and started to move – '. . . only . . . well . . . no money, mate.' Winnie shook out a grubby handkerchief. 'Ain't 'ad no letter from 'ome fer two weeks.'

Joyce moved forward. 'I got tuppence, but wot's the use if on'y 'alf of us is goin'? 'Sides, I don't really want to go now.' She tried not to glance down at the frock.

'So . . . that's four can go and two can't . . .' I was thinking aloud. Those sausage-ropes of long division hadn't come in handy yet, I reflected. They didn't *care* what got left.

'We gotta extra tuppence, 'Ild . . .' Pat was jogging at my elbow; excited chattering broke out . . .

'That's five can go . . .'

Leaving one outside.

.

We all stood pressed against the rusty railings. It was mostly the backs of tents, but Connie swore she could see the edge of a moving swing-boat. A thin little man was standing by the large open gateway taking tuppences and dropping them into a china bowl before picking up his rubber stamp and dabbing it on people's hands. And now no more people were waiting. The man got up off his chair and stretched himself. He'd seen us. 'Nice day, innit . . .' Winnie's coppers jingled into the bowl; the rest of us jostled nearer the table. The man stamped a purple star on Winnie's wrist, but it was Joyce he was staring at. She burst into tears at just the right moment; Jessica had moved nearer the bowl – she flicked her hand delicately; coins jangled, but not hers; the man stamped again, still staring after the pink taffeta with trailing paper.

We were in.

It didn't take us long to find out that not a single thing was free. 'Bloomin' cheek, takin' our money away for nuffink!' Winnie'd lost all interest in the hoopla stall, and none of us had a single penny to roll down the 'Win Yourself a Fortune' funnels that pointed so temptingly to sixpences and half-crowns. Cakes and lemonade were tempting but costly. There were only the swing-boats left. We wandered over to their corner, the red, yellow and blue fancy paintwork cheering us. 'Like on 'Ampstead 'Eath, innit . . .' said Winnie as we watched the gaily painted boats pendulum to and fro, the long ropes with the coloured furry ends clutched tightly in the hands of the lucky children. 'Cor, some of 'em's scared, Mister, pore lil things . . . need a bigger girl in there, they do.' The man didn't seem to hear; Winnie sighed. ''Ow much fer a go, Mister?'

'Tuppence each,' said the man as he bent to raise a long pole. We watched as it touched the curving bottom of the moving swing-boat: scrape, scrape, up and down – the man held on till the swinging ride had stopped. Two little girls climbed out on to the bright yellow steps. The man wiped his brow; Winnie nodded. I wished I hadn't moved along to the last boat; they were talking about something.

'All me fam'ly's in fairs,' Winnie was telling him. 'Ain't that right, Rachael?' – she turned to me. 'We're fairground ourself, ain't we?' I stood amazed at my new name, nodding to shake it in rather than to agree.

The man came over. 'All right, kids, two of yer in the boat an' four wiv the poles. A bloke's gotta 'ave some breather. Know where the beer is?'

We shook our heads, but he'd already lost interest in our faces. Winnie was thrusting Pat and Connie into a swing, telling them how to cross the ropes and pull. Soon they were happily swinging. 'Better stop them two now' – Winnie pointed to the adjoining boats. ''E'll be back soon an' we won't get a ride, see. 'Cause why? 'Cause there ain't no beer around.' Together we struggled with our long pole, Joyce and Jessica copying. Crumbs, it was heavy! And when that thick-shod boat bottom crunched against it I was nearly hammered into the ground. But Winnie hung grimly on, already understanding that you just slowed it down. She ignored Jessica's roar of laughter as I scraped myself up off the muddy ground. 'Not down. *Up*, yer silly ninny, *up*!' Winnie's red face puffed the words at me, and with a long shuddering '*dj-ah-ahrr* . . .' the boat was finally brought to rest. 'Blimey – whew!' was all she could say as two worried-looking kids hurried away down the steps as fast as their little legs would carry them. 'Come on, Rachael!' We climbed into the hanging boat and exchanged furry rope-ends. We pulled and were soon swinging higher and higher. Winnie stood up for an even longer pull: 'An' when 'e comes back, yer talks Cockney, *Rachael*!' I couldn't nod, it would spoil the pull, the smooth sharing timing . . . So I yelled . . . something. 'Yea, s'orlright so far' – my turn to pull. 'Nah, more shoutin' . . . but try not ter say nuffin' . . . an' if yer 'as to . . . you're '*orses*.'

The ropes scraped, hers slackened, mine now – what had she said? 'I'm what?'

She sat back down. ''Orses. Up on yer toes in a bally frock.' '*Whoomp*' went the boat, and up, me now, me, Rachael of the bareback horses – crumbs, Winnie couldn't half think them up! Winnie grinned, I smiled back, my grasp sunk sure in the coarse thick mane. Ballet could wait. The horse was enough. A jarring stumble, just the bumping crush of the man's long pole. The grasp in my fingers already knew rope-ends.

We sauntered towards a big white tent. Brassy music like they play in parks on Sundays was coming from it. Something else joined in. Men's voices. 'All through the night . . .' Oh crumbs – pennies – and four o'clock, and our eyes watching only a hand turning the front-door latch . . . Too late now.

'I'm fed up with this silly old Feet anyway,' declared Jessica.

'So'm I,' we all decided together.

At the gateway only the empty table waited. We stared unbelieving. 'Bloomin' cheek! *Anyone* can get in! For nuffin'!'

Mrs Sleweslin's brown-and-yellow-frocked shape buzzed in and out of the dining-room. Pat and I were to have only milk and a digestive biscuit. The clatter of cups and saucers. A dropped spoon. Pat's head hung low over her milk and mine tried to do the same. But the angry buzzing waspy shape moved from kitchen to dining-room. Knew all about it, she did. All about The Fête. Oh the shame! Never in the whole of her life . . . More rattling in the other room; the man murmured something. The buzzing went on. Never again could we be trusted outside the door. What sort of home did we come from? I stared into the milk, seeing little solid bits clinging to the side of the glass. The voice rose: 'No! It's the eldest one. A bad influence.' My face felt all red. I peered harder. Milk wasn't a solid white liquid, not like water; now water was colourless but solid, it didn't have little tiny hardly seeable specks that clung. 'It's my best I've done, to be sure. But *Gangs!*' My attention drifted back to the digestive biscuit. They didn't understand. It hadn't been any use trying to explain. Fancy saying 'Explain yourself!' and then buzzing about and not caring that you were trying to. 'Not even *sorry* . . .' She'd ignored the tears and sorries, treated them as if they hadn't ever been said. Believed they hadn't, even. 'There's no more playing out for *her.*' The biscuit broke under my fingers; I scraped up the crumbs and sat holding them. The buzzing was quieter now. The sound of water filling the kettle. I looked up, trying not to let myself shake with the crying.

The man's face looked kindly. He put the kettle on the range and with one last, almost sorry, glance went back to where the buzzing sound grew again. Pat's hand crept over to mine. We sat at the kitchen table together, crying quietly. We'd been naughty and we knew it. Why didn't she hit us? Why didn't she hear us? Oh, why, why, why . . .?

The relief of being back in school was shared by everyone. We were sick of the long holidays, glad to be away from those imprisoning, seemingly topless mountains, the black choking dust of the coal tips and the endless rattling of the clanging iron buckets. But most of all we enjoyed just being ourselves among our own kind, the English evacuees, hearing from our teachers the spoken English we knew, reciting the poems as they would have us speak. Even just speaking it badly among ourselves, it felt right. School, with its scratching pens, timetables, difficult spellings and blue-check dusters, was where we wanted to be. Even Winnie had sobered down, head bent over her books, tutting over ink-spills she'd never bothered about before.

Yes, we were glad to be back under Miss Daley's watchful eye. Miss Daley, who'd been somewhere called home, had brought something of it back with her. Those shoes had walked London streets. That costume was surrounded for ever by London air. Her very hair and hat had been touched by London rain. We'd collected a sort of quiet pride about our Miss Daley. Inside her school everything was ours. The things we knew or didn't know were marked in red ink, whilst outside there seemed to be an endless maze of differences with no red ink to mark the way. We needed school, and we needed it to be ours; it was for many of us linked with all the foggy memories of places called home.

Chapter 17 ~~~

The smooth-worn seat of the lavatory felt cool and solid to my naked bottom. I'd wanted to wee for ages and ages, yet the cold darkness had kept me lingering on the edge of sleep till I could wait no longer. It took me a little time to realise that something was wrong, though. My nightie – had I rolled it up? Of course I had. No, it wasn't my nightie, it was my feet. They weren't cold.

Nor had they touched the furry woolly rugs. A slow drowsiness was coming; never mind about that now, sleep was claiming me . . . sleep . . . Suddenly I was shocked awake. Had I walked in my sleep? I felt the wetness, still warm, clinging to the back of my nightie, my hand raced down the bed, felt the damp patch underneath me. All sorts of mixed feelings were blotted out at the thought of what Mrs Sleweslin would say. I felt myself begin to tremble lying there in the dark wondering if I should go and tell her now – get it over with – be punished. But the house was sleeping; no sound broke the still silence within it. Then suddenly the familiar wail of the air raid warning shrieked its high-and-low sound around the valley; Pat stirred sleepily.

'Pat! Pat! It's the *warning*!'

She sat up, rubbing her eyes. 'Eh . . .? But it's *night-time*, 'Ild . . .'

Sounds from the next room. More sounds from the street. Doors, windows being opened. Shouting men: 'Take cover! Take cover! Put that light out. Put that light out. Take cover!'

The wail began to wind itself down. Up high in the sky the droning buzz of a thousand bumblebees coming from a long long way away. Our door opened. No light on the landing. The dressed shape of Mr Sleweslin lifted Pat from the bed. 'Come on. Don't worry, bach, I've got you safe.'

They were gone. Gone out into the darkness, and I was left. Nobody had got me safe. The buzzing was getting louder. A sharp rattle of the door-knocker, shuffling feet in the street: 'Under the stairs – take cover under the stairs – it's enemy planes.' The voice hadn't waited for the door to open, it had moved on up the road, rapping and calling the same thing at other doors.

'Dew! Dew! There's a business!' The man's voice down there in the passage. I cringed down into my wet patch. The Germans, maybe Hitler himself, they were up there. Oh God, dear God, I'm frightened! Take them away. Please, please, take them away. 'Come on, girl. Never missed you in the dark . . .' Mr Sleweslin was reaching out for me. Great big sobs burst out of my shaking fearful body; the wet nightie clung to my back like an evil burden. 'There, there, no need to cry, bach, it's safe we are here, see, safe.' The man carried me swiftly down the dark stairs. I tried not to cry; the effort was a strangled choke. 'It's a terrible state she's in, Mam.' The man had sat me in his big basket chair. I was trying to speak – trying to say all I felt about being saved. But the wet nightie was being replaced by a knitted blanket thing. 'Shock. There's shocked she is.' The man had turned his back, was making tea. The lady shushed and murmured; Pat started to cry. 'Dew, Dew.' The man comforting Pat; dry sobs still shaking themselves out of me.

A hot drink. I felt quieter. Now I could say 'The bed . . . the . . . bed . . .I've been an' wet . . .' – tears I didn't know were left inside me rained down my cheeks.

'Shocked,' said the man again, his eyes kinder than I'd ever seen them.

'And you saved me.' The tears rained, the sobs wobbled my words. But I still had to say them. 'You came back. You never left me alone, not like – like Mr Bryn did. You . . . saved me too.' All the fear had washed itself away, I was still crying my blessed thanks to the man.

Why didn't he say something? I raised my face to see and saw his stricken shocked look. A rigid stiff face. That was looking at me. 'What? What?' The lady was angry – behind me somewhere and angry. Pat was being led from the room.

'It's under the stairs . . . the warden . . .' The man sounded as if he was talking to Pat in his sleep.

Mrs Sleweslin bent over me. 'Tell me, girl. Go on, say it. When? When?' The voice was tight, as if holding back a terrible anger; I shrank into the chair, too fearful to cry now. Words tumbled out. Words that told of Mr Bryn taking Pat away on the night of the big thunderstorm. How he'd saved her. I'd heard him say so. And how I'd waited and waited to be saved too. But he hadn't come back. No one had come. There was no sound when the tumbling words ceased. But somehow the man was back in the room as if he'd never left it. They were staring at me with cold, hard faces. 'That's not true! You are a wicked little girl.' The lady's voice harsh like rocks, cold like the glitter of a dinky-curler that had slid out from under her frilled sleeping-cap, a cap she suddenly pulled off and covered her face with. But if she was crying I couldn't see. She'd turned away, leaving me to stare miserably at the hard metal clips. I couldn't say anything at all, but I did see how she'd taken that frilly softness to cover her face.

The All Clear was sounding; Pat was in the man's arms. 'Go to bed.' The lady was upright, tying the cap over the curlers.

*

The night warning had set the housewives chattering on doorsteps. Real Germans had flown over their mountains. Out in the streets they'd been watching. Mind you, it was said that a certain big town away to the coast had been the target. Whispers and shaking heads. They'd had to turn back. Oh indeed yes, lost they'd been. Lost in those mountains. The wardens. Late they were. But brave. Indeed yes. Even the children talked and laughed about being stuffed under the stairs, under beds, or forgotten altogether. Some of them had crept out to join their elders on the pavements. To look up, search the sky. But there'd been nothing to see, just the noise, louder and louder.

Yes, there was plenty of talk. But not in our house, not where I was, it was as if I'd been made invisible. After school the dreadful slow walk back to Mrs Sleweslin's; the long evening to be lived. But Mrs Sleweslin was out. The man listened to our Grace. The man puffed his pipe whilst we washed up at the sink. Then she was back. Hat and coat still on, she beckoned the man. They went up the long passage into the front room. Pat and I sat on the stools and waited. Waited for the relief of bedtime.

Next day, another morning. More silence for me. Yet I hadn't wet the bed.

Still the same old chatter at school. The night raiders. Only our teachers seemed to be outside it; they acted as if there'd never been a warning.

At tea time there was only one place laid at the kitchen table: one place for *me*. The thin bread and butter with its spoonful of jam on the side of my plate, a piece of the apple tart we'd had for dinner, scalding-hot tea. Just me and Mrs Sleweslin. Pat was in the garden. The man had taken her there with a bright new blue ball.

The lady said, 'Eat your tea. It's upstairs I'll be. You're to come there' – she was at the door – '*when you've finished.*'

A numb sort of feeling grew inside me. What was happening? What – oh please, please, what? The bread and butter must be eaten. I choked it down. Now the pie, and tea. My mind had made itself up. It was time for the punishment. I was to be caned or something in that bedroom. I went up the stairs on trembling legs, glad that I'd washed up my tea things first. Now there was only the caning. It would hurt. I tried to pretend it didn't matter, and no, I wouldn't be a baby and cry now. I'd earned this beating. And after it was all over I'd be different. I tapped on the closed bedroom door. It opened. The lady pointed to my best blue coat. She was closing a packed case. My case. My eyes searched for Pat's case. Mum was coming, she must be. A look at the lady's face. No other case to be seen. Only one powder-blue coat. Words, as we went down the stairs. 'Best for everyone. Mrs Jones is expecting you. All arranged it is.'

The front door was open; she gave me my case. 'Just over by there, next to the ivy. Sixteen it is.' The door closed behind me. I stood on the pavement strangling back my longing to cry out, to beat on the shiny door. Pat, oh Pat! Let me be with Pat. I'll do whatever you say. Just let me be with Pat! A tear trickled. I wiped it away with my hand. I moved slowly, across the road to the side with the ivy-covered wall.

Steep broken steps led up to a long bare garden. A mud path set with stepping-stones took me to the dirty-green door. Three blank-eyed windows with yellowing lacy curtains silently ignored my coming.

The knocker was rusty and stuck as I lifted it. I rapped on the door with my fingers. The silly knocker fell, suddenly making me jump with its dull crunch. Footsteps on lino. The door opened a few inches. A grinning face, a face I knew. Bridget, a Cottage Homes girl. I tried to smile. She chuckled, pushed the door to a narrower slit and called:

'It's *her*. She's here. Shall I let her in?'

Chapter 18 ~~~

Mrs Jones looked tall. She sat, still wrapped in her overall, by the glowing fire in one of the three wooden armchairs that were grouped around it. Her faded pale hair was held in a bun at the back of her long thin neck. Grey eyes, wandering lazily towards me – over me – then past me to where Bridget stood. Mr Jones, grimy with coal dust, lay back with eyes only half-opened, his huge hands clasping the wide leather belt that fastened in a big metal buckle. His thick stripy shirt had no collar and the sleeves were rolled back, showing short black-hairy arms. Nobody had said anything yet, but Bridget gave a giggle. A slow smile started on the lady's face; I smiled too. But her smile was going past me –

I looked to see where. Bridget's mocking stare dared me to keep looking. I turned away, seeing the oilcloth-covered table, four straight-backed wooden chairs, a cupboard and a shelf that held crockery, the lino-covered floor with a strip of coconut matting in front of the range, a high strip of small windows, a high mantelpiece. Two vases with an alarm clock. Papers and letters stuck out from behind the hanging mirror. Still nobody said anything. The man heaved himself up out of his chair, hoisting his trousers, tucking in the thick flannel shirt. Surely I'd come to the wrong house? They didn't expect me. They were waiting for me to explain. Yet Bridget had called 'Shall I let her in?' I felt the edge of that panic again – what if they *didn't* let me in, where could I go, what would I do? I'd pushed at the door fearful of the all-alone-belonging-nowhere feeling. The giggling girl had known what I'd do; she'd let go of that door at just that moment and I'd crashed into the passage and fallen on to the bottom of a flight of stairs. Her laughter was quiet, not friendly, not to be shared; her face was a blur in the dark passageway, but she'd stood with her back to the closed front door as if defying me to get out of it.

'Please, is this Number sixteen . . .?' My voice had decided that it would ask; my mind was ready to listen to the instructions that would tell me of my mistake.

'It *is* Number sixteen, *Miss*. Let me have that case. There'll be none of *their* fancy ways in this house. It's once you'll be told, see . . .' The man had taken my case. His coal-rimmed eyes, still hooded by the heavy lids, weren't showing the windows of his soul; a jerk of his head was to be obeyed.

Out into the dark passageway I went. Another command, grunted this time. I climbed the slippery lino-covered stairs. He brushed past me on the square of landing, opened a door, put my case inside and pointed to two hooks on the back of the door, a row of nails on the wall. And left me.

Two long windows reached from the low ceiling to the floor. Only the lacy curtains hung there; the floor was only partly covered with lino, the rest was bare boards. A low chest. A case. A bed that seemed low enough not to have any legs. A chair. And that was it. A hairbrush, comb and framed picture stood on the chest, whilst a nightdress-looking thing was folded on the chair. Three of the nails held frocks, Cottage Homes frocks – one checked, one flowery and one plain.

I stood there wondering what to do, but already my fingers were unbuttoning my coat. I hung it on a proper hook behind the door, then I crept to the windows, peeping at the Sleweslins', looking for some sign of Pat: Pat who would surely run out at any moment, Pat who must know by now that I'd gone. I took off my glasses to wipe away the tears. She wouldn't come, they wouldn't let her. And oh dear, I didn't want to stay here, I had never liked Bridget Connors, her tilted eyes and curly hair framing a wide freckled face that mocked so easily. 'Merry Bridget' her Cottage Homes friends called her. But once in the quiet cloakroom I'd heard what Miss Daley had called her, and of course to her face: 'Malicious'. I didn't know what it meant, but it fitted her better than Merry.

A sound behind me: 'This is *my* place, and you better remember it, see.' Merry Bridget stood there, hands on hips. I nodded. 'Crybaby. Pee-the-bed. Well, you just do it on me and see what happens' – I didn't know whether to nod or shake my head. 'You gotta come downstairs now. They're wonderin' what you're up to.' She glanced around the bare room. 'Better open that silly old case.'

'I don't know where anything goes yet,' I said, anger making me bold. But she was snapping open the locks. Neatly packed clothes swirled all over the room.

'There. That's only a *start*!' She was gone, slamming the door behind her.

Astonished and angry, I picked up my clothes and put them back inside the case. It was then that I missed the doll. Frantically I searched the bare room, desperate to find the little green-dressed doll that was mine; she'd be smashed but I had to find her, I had to. It took me a long, long time to accept that she wasn't there. Never had been and never would be. I huddled down on the end of the bed and cried like a baby. Cried for a doll that had never been mine.

There wasn't any bedtime, the ticking clock needn't have been there really. I sat on the straight-backed chair drawn up to the kitchen table, studying the faded marks in the squared oilcloth. The uncle – Uncle Emrys – had gone for his drink at the Workmen's Hall. His big empty chair shielded his big heavy working boots from the bare light bulb that lit the room. Bridget was in the middle chair facing the fire, legs doubled under her, writing a letter. A letter was also being written by tall, thin Auntie Gwen. Now and then they exchanged the letters and whispered together before exchanging them back. Sometimes one of them coughed and I'd look around. But it was only to meet a sort of who-d'you-think-you're-looking-at stare that waited there for me.

I stared at the wooden skirting that came more than halfway up the wall. It was varnished. Scratched and chipped in places. But the sworls were interesting, so were the pretended knots that real planks truly had. Green shiny distemper went up to the windows. Blackout boards pegged side by side, one two three four. Each had four pegs. Now multiply that by four.

I yawned. A sigh of irritation behind me. Where, I wondered, was the sink? The lavatory? And was that the door to the scullery or the yard? Auntie Gwen was shy of me; I could feel her peeping now and then. I'd smile at her next time. The sound of tearing paper. Bridget receiving an envelope. Writing on it. Auntie Gwen going to the under-the-stairs cupboard. A coat. No, two coats. Bridget getting a jug; a greyish tea towel to cover it.

'It's not afraid to be left you are?'

I looked at the grey eyes, shaking my head. 'Please – where's the lavatory?'

Bridget shrugged into her coat. Impatient fingers waved to the other door I'd been wondering about. 'And be careful. No lights. It's heavy fines for that. You can go to bed if you like. There's a rubber sheet on your side and it's washing the wet sheets yourself. So . . .' She shrugged. They exchanged smiles and went to the front door; a slam and they were gone.

I lifted the latch and found myself in the scullery. A sink and a copper and a long tin bath. Rubbing-board and two buckets. Another door. An iron lock-thing on it. An outside door, then. But no blackout over the tiny window.

Quickly I pulled the door behind me shut. The darkness closed all around me. I was afraid, but I had to find the lavatory. My hands raced around the feel of the rough stone wall – a sigh of relief as they felt wood. Now fumbling for the latch. Lifting it . . .

The door wouldn't move.

I tried again, panic racing through me. *Was* there someone in that dark scullery besides me . . . ? I raced back to the kitchen door. Opened it. By its light I'd see. Heart racing, I forced myself to look. There was no one. I looked at the door that wouldn't move. Bolted at the top. Tempted to leave this friendly light to show me the way, I ran and leapt for the bolt. Now back, to close myself in the empty darkness again. Nothing there. Nothing there. Lifting the latch. A small moonlit oblong yard. Steps going upwards. I forced myself to climb to find the place. Yes, there it was, outlined in the moonlight. A shed like Carrie's. Leaving the door open, I found the hole in the wide seat. Eager to be gone, I weed as fast as I could. Raced back to the open house door. Entered the darkness. Made myself stay to move that bolt upwards. Then scurried for the light of the living-room. Sat again at the table and waited. Four fours are sixteen. Twenty-four squares across the table. How many along it?

How did I go to bed? There were no blackouts. No lights. Nobody to ask. But it was a quarter to ten. They'd left me so that I *would* go to bed. I hadn't known how afraid I'd be all alone in a night-wrapped house. A quick dash along the passage? No. *Walk*. Walk because you're *not* afraid. My heart was, though; it beat its fear against my chest and hammered as I carefully climbed the stairs. The bedroom was lit by moonlight. Those plain yellow-washed walls were all lacy now.

The worst part of being alone is taking off your clothes. They have to come up over your head. And then you can't see. You breathe faster and faster. And then you sit holding a pale nightie. It's got to go on. Yes, it's got to go on. You have to cover your head again.

Saturday morning. A dry bed. Bridget shaking me awake. I sat up, saw the candle-stub in a saucer on the chair by her side of the bed. 'You got cat's-eyes?' she said, brushing her hair.

'I didn't know the candle was there. 'Sides, there's no blackout.' I didn't really want to talk to her, she was only mocking me anyway.

She laughed. 'You haven't guessed, then?' Her eyes went from the bed to the two windows. I shook my head.

'Well, I'm not tellin', see. An' you better get up. Or have you gone an' peed?' – she ripped back the covers and pulled me off the bed. 'Huh!' She was disappointed. 'You *will*.' Now her certainty had me worried. 'Come on, give me a hand, Four-Eyes!' She was dragging the grey blankets back up the bed; there wasn't a topsheet. 'You hear them last night?' I shook my head, wondering what she meant. A slow smile spread over the wide face, tilting the brown eyes impishly. 'He gets drunk,' she whispered. She walked back to her side of the bed. 'That's *your* side, see, you can't come over here at all, it's mine. The whole place is mine really, but she gets extra money for having a Pee-the-bed. And sheets too. But it's me that's gotta put up with you and I don't even *like* you, so *there*!' Her invisible barrier had taken the side of the room that had the chest, chair and nails, leaving me my side of the bed with its thick red rubber sheet showing beneath the edge of the blankets and two coat-hooks on the door. 'Here's your old case.' She sent it crashing across the room. My folded-yesterday school clothes flew after it. I cowered against the door. Her show of dislike and bad temper was covered all the time by either that smile or a treacly chuckle. Merry Bridget enjoyed her feeling of dislike.

The door burst open. Uncle Emrys stood glowering around the room. Bridget was tidying the top of her chest. A sweet smile over her shoulder to show she was really quite busy.

The man seized my arm. 'There'll be none of that bad temper here. Now get dressed. It's downstairs, busying yourself with the cleaning. It's not room for *ladies* we do have here.' He'd released me; I backed into a corner, nodding.

'I did tell her, Uncle Emrys' – Bridget managed to draw his attention to the spilt case, the heap of clothes.

But the man's look was one of amusement. 'Oh, Bridget, Auntie Gwen's made the coffee. Come before it gets cold, bach.'

'Yes, Uncle. Soon as I've helped.' Bridget was meekly sweet.

'Leave her to learn the hard way,' said the man. They went away, leaving me bewildered about what had been going on.

Downstairs in the kitchen they sat round the fire in the wooden armchairs. A cup of cold coffee beside a plate that held long-ago-made toast. There was nothing else on the table, and their stares made me feel like a stranger just arriving. Nobody would think I'd been here since tea time yesterday. My 'Good morning' was a habit. It just happened. Bridget made a choking sound. I sat at the table and said my Grace. There were more titters and chokes, but I didn't look up; after all, I was late joining in their day. The toast was hard and leathery. There wasn't a knife, so I did the best I could with my fingers, aware of the peeping. I felt the shyness coming back. Now they were all staring. I asked if I might please leave the table.

'Can't take it *with* you, can you!' the man snapped. Bridget and

Auntie Gwen were pleasing him with peals of laughter. I tried to smile, but the man wasn't interested. Nobody was.

I left the table – at least, I stood up and pushed my chair back, collected my dishes and went to the scullery, where I washed them in cold water. Went out to the shed and came back to stand and wait to see what we had to do first. I stood there by the table. Not a head turned. Should I sit? No. You had to be told to sit down. Somebody would say something in a minute. I waited. And waited. They smiled among themselves; no words passed between them.

Perhaps I was standing in the wrong place?

Should I move nearer to them? No, better ask first. 'Please, what shall I do?'

Bridget's head turned to stare. Auntie Gewn looked as if she'd just woken up; her hand went to a coal-dust-looking smear just under the edge of her eye. The man yawned loudly and turned his back even more towards me. He whispered something to Bridget, who nodded, giggled, and bent to Auntie Gwen. They all looked up at the row of windows as if the answer would come from there. Uncle Emrys stood up, snapping his buckle. He went to the cupboard and threw out some rags. 'You do the putting-on, Bridget.' Auntie Gwen was touching the smudge on her face again, but she'd turned away to do it.

Bridget got up at once. 'Thank you – the windows are my fav'rite 'cause they shine up ever so nice if you rub hard.'

The man took the kettle and went to the scullery. He returned with a steaming bucket, a bar of soap and a cloth. 'There you go, Bridget, plenty of soap now . . .' Bridget climbed on to the table and began to wet the windows.

'Please can I help?' I asked, bending eagerly to scoop up the waiting rags.

'Of course!' They all said it at once. I felt silly. Daft as anything. But they were laughing as if amazed at something. Bridget was rubbing the bar of soap up and down on the glass, being all Merry again. I stood red-faced, clutching the rags. 'I'm sorry, but I've never done windows before. Do I shine them now?' I asked.

There was a sort of hush while they took deep breaths. The man pulled out a chair and swept a mocking bow, sending the other two into fits of giggles. 'Yes, *now!!!*' – he'd shouted the words clear and separate, so close to my ear that I jumped away from him. But seeing the way his face was turning red under all that coal dust, I hurriedly climbed on to the chair. Remembered my shoes. Got down and took them off. 'Oh Dew! Oh Christ!' the man thundered. Auntie Gwen and Bridget were laughing in great gasps, but *he* wasn't; he kicked my shoes clean across the room. A mistake. I'd made a mistake. Climbing on to the chair again, I wondered about standing on the table. Shouldn't there be paper? After all, the oilcloth seemed to be the tablecloth. Or maybe that was wrong too.

My first rubs at those windows were soft stroking things. There was a silence behind me. I could feel them all looking. I tried again, harder this time, up and down, up and down. The uncle sighed. Bridget was stifling her giggles with Auntie Gwen. I daren't stop, though, better try going across from side to side. My rubbing got harder, but the cloth kept getting caught up on the long drying strips made by the soap. I longed to turn, to ask how, but the stares had me fixed there. The soap *wouldn't* come off; it only changed its shape, smearing and twisting like paths across the glass. My rubbing was going round and round, faster and faster – it had to, the soap on the other windows would be drying. At last I moved to the next window. The smears on the first one had spread to a sort of all-over cover; no amount of rubbing changed it. I felt hot, getting near the fire end now, refusing to hear the whispering and tittering, ignoring the man's grunted swearing.

At last they were finished. I climbed down and looked up at them. Crumbs, they'd looked better than that before we'd even touched them!

'Out of it!' Auntie Gwen was sending me out to the scullery. The door was open on to the narrow yard. Bridget came too and smeared the soap on, making signs to someone inside. Someone who'd got a *damp* cloth and was busy with it on the messy windows. The nearly-smiling face of Auntie Gwen.

Now Bridget was getting off the chair. I went to climb up. 'Wait till they're dry.' She took the chair away.

'But . . .' I pointed up to where the inside cloth should have been. *It wasn't there.*

Bridget grinned. "S'arder when they've dried, see. An' *you* gotta learn the hard way, now ain't that right?"

I nodded. 'But that's silly . . .' I began.

She came towards me big and eager. 'What's silly, eh?'

'Rubbing in soap, that's what, it's not the way . . .' my words were gabbled because I didn't really know if I was right, I was just hoping.

The hard thump on my shoulder sent me sprawling against the wall. 'Yeah, *innit*. Just the same, Four-Eyes, you'll *do* it, see. You'll do it or *else*.'

Holding back tears of misery and anger, I waited till the windows looked dry. Then I claimed the chair from the scullery and set to work on my useless rubbing, the back-aching, arm-breaking polishing. Inside they watched and nudged, giggled and drank from steaming cups. There *was* a cup for me; Bridget pointed to it on the table's edge. I began to climb down but a waving hand kept me up there rubbing and polishing, seeing only smears and more smears. I even tried to breathe them off.

Suddenly Bridget was up at the inside of the window pointing to a place. I rubbed furiously. She nodded her smiling face. Turned to the grown-ups for their nods and smiles. I smiled back. They were pleased. Now Bridget moved along the far end. Another place. Hurriedly dragging the chair, I climbed up and rubbed at it. Then another place. And another. Everyone was smiling, everyone was pleased. And although I could still see the swirling smears, I thought that at last – well, I must be doing it right.

Then Bridget clapped her hands and spread them wide. I nodded. She nodded back. I pointed to the coffee. She pointed to the coffee. 'Shall I come now?' I mouthed the words.

'Yes!'

Oh, I was pleased. Pleased that I'd pleased them all. Glad to be able to go inside there and even drink the coffee, perhaps sitting at the end of the table nearest to them.

Only there was something wrong with the back door.

I pushed and pushed. It stayed firmly shut. Silly me! The bolt. Someone had bolted it, forgetting I was still outside. I knocked hard. Then harder. They must have the other door closed. Hearing through two doors, and no proper knocker to hear from – well! And they were talking, or I supposed they must be. Someone would come presently. The coffee cups would be empty and they'd see mine still full up, waiting like me. Only I was out here and it was in there. They'd be sorry, but we'd laugh about it. Yes, we would. A cold gust of wind reminded me of short sleeves. I looked at the goose-pimples. They were taking a long time to finish that coffee. I sat on the chair pulling up my legs, tucking them under

111

the thin cotton of my Saturday frock. It was bright red. Tiny dark-blue flowers with yellow centres. Five tiny navy-blue bows down the front of the bodice. I liked it. Pat liked hers too. Pat . . . what's she doing? Is she missing me? Is she wearing the same frock as me? We were always dressed the same. To show we were sisters, I supposed. First of all when Pat was younger I'd been dressed like Roberta, but then Roberta grew so fast, leaving me far behind, far enough to be dressed like Pat.

I shivered. Crumbs, it wasn't half cold out here! Surely they'd forgotten me? I tried tapping the door again. My feet were cold. Of course! I'd left my shoes inside. The white cotton socks! I looked at the dirty black soles . . .

A tapping. Where? Yes, *there*. I'd spun round, looking up to the windows. There was Bridget beckoning. I pointed to the door. 'It's locked.' She put her hand round her ear; her gaze was questioning. 'Locked!' I mouthed, rubbing my arms and nodding towards the door. She turned to look back into the room. I moved nearer to the door. Now someone would come. Ooh, I was freezing cold!

Bridget signalled that she couldn't understand. Making sure she was watching, I tried to open the back door. It opened at once. I stood staring first at the open door, then back at Bridget, Bridget who was laughing and screwing her finger to her temple. I looked away, picked up the chair and went inside. Bridget was jigging up and down, my shoes on her hands. 'Look, betchoo think they're gloves!'

Her voice. I hadn't liked the things she'd said with it. But her tone was light. Friendly, almost. I joined her laughter. But too late. She'd stopped. That silly '*he-he-he*' sound was mine. No wonder they were all staring. I swallowed the pretended laughing noise, feeling my lip begin to tremble, surprised that it was tears that wanted to come.

I took a deep breath. 'The door. It *was* locked.' But from their faces came a 'wonder-what's-up-with-her' look. 'It *was*,' I whispered. Bridget shook her head. Then Auntie Gwen. I looked at Uncle Emrys.

'There's *lies* you're telling, my *lady*.'

I'd never heard 'lady' said quite like that before. I stared at him. Lies? Lady? *Me?* The room was silent.

'It *is* lies.' His face was telling me what it wanted me to believe.

I felt my head shaking itself. 'No it isn't! I tried. Honest I did! I tried an' it was . . .'

'*No!!!*' he shouted, halting my shaky whispered words. I felt myself going red, wanting to nod, to say yes, to say anything he wanted. But I couldn't.

'A man wants his dinner, woman!' He'd finished with me. Auntie Gwen and Bridget, chuckling now, went out to the scullery. I couldn't help looking at him, but he didn't mind. He even smiled with his red, red mouth that I didn't like. Bending down, I put on my shoes; heard him chuckle. Stayed there hunched on the floor till he roared with laughter. Then I fled. Along the passage and up the stairs to press myself tight against the window. To shiver and cry softly. To wonder and wonder what was happening to me.

Chapter 19 ~~~

'Dinner!' Bridget's call up the stairs. A sick feeling deep down inside me. I had to go down there. I had to. My fingers released the edge of the curtain and touched the blue of my best cardigan. I'd been so cold. But no one had said I could put it on. And you did have to be told. Children had to be told everything they did. They couldn't ever do as they liked. And I'd done just that. Should I take it off? Put it back inside the case?

Footsteps on the stairs. Bridget in the doorway. 'Ooh, I *say*! My, ain't we posh!' Her loud voice must have reached all over the house. I began to struggle out of the pale-blue warmth. She was across the room, pulling it roughly back up my arms. 'Oh no you don't. This is too good t'miss. *She's* comin'!' Her call was for downstairs as she forced me on to the landing. I stopped struggling. It wasn't any use anyway.

Auntie Gwen was spooning out potatoes at the table. Uncle Emrys, already served, was taking great forkfuls of food and stuffing it into his red mouth. 'Dew!' Auntie Gwen's quiet remark as I stepped into the room.

Bridget pushed me further in. 'Sunday best every day, it seems,' she sneered. Whatever the uncle said got swallowed with a great mouthful of food.

'Jesus-something-or-other' came next, food spilling down his chin because he'd been unable to talk and eat at the same time.

A sigh from Auntie Gwen. 'Sit by there. My patience is going fast.'

Potatoes splattered on to my plate. Fingers plucked at the pile of jellied brawn. It flapped on top of the hot potatoes. The jelly began to dissolve, leaving flakes of different-coloured meat to be covered by a splodge of yellow soggy cabbage. My stomach turned over as the water met the jelly; I closed my eyes, not wanting to look; Bridget was quick with my eye-closing bit: 'It's *Grace!*' she shouted. I could feel them staring, but it was my own fault, I shouldn't be late, then I'd be saying it with them. But here I was having to thank God for this wet-looking mess that – wanted or not – I was about to receive.

They were silent.

'You hear that, Bridget? Hear it well, then. You too, Emrys . . .' Auntie Gwen sounded playful. A splattering guffaw at the other end of the table stopped me from looking up.

'Yes, Auntie Gwen. Ever so sweet . . .' Bridget was trying to make it sound like me talking.

I picked up the fork and waited. There wasn't a knife. Hurried scraping sounds told me Uncle Emrys was close to finishing. I still wouldn't look at him. 'Here . . . a knife for you, my *lady*.' He was leaning down the table pointing the blade towards me – a dirty used blade, one he'd put into his mouth often.

I hesitated. The knife came nearer. Reaching for the handle-end, I took it. They cheered. 'Oh, la-di-da!' sang Bridget.

I put down the fork. 'Please may I . . .'

Looks of enquiry. '. . . take the table somewhere else?' Uncle Emrys was highly amused at his joke.

I smiled weakly. 'Er, wash the knife, er – please.' I rose ready to go and do it.

'It's clean. *Clean*, you hear me! Now you do get and use it.' He was very angry. Very angry indeed.

'Cheek!' said Bridget.

'There's flagrant *cheek*. It's over there she'd be getting that from.' Auntie Gwen was talking angrily about me.

I looked down at my plate. Not hungry. Wanting only to drop that dirty knife and run.

'It's every morsel you'll be eating, girl. Or sitting there till you *do*!' Uncle Emrys was towering over the bowed heads, hoisting his trousers, tucking in the shirt. I nodded.

'Eh? What?' He looked up again quickly.

'Yes, Uncle Emrys.'

I had to start. Trying not to use the knife, I managed to scoop up the first mouthful. Squashy wet greens with unexpected lumps of the melted brawn meat. Fighting back the sick feeling, I tried the potato. Watery on the outside, it ran through the prongs of the fork till at last a lump stayed firmly on. It was raw tasting, hard, uncooked. I forced it down. Feeling the watchful eyes. The silence. Slowly I went back to the now-cold cabbage. It was horrible. All of it. Their plates were clear. They'd finished. But how . . . oh God, *how*? More forkfuls. More swallows. Don't be sick. Not much more now. The last to come. I scooped it up, swallowed without chewing or tasting, laid the knife and fork down on my plate and thankfully said Grace.

'Here . . .' I told myself, '*again* I'm wrong.' I'd forgotten they were waiting to allow me to catch up so as to say Grace with them.

'Can we go now?' Bridget was asking me. I looked bleakly round the table. They were all waiting to go, but *I* couldn't tell grown-ups to go. Still they waited. All looking and wanting me to say yes. Under the table a swinging foot kicked me. '*Can we go?*' Bridget's demand brought her face close to mine. I shrugged, looking to the grown-ups. But they shrugged too.

'Oh, *blow* you!' Bridget swung another kick.

'Stoppit . . . you stoppit!' I told her shakily.

'*Temper!*' Uncle Emrys was warning me. 'CAN WE GO NOW?' His bellow flew down the table, my silly head nodded and nodded. 'PRAISE BE TO HIM UP THERE!' he stormed, and everyone said it after him except me.

'*Say* it!' His voice was like a dart. I swallowed noisily.

'Praise be to Him up there!' I'd said it. Their Grace, I supposed. But they were laughing again. I felt ever so sick. And something had gone ever so wrong too. Suddenly I was running for the shed, hands clutched tight over my full mouth.

Bridget and I did the washing-up. Behind us the copper filled with water roared as we stopped now and then to feed the fire-hole with wood and cardboard.

Saturday afternoons we had baths. But first – or rather, second after the washing-up – there was the chicken-mash to mix, cooked potato peelings and some sawdust-looking stuff, messy and smelly. And where the chickens we'd mixed it for were, I just couldn't guess. There was only one towel hanging on the scullery door. We'd wiped the washing-up with it and now we'd dried our hands and arms from the chicken-bucket on it. I didn't feel clean really, that sticky mess seemed to layer itself right into my skin and the wet grubby towel hadn't helped to take it away either. Bridget hadn't spoken since Auntie and Uncle had gone out to do the shopping, but now she was staring at herself in the mirror that hung over the fireplace, looking first at one side of her face, then the other. She'd brought the wet sticky towel in to dry on the fender; steam that smelled all stale rose from it.

The clock ticked away empty time. I sat at my usual place, the table, wondering if I dared hope Mum would come. But it was nearly five o'clock now. Too late.

'Come on, Lazybones, we better get the bath ready, *She's* a proper . . .' Bridget had stopped herself from saying whatever it was that *She* was, but I felt the dislike in her voice. Had she really been talking about Auntie Gwen?

We laid the long tin bath in front of the scullery sink. Bridget had got a bar of hard yellow soap out of the sink cupboard, and something that looked like a worn-out dishcloth. 'Put a bucket of cold in there,' she ordered, and was gone.

I turned on the tap. Wondering. That smudge on Auntie Gwen's face – it hadn't been coal dust or soot but a bruise, and I'd never seen one on a lady's face before, not ever. It must hurt, 'cause she kept on touching it. Oh crumbs – the bucket. I turned off the tap, tipped out some of the water and tried to lift . . . too heavy, now what? A saucepan. I baled away till the bucket was light enough to lift. There, that was done. But that bruise?

Bridget's running feet down the stairs: 'They're back!'

'Copper ready?' Auntie Gwen dumped the heavy bags on the floor.

'*And* the bath. I've done the chicken-mash too' – Bridget was helping her to take off her coat.

'*You!*' Uncle Emrys was talking to me.

'Yes, Uncle Emrys?' I half-looked at him but turned away from his long hard-slitted stare.

'Put the food away. *Move!* Earn your keep – *lady*.' My cheeks

116

stung red; he knew I didn't know where anything went. I got up and looked into the shopping bags. He got up and went upstairs. Bridget was half-turning her head:

'She's nosing through yer bags – be all over the village it will – yer business . . .'

Auntie Gwen leant in the doorway. 'Not before I know theirs it won't.'

Bridget smiled as the scullery door slammed. 'You having your bath now, Auntie Gwen?' she called sweetly.

'I am.' The answer was muffled.

'Silly old . . .' Bridget gave me a sly look, then began putting the rations away. I went back to the tired oilcloth.

Bridget bathed next. I heard the lid thump back on to the empty copper. 'There's your towel when Merry's finished.' Auntie Gwen, pale and damp-looking, was rubbing her wet hair on what I'd thought was the tea towel.

'Yes, Auntie,' I said, looking at the much-used greyish thing.

'Go on . . .' Bridget came running in, rubbing her hair on a similar bit of rag to Auntie's.

'No . . . I'll go, better to be sure she's clean.' Auntie Gwen followed me to the bath. Greyish water twice used and on it floated the dishcloth thing. 'Oh, there's slow you are!' Her prod was rough. I finished undressing and stepped into the nearly-cold water. Scum marks fastened themselves to my legs like garters. 'Oh, come *on* with you!' She pushed me down, scooping water over my hair, rubbing in the hard bar of soap and then more water; a slosh round with the rag and I was out. Finished. The chickeny towel dried my scum-smeared body, and now she wrapped it round my head. 'Get yourself dressed.' And she was gone. I brushed off the crumbly scum with my hand. Now to put on my week-old underwear. The first time I'd ever felt dirty after a bath.

The bus had gone, taking Auntie Gwen and Bridget with it. Uncle Emrys crossed the road to go into the Workmen's Hall without so much as a backward glance at me. I turned away from the bus stop and stared into the gathering dusk. Maybe I'd go and call for Winnie. Her lady didn't seem too bad. My feet started the walk. But at the end of Winnie's terrace I stopped. The deserted, quiet look put me off. Somewhere near the middle, in one of those silent houses, Winnie would be doing whatever Winnie did at this time on Saturday evening. I tried not to think of Pat, who'd soon be finished undressing her doll. I didn't want to think about things like that: me who'd promised to take care of Pat.

I wandered back to the bus stop. It was getting darker now; already the mountains looked like great black lumps. I looked up at the sky. You could see night coming, it was like a big for ever cloud that just went on and on like the miners' choir when they sang 'All through the Night'. Now I remembered how Mr Bryn had sung it in Welsh and Pat had thought he was singing 'Ah! Feed an' 'orse!' We'd laughed afterwards.

I'd been walking up the hill all this time, walking away from the coming night. But sooner or later I'd come up against a mountainside and night would overtake me. Besides, I'd never gone farther than the chapel. Small as the village was, it had its different places. If you lived in one part you hung around there, played there, stayed there, because just up the road this way or that you'd be a stranger. Not that you weren't always a stranger anyway. It's just that you had to know how far your bit of the village extended, and only on Sundays did we ever go up as far as the chapel, the same as on school days when we went the other way as far as the school. So there was the main street, a couple of terraces, some back alleys, the pit-props, the bit of waste ground, and of course the nearest mountain. But grown-ups would send you out of the alleys, the terraces, and off the pit-props. So it didn't leave much really.

I'd reached the vicarage, opposite the end of the waste ground, where a few sheep huddled together bleating in the cold wind. I wondered why nobody bothered about them, not even when it rained. Where were the shepherds? Those kindly men in smocks with long crooks that watched the flock? Not here. We hadn't seen a single shepherd since we'd arrived.

I crossed the road and walked down its other side, slowly. There was nothing to do, nothing to hurry for and nowhere to go. I paused at the post office, fearful of passing too close to Mrs Sleweslin's shiny door. I stood for a little while trying to pluck up enough courage to do it, but something inside me didn't want to go *near* that door, not ever again. I recrossed the road, glancing up at Pat's bedroom window as I passed the house. She'd be in bed now, all lonely. Her second night alone. I shuddered with the cold. It seemed much longer than that somehow.

I wandered back to the bus stop. I'd stand there. Pretend I was waiting for a bus. Pretend I was a grown-up now and waiting for the bus to go home, back to where I belonged.

I stood still and ladylike for ages. The game of pretend had given me a handbag and a case. It had even made me rich enough to have a watch. I sighed like a grown-up, soft and low, pretending the bus was late. Miss Daley had stood here and waited like me for a bus to take her to the place where she would get a train. Only she'd been Miss Daley and there had been a bus; I was me and there wasn't going to be any.

The lady things melted away. It was quite dark now. My lady hands sought shallow coat pockets; my legs stung in the cold of the wind. Crumbs, it was cold! Before the war, that's what I'd think about. Running. Running to get indoors before the chips got cold. Lovely golden chips soaked in vinegar, the newspaper all soggy with it had burned quickly in the fire. And when Mum came home . . .

I leant against the alley wall and tried not to cry. Ten o'clock seemed to be an awfully long time coming. But that faint chugging sound was the bus. It must be, there wasn't anything else that sounded quite like that. I was hurrying through the dark alley to Number sixteen's front door. At any moment the bus would come slowly round the sharp curve, a dim pair of slitted eyes feeling its way through the everywhere dark – like I was, up the broken steps waiting at last by the side of the rusty knocker you couldn't trust.

Auntie Gwen and Bridget would be here soon. People had got off the bus; its dim shape was standing still. Now it shuddered and moved slowly forward then backwards, turning round to go away. Two shadowy shapes were coming across the road: Auntie Gwen and Bridget.

'Ooh look, it's a garden gnome.' Bridget's giggle.

Auntie Gwen was fumbling with the big iron key. 'There's cold it is! Dew! Glad to get back to the fire.' I followed them quickly inside, glad to be with the light again, seeing and feeling the comforting red glow of the slow-burning coals.

'I'll make coffee.' Bridget put two cups on the table. Still wearing her coat, she measured out the condensed milk and bottled coffee. Three people, two cups, one from three is two, they weren't seeing me, I wasn't here, all they'd seen was a garden gnome, my whispered 'Good night' was unanswered. I looked at the two backs huddled over the fire nursing cups of coffee. 'Look at me. See me. I'm here.' A voice inside me that couldn't get out. I went up the dark stairs to the cold, dreary bedroom. Still wearing my coat, I knelt down by the bed. But not to pray. I cried against the red rubber sheet that had brought me here.

Chapter 20 ~~~

I awoke on Sunday morning with the feeling of being late. Bridget was still fast asleep and there were no sounds in the house. There had been sounds, funny crying laughing sounds. But that had been almost a dream, deep and dark inside the night. I got out of bed, thankful that my part of the sheet was dry. The springs made a little sound, recalling a bit more of that dreamy awakeness. Another bed with lots of springs, sounds of a struggle, quiet yet there all the same. I dressed quickly. There had been a bruise on Auntie Gwen's face, and he got drunk sometimes. Did that mean a fight between grown-ups in the middle of the night?

I opened the door quietly and crept downstairs to the warm kitchen. The clock was gone and the kettle stood in the hearth. I lifted it on to the top of the range. Still the feeling of lateness was urging me to hurry. I washed at the kitchen sink, the icy-cold water bringing me fully awake. The hard yellow soap left me with stinging eyes and a Wash Day smell, but the towel I stared at in surprise. It was clean.

Back inside the kitchen I felt the kettle. Still cold. Perhaps it would be hot enough for a cup of coffee by the time I was ready for going out.

I had to stand on tiptoe to comb my hair. Then, without thinking, I sat down at my usual place and stared at the oilcloth-covered table. Did men hit ladies? I didn't really think so. Boys were rough. They could easily forget you were a girl and land you a thump. But a man wouldn't forget.

The kettle still wasn't hot. I'd have to go. But ought I to wake Bridget first? I had to go upstairs for my coat, my best shoes, my hat. But creeping quietly upstairs in my socks, I knew that nothing would be worse than Bridget's mocking. No, she could stay asleep. After all, I'd never seen her in chapel, and if she went to church – well, they'd all be awake by then, surely.

Back in the kitchen. The sooty kettle was beginning to feel tepid.

But I was ready to go. A drink of that icy water would have to do for breakfast.

At the front door, quietly easing the bolt, slowly turning the big key, the same key that had locked me out last night.

Now what? I couldn't lock them in and take the key with me. I stood wondering what I should do. Lock the door and put the key through the letter-box? It was the best thing I could think of. I stood and listened to the dull *clunk* as the key fell on to the passage lino. A surge of happiness met me at the bottom of the steps. Nobody had locked me out, nobody had left me to roam dark, lonely, deserted streets. *I'd* turned that key – and it was daytime.

A few people wearing their Sunday best, just like me, were on their way to places of worship. Far up the hill I saw Pat and Mr Sleweslin about to turn the bit of road that would take them out of sight. I hurried. Even ran some of the way. Arriving breathless but happy outside the chapel. A peep of Pat's straw hat through the going-inside people; a huge sigh of relief, not late after all and the nearness of Pat again.

Inside I walked quietly to the row where Mr Sleweslin was guiding Pat. She turned. Her smile was quick; her hand nearly-waved, but the man had seen; he looked at me and shut his little gate with a click. His arm waved me towards the back. At first all I could do was stand there looking at him. Then someone tapped me on the shoulder, they wanted to come past? No, this man too was sending me back. No, he was *taking* me. Leaving me now, to choose between the two long rows that had no gates, no pens – rows that belonged to nobody, rows that were always empty. Fighting back the tears, I crept inside the last one, the one right in front of the doorway. There was no book, just the bare ledge. Behind me the doors were closed, everyone was here, down there in front of the little organ. A few heads turned to stare at latecomers. Or was it at *me*? Me who stood all alone some six rows behind the rest of them?

The service began. Nothing I could understand, but at least Pat was in here. In her usual place. *Their* place. Where I couldn't go any more. I felt my cheeks stinging all red and hot – why hadn't I guessed this bit? Their house and God's house were theirs, and I wasn't a part of either of them now. But they still had Pat and I'd promised, hadn't I? Promised Mum. No, I didn't begin to understand the service, but I knelt and stood, listened and watched, and waited for the end.

★

Somewhere inside, Bridget's laugh. I wouldn't knock again. She knew I'd already knocked, forcing the rusty knocker down, and now stood here waiting. Uncle Emrys answered my knock. 'Look you! Look who's here!' he called along the passage. Bridget and Auntie turned to look. 'It's the psalm-singer.' They laughed.

'Looks more like the dog's dinner.' Bridget's eyes swept briskly over me. 'She's a sly one, eh? Creepin' off at crack of dawn. Didn't pee the bed, though.'

Auntie Gwen interrupted. 'Oh, not on the *Lord's* Day, she wouldn't pee at all on the Lord's Day.' Uncle Emrys roared with laughter. I felt the heat of the kitchen stinging my cold face, tears spilled down to cool it; they were all laughing, all looking.

'Weeping buckets saves using 'em, eh?' Uncle Emrys settled behind his paper; Bridget and Auntie Gwen whispered and bent over pots on the range.

'I'm sorry, I didn't know whether to wake you up or not, but I left the kettle on' – the words raced out, but nobody anwered. I felt a big shudder all over me. It wasn't any use. They wouldn't answer. Not now. Not ever.

'She's wet the bed! She's wet the bed!'

Wriggling out of the nightie, shivering with fear and cold. The footsteps coming upstairs. Auntie Gwen and the gleeful Bridget had come to see. 'There's a dirty bitch, it's washing it you'll be, so hurry yourself, girl.'

Dressed, I hurried to the sink. 'It's cold water you'll be using; there's soap.' Auntie Gwen was sipping from a cup.

Rubbing frantically into the icy sheet. Now the nightdress. Time to rinse. And rinse again. Find the pegs and run up the long garden. The sheet and nightie waved in the wind like flags telling their own story to those who lived this side of the road. Maybe Bridget wouldn't be first with the news after all. But I wouldn't care, nothing would make me care; head down I hurried up the hill, suddenly finding that Joyce was there just in front of me. And the loud shout from behind: Winnie! Arm in arm we skip-stepped to school – I was me again, all the misery just vanished, out came the knotted-clothesline skipping-rope:

'All-in-to*gether*, girls, this-frosty-*weather*, girls –
When I count *twenty*, rope must be *empty*!'

122

Faster, faster, went the rope; I was last to run.

Uncle Emrys on the late shift. Cold meat and potatoes for dinner on Mondays; luncheon meat on other days. Bread-and-dripping or jam at tea time, and me free as air to leave the whisperers by the fire, to find any of the Gang who'd managed to get out. Together we explored the village, mostly by the back alleyways or mountain slopes. Up at the top end we found the rougher kids who'd chase us away from the slummy-looking cottages that were built right into the mountainside, whilst farther round the hardly used roadway was a deserted chapel with broken windows. Slag heaps too that had leant themselves on to the mountainside. It was dreary. Even worse than our end. But night came soon now and one by one, starting with Connie, the Gang would have to go home. It was Winnie and Joyce who took turns staying later than they should. Then I'd be left all alone. Yes, I'd *say* I was going home. But I was only wandering the silent streets and, as I got braver, huddling on the grassy mountainside. There I could be me for a little while longer.

The last day before we broke up for half term I went to visit Carrie. There'd been no more air raid drills and we'd always waved to her from the end of her street. But the need to see her was growing. Perhaps *she* could tell me what it was that was so wrong inside me? Only to her could I ever begin to try and explain what it was like being me with the Joneses and Bridget. Or was it them being with me?

We left school half an hour early, and my friends sped off to try and get an early tea, to please their aunties this way or that in order to get out either earlier or for longer.

I went along the back alley to Carrie's. My knocking and calling brought her hurrying. Big warm arms held me tight. Soon the tan tea was made and out of a tin came the big chunk of seedcake. 'There's thinner than ever you are. Come on, girl, eat up – eat up.' We sat by the hot fireside, unable to do more than be just glad to see one another.

'There's lucky you came today, bach.' Carrie nodded towards a bulging bag. 'It's going away for a few days, see. Getting things ready, takes time. But there, bach, it's *good* to see you. Now tell me all about the goings-on with that Gang of yours.' Carrie didn't seem to want to stop talking and I felt so contented to let her, to drink the tea and munch the seedcake. Dear Carrie, it was like it always was, she made me feel so happy. I glanced round the room. There'd been some changes. The broom had swept the floor. And the tablecloth wasn't so crowded with the jars and tins. 'Oh, it's *tidying-up* I've been, bach, best to always come back to a tidy house.' I felt a prickle of dismay, Carrie really *was* going away. She meant it. I chewed slowly on, wondering what to say. 'There. Don't look so gloomy, bach! It's only a few days, then I'll be back, see!'

I nodded, smiled, longing to ask *how many* – when – where – why – but the words didn't come. 'I've got a new billet.'

Carrie raised surprised eyebrows. 'Oh?'

I nodded, eager to go on. 'Yes. An' they don't mind if I come out, not ever they don't, 'cept Saturdays when it's the windows and bath time.'

'Well bless my soul. You'll come to see me sometimes?' Carrie's surprise had turned to excitement . . . I was nodding and nodding . . .

I glanced at the bag; Carrie did too. 'We'll *all* come and . . . and . . .'

But Carrie wasn't really listening, she was staring up at the jumbled mantelpiece. 'Been saving, I 'ave – saving all these years, like. Hard it's been, getting the money together, but it's all right now, see, I got the money safe, all of it. Carrie Thomas can go and stand with all the grand folk round the Monument. They do say *all* the names are on it, bach!' The sudden pride in her voice wasn't for herself, she was happy and smiling, reaching for the kettle teapot. No, that pride was for the names on a monument.

'More tea?' It splashed into my cup. 'There's some . . . eh . . . don't come back from the war you know, bach.' I nodded, thinking of us and our labels, the long way we'd come.

'But there's *good* it is that you'll be coming. We'll have one of those singsongs, eh! Soon as I get back. Tell the others, bach. There's a big seedcake I'll be making . . .'

She said other things too. About the fresh air and how it ought to be doing me good. A bit more food, perhaps, but there's nice to be able to play on the mountains. Living with grand folks isn't right for youngsters, it's a bit of love and a lot of fun that makes a happy child. But food too, mind, short though it might be in some homes. Love took care of everything in the end. 'It's being wanted, see, bach.'

*

'Oh, 'Ilda! An' we got it all ready an' all.'

I looked from Bridget to the bare table. They must have cleared it away. 'Oh, I'm ever so sorry. But I'm not hungry,' I said, 'so it doesn't matter. But thank you.' I swung my school hat by its elastic, coat folded now over my arm.

'You *sure*?' Bridget sounded concerned.

I nodded.

'*Quite* sure?' Her face looked really interested.

'Yes, thanks.'

'Quite, quite, *quite* sure?'

'Yes, thanks. Please – I'll go and put these away.'

'Hurry up. We're going to play a game. You like games, don't you?' Bridget's voice called along the passage.

'Er, yes, I suppose so,' I called back, wondering what she meant. She and I had never played any games.

I went back downstairs to find Auntie Gwen and Bridget sitting at the table. Arms folded. Just waiting. Waiting for me, I supposed. I sat in my usual chair. Smiled, showed I was ready to play. They smiled back. But sat still and said nothing. I waited.

'Shall I get the game for you?' I felt worried but didn't really know what about. Bridget giggled. Auntie Gwen sat arms folded, unsmiling. They weren't going to answer me. I sighed inside myself. Stared at the oilcloth. Waiting. Only the ticking clock, the thud of a falling lump of coal. Then I saw the gentle nudge from Auntie Gwen to Bridget. Now. Now they were going to get the game. But nobody moved. I looked at them. They stared ahead. Past me. We sat like that for ages.

Then Auntie Gwen said, '*I'll* get it tonight.' She was getting up.

'Oh Auntie, you must let *me* help.' Bridget was out of her chair.

I smiled at both. 'Can I help?'

They didn't answer. Auntie Gwen smiled as they went out into the dark passage. I smiled back. 'You wait there.' I nodded, wondering about the coming game. I glanced at the clock. Seven-thirty. We'd already waited over an hour. But I didn't mind. I'd seen Carrie. And I'd keep it a secret too.

Oh crumbs, I'd have to go to the shed. Still, if I hurried . . . I ran all the way there and back. They hadn't come back with the game yet. I sat at the table to wait.

At a quarter to nine I knew for sure they weren't going to come back. I got up and looked in the under-the-stairs cupboard. Their coats were gone. They'd planned to leave me waiting and waiting for a promised game. I looked around the room once and took myself off upstairs to bed. It'd made me sad, but I didn't cry. Without really knowing what or why, I had the feeling somehow that maybe that had been the game.

Carrie's stool stood emptily by the front step of her home. Each day we'd race to the corner of her road. Then the first one to arrive and look would slow to a walk and we'd all know. Yet it was over a week now, a whole ten days since she'd been sitting there. We walked on down the hill, disappointed. The weather was much colder now. Grey mists rolled in over the mountains and the drizzling rain came almost daily. And we hated it, or at least the rest of the Gang did. For them it meant staying in under the watchful eyes of aunties who were concerned only about getting damp coats dry and mackintoshes put to drip over the sinks. 'Always thinking of tomorrow' – I'd spoken my thought aloud. But today it hadn't been raining. Well, not yet. The mists were coming, though, and by the time we got home for tea there'd be that teeming rain. And for me later the empty wet streets that waited for my wanderings, those dark lonely walks that nobody could share.

The Joneses and Bridget lived around the fireplace, or if Uncle was 'lates' or 'nights' in the pit they might go visiting Auntie Gwen's sister. But that key always went with them, even if it was raining. Perhaps they thought I visited someone too, 'cause they'd lock me out, raining or not. But tonight I would come back up this hill. It'd be so dark that no one would see me up here where I didn't belong. And I'd go the back way to Carrie's. Sometimes people got curious if they heard a door being knocked on at night.

I went home to the bread and jam. Uncle Emrys was on the late shift. After tea I washed up. Letters were already being written round the fire. Bridget's sister was sending her a parcel for Christmas and a length of material to have a new frock made. Auntie Gwen's excited voice had let me know the secret, though I think Bridget liked that part best of all.

I never got letters from my mum now but she was writing to Pat, or at least I thought she must be because Pat sometimes brought me threepence on Mondays.

Auntie Gwen and Bridget didn't look up as I put on my coat, and we never said anything like goodbye or so long.

I closed the front door quietly, locked it and put the key through the letter-box. Chill drizzling rain spattered my face and legs. My shoes squelched messily each time I missed one of the invisible stepping-stones. I reached out for the first step. Now the second. Careful of the third – it rocks; my hands were now on the cold wet walls guiding me down the rest of the steps. The night was inky-black but I'd at least got somewhere to go, something to hope for. But I was afraid crossing the waste ground – one of those silly sheep would bleat eerily or, worse still, rise up and rub against me, making both itself and me stiff with shock. The steps up over the iron bridge were slippery, the railings dripping wet and freezing cold. And underneath rushed the dark river, splashing and gurgling in a wider dark. But I was across now, passing round the bottom of the huge coal tip, the allotments clotted with little sheds, sheds that blended into the blackness. Only the fence to guide me. But that meant walking close to it: walking in those clumps of wet reeds. The first brush of extra wetness made me shiver as water ran freely down my legs, soaking into my shoes; I remembered the day when we'd lifted our faces and opened our arms to the rain, tried to feel that gladness again. But it didn't come. Rain is different in the all-alone black stillness of the night. I walked on. One hand to feel the way, the other tucked inside my pocket. Not long now. Everywhere seemed farther away at night. The fence was turning a sharp corner, I'd have to let go of it now, cross the rest of the way to the alley without its friendly all-along company. I felt the rough pathway under my feet. Now I could hurry. Almost run if I wanted to. But I mustn't lose the path because then I'd lose the alley. Carrie would be there, of course she would. A few days wasn't nearly two whole weeks. And that empty stool – how silly we'd been – who'd sit outside in freezing weather just to wave at us? Yes, Carrie had been back *ages*. And she'd waited for us to come to her warm kitchen where the tea was ready and the seedcake baked. I was in the alley now, guessing mostly about how near Carrie's gate was. Glad that hers was different from all the other gates. *There!* My hands explored the rusty bed-frame. Next to find my way through the long tangled grass, skirting unseen hazards of old wire and spongy stumps. The darkness of the shed to pass as swiftly as I could. *Now the door.* I stood for a moment to get my breath, wiping a wet face with wet hands. Now a smile all ready for when the door opened. I tapped quietly, listening to the dripping rain. Better knock again, a little louder this time. 'Carrie! Carrie!' at the crack of the door. The window. Yes, tap on the window and call too, of course, so she'd know it was only me. Now I was pressing my face against its wetness, calling and tapping again. All was quiet. I stood there knowing. The stillness behind that window was empty and dark. And Carrie just wasn't there.

Chapter 21 ~~~

Bridget was very Merry. The postman had brought a parcel from her sister: the dress-length had arrived. There were two dressmakers in the village and Auntie Gwen was taking her this very evening to be measured for the Christmas frock. I sat at the table and watched the lovely soft clover-coloured material being draped this way and that. 'There's beautiful cloth, Emrys . . . Must've cost a packet of money . . .' Auntie Gwen held the cloth against herself; its colour seemed to brown over and make her look all yellow, but her grey eyes sparkled. 'Now where would anyone find such cloth at times like this?' She was pressing it closer to her body, stroking its soft woolly look.

'Aw, put it away, woman! Makes you look consumptive!' Auntie Gwen looked angry but said nothing as she hastily folded the cloth back into its brown paper; I bent my head quickly over the bread and jam. 'Suits Bridget, it does . . . suits her to a T' – Uncle Emrys was looking at Bridget as he spoke; she gave him a sparkling smile. Auntie Gwen sipped her tea noisily, not caring about anyone, not even Bridget; she got like that sometimes, I don't think she knew that anyone saw it. But Uncle Emrys did; he liked to make it happen too. I knew what he'd do next. Talk to Bridget and pretend Auntie Gwen wasn't there to hear. He was doing it now. 'It's a treat you'll have coming Friday too, bach . . .'

Bridget nodded, glanced sideways at me. 'Yes, Uncle. All us Cottage 'Omes children are gettin' our Christmas presents just like we was still in the 'Omes, only we're not.' She paused. 'Being a orphan at Christmas is . . . well, it's not like *some* kids, is it?' – she had a whining, sly sound hidden in there somewhere –

Uncle Emrys patted her shoulder. 'There there! Well, it's off I am now, take care you don't slip on the frost.'

''Bye Uncle . . .' It sounded as if he was the last person to step off the world and leave her on it.

The door slammed behind him. Auntie Gwen woke up out of her daze – 'Oh, *gone*, is he?' – her voice pretended it didn't mind.

'Yes, Auntie. Shall we do the washing-up first . . .?' Bridget was reminding Auntie that they were going out and that washing-up took time.

'I'll do it,' I said, knowing that they'd ignore me.

'No, Bridget, let the *lady* do it. And she can make up the fire too.'

I made myself move fast without actually running. They were getting ready and I wanted to be out first, or what would I do with the key?

I washed most of the damp coal dust off my hands, feeling its gritty hardness still lying under my nails. Bridget had at last found a clean petticoat. She was pulling on the red jersey, still being a little orphan girl. It slowed her up a bit because she had to look sort of wistful.

My coat, still damp from last night, covered the warm me with its chill. Uncle Emrys said there was frost. Maybe it'd freeze my coat stiff and the cold wind would blow away the frost leaving it nearly dry, like yesterday's sheets. A dry coat would be nice. I let myself out into the freezing night.

Carrie's? Yes, I'd go the long way, right round the village, upwards past the chapel. The dressmaker for Bridget's Christmas frock would have to live on the hill that went up to the school, wouldn't she, and that's where Auntie Gwen and Bridget would be going. Still, it didn't matter, I'd got plenty of time and they wouldn't really care about anyone who wasn't Bridget the orphan with a married sister who sent posh cloth and sometimes parcels that were almost a secret.

I'd passed the Welsh chapel. I looked at the place with mean eyes. Shrugged.

Passing the pithead now. Loud puffing panting breathing; dull clanks; tearing shrieks of metal chains; railway wagons filled with black chunks of coal. A dirty, ugly place. Yet that's where all the cheerful fires came from, the glowing red-and-yellow coals that warmed and cooked and made the great trains move. And above and beyond all this – crumbs, what a lot of stars there were! And the moon – how lovely it looked with that halo round it: a halo tinted with all the colours you could imagine; the more you looked, the more colours there were. How clear the sky was, too, just full of that twinkling starlight!

Ouch! I'd collided with the fence.

Back in the dreary street. Houses high up on a bank on the other side. A little school to walk past. Some more houses, both sides now. Then a sudden bend in the road; mountain and slag heaps walled the way. Now the deserted chapel. I hurried suddenly, afraid of the broken windows, the deep shadows cast by the tall unwanted building. I was running, lonely and scared, running from the shadows. They were far behind me, but I kept on running. Must get to Carrie's. Houses again, blank and grimy, uncared-for and no wonder. The tips towered up behind them, layering everything with the gritty black dust; dust that crackled under my hurrying feet. A dog barked noisily. I glanced about uneasily, couldn't see it, the barking ended with a sudden yelp, a man bawled something, a door slammed. All was quiet again.

The stool was still there. My hand touched its cold seat, thick and grimy with coal dust. I didn't use the knocker; someone might come from one of the next-door houses to see who was knocking. My knuckles met the gritty windowpane, tapped gently. I waited, even though something inside me was telling me she wasn't there. I hunched on to her stool. Why couldn't I cry? My throat hurt, my body shuddered. *She's not coming back.* I whispered it now, making myself hear. Now the pain in my throat would turn on the tears. I waited for it, waited a long time. Then I got up and walked away.

Chapter 22 ~~~

Uncle Emrys stood watching the kitchen being got ready for Christmas: Auntie Gwen wetting the lino with a soapy mop, Bridget climbing down off the table away from the fresh-washed windows, me climbing up, rags in hand, to shine the glass. There hadn't been any soap smears for some time; soap wasn't so easy to get now. I ignored Bridget's face-pulling. She was outside now, washing the other side. I polished on, trying to get ahead of her. But washing is quicker than the drying part; she drew level with me at the third window, grinning and pretending to be washing my face, throwing the wet cloth hard against the glass. Uncle Emrys grunted. 'No sense of fun, it's a born misery,' Auntie Gwen decided. I climbed down off the table, carefully crossing the wet floor to get my coat. There was whispering and grown-up smothered laughter, but I didn't look round. Bridget came in from outside. I passed the scullery sink, knowing what she'd try and why, but I had it draped over my other arm; her snatch missed and that bucket was only half-empied; she couldn't leave it. I'd timed it just right, got it all worked out before it ever happened.

The yard door slammed behind me. Me, the chair, and the rags. I climbed up and rubbed the wet glass dry. Now the driest cloth to polish with. Three shapes down there in the kitchen – don't look, don't listen, move along now, down off the chair, back up again, just polish away, don't think about the two shapes standing inside because at the next window there may be only one. But always at the last window there'd be three again – giggling . . . watching . . . waiting . . .

There, all finished now. *Don't* look at Bridget on the table pointing here . . . there . . . where . . . leave it, it's all part of the game. Put on the coat. No, don't try the door, it *is* locked, quietly locked so you won't hear; they have to play this part, it's not like the soap, it's the real bit, the bit that matters.

I sat on the steps. Cold damp stone like the facing wall. The icy wind wasn't so bad in the shelter of the steps. And I could rest my chin in my hands and not have to look anywhere.

They took turns to peep. Turns to tap the glass. I supposed they even took turns about who would bolt or unbolt the door and how long they'd leave me out there waiting. They waited in there for me to guess *when* that door would open to my touch. But I didn't try to do any more guessing now. It was their game.

'You don't need a coat to clean windows, *lady*!' That's what he'd shouted the first day I'd taken it. I'd stood there holding it, afraid he'd make me put it back. '*Well . . .?*' He'd gone to sit in his chair; I walked towards the door.

'I know. It's for the waiting part.'

★

Sounds now from inside the kitchen. The scrape of a chair. Voices talking, almost calling: 'This way a bit. No, too far. Yes, that's it.'

A silence.

'Green and red? Yes, over here.'

'The scissors? Over there.'

More moving around. They hadn't unbolted that door though. I'd got a sort of feeling about it by now; sometimes I'd even gone away because I knew they wanted me to; it was like that today as bits of crepe paper floated past the glass panes untouched by the cold wind. Already my ears were stinging with pain; the upturned collar didn't help, my neck was too long. The plaits. Undo them. See if that helped. It didn't. I came out of the shed blinded by the windblown hair – crumbs! That wouldn't do. What about a bun sort of thing? My fingers dragged hair down low on my ears. Now tie it at the back. It worked! The sudden warmth made my frozen ears throb worse than ever. I sat in the shed and waited. It wasn't too bad after a little while. Better go and hope to meet Winnie. It was so cold I wondered if she'd come out.

It was then I heard the first stray scraps of sound blown on the shivery wind. It was music. A band somewhere. The sound of carols. I left the yard. Followed the sounds. Huddled myself into the doorway of the Workmen's Hall, never taking my eyes off the black-coated figures with peaked caps and red braid, trumpets, drums, a harmonium, a huge great curly brass thing, the long silver bent pipe that hands moved up and down whilst lips blew air into them.

But the carols! Those sweetly soft tunes we'd sung from the very first beginning of Infant School: 'Away in a Manger'. 'While Shepherds Watched'. I listened there outside the Workmen's Hall, huddled against the cold. Softly singing the ones I knew. My voice gradually got that special sound. The sound that's always there. Waiting. Inside a Christmas carol.

Bridget wearing the new clover frock, her hands tearing at a brown-paper parcel – the flash of a pink-backed mirror, a disappointed sigh as she fingered the matching brush and comb. 'Oh, *you* awake! Come on, get up, it's Christmas! Look at my frock' – she spun herself around, a swirling smiling girl holding a hairbrush.

I sat up. 'It's ever so nice.' It was. I'd never seen a little girl's frock with long sleeves before, and such pretty softness.

'Bet you wish it was yours!' Bridget stroked it.

I nodded.

'But I got lots more yet – and you haven't even looked at your stocking.' She was tearing at another parcel.

I turned to where the stocking hung, still feeling the faint surprise that it was a sock belonging to Uncle Emrys; he'd given us one each to hang up last night.

'Well, go *on!*' Bridget was getting impatient.

I pulled the sock off the bed-knob. 'Happy Christmas!' I said, and began to pull out the first surprise. A magic painting book. Now a cut-out doll book. A dark check pixie hood. Two pairs of socks. A Father Christmas hankie. A chocolate Father Christmas but he was mostly in pieces, only the bright silver-and-red paper told me what it was. Now a folded envelope and inside a half-crown.

Bridget swept all her presents together. I stared dumbly at the soft pink slippers, the sewing set, the big story book, two smaller ones, paints, two red rubber balls, a skipping-rope and a whip and top. All Bridget's. I couldn't believe it. But they'd been on her side of the bed. Father Christmas never got mixed up, not like this he didn't. But I'd wanted a proper book so much.

'You got something else to open yet. I hid it under the bed.' Bridget was friendly again.

'Oh – oh, did you?' I leant over, excited. Here was the real Christmas; Bridget had only teased me. She waited by the door whilst I undid the string of the brown-paper parcel. My heart fell like a stone. A pair of plimsolls and a toy watch. There was writing: 'From Auntie Gwen and Uncle Emrys'.

So I'd got presents, hadn't I? And I'd need those plimsolls in the summer. It was very kind of Auntie Gwen and Uncle Emrys. It meant they must like me a little bit. Didn't it? And Father Christmas had done his best, I supposed he always gave orphans a bit more.

I got up and dressed, picked up all the paper and tidied the bed. Pat! Little Pat all on her own. Was she too undoing a stocking, thinking of me and Mum? Would she be in church today?

At school I'd made a comb-case. I took it from where I'd hidden it at the bottom of my case and went downstairs.

'Happy Christmas, everyone!' Bridget was chattering and laughing, so they didn't hear me.

I went to Auntie Gwen. 'Thank you for the present. I've got one for you' – I held out the comb-case.

'Oh . . . oh . . . but I've got one already.' She was holding pink felt towards me. 'Bridget made it' – a smile going past me – my arm still stuck out towards her, the gift that wasn't wanted didn't want to be refused . . .

'Give it to someone else,' Auntie Gwen said without looking at it. Somewhere behind me Bridget was thanking her for the slippers; giving a parcel – now another – to Uncle Emrys, who'd just come downstairs. I faded myself away from the fireside. 'Oh – there's lovely, look, Emrys! A cardigan!' The navy-blue wool was being held up, looked at, admired. 'Hand-knitted it is too, there's good your sister is, bach' – a big kiss landed on Bridget's waiting face.

'Now *there's* a pair of socks, that's *real* socks, Gwen, just like my mam used to knit they are! There's golden-hearted . . .' – he was hugging Bridget.

I'd stuffed the comb-case down my frock. Nobody would want it anyway, the chatterers around the fireplace had so much already.

I'd better wash.

It was cold in the scullery. Colder in the shed. The misty rain was already coming down off the mountains. I hurried back inside, washed my face and *let* the soap sting my eyes.

The front door slammed. Had someone gone out?

'It's for *her*.' Auntie Gwen's voice. I dried myself quickly. The way she'd said 'her'! Feeling a bit shy, I went back to the kitchen. 'There's your sister been to the door, brought some old doll. Sent up from home she says.' I took the box, peeped inside. Last year's doll, the one Father Christmas had brought to Auntie Vi's. Oh, there was a letter too. A letter from Mum:

Dear Hilda and Pat,
    I am sending the dolls you left behind when you left that last place you was at. The lady there came to see me and brought them with her. She was very nice but don't know where you are now and now she's moving away. I am coming to see you soon. Be good girls.
                        Your loving
                        Mother

The excitement bubbled up. I'd got my doll, and Mum *was* coming! It *was* Christmas!

*

Dinner under the crepe-paper decorations. No Sunday school this afternoon. A silence round the table that made me wonder. Had something happened this morning while I was at church?

Bridget suddenly looked at me, looked quickly back at her plate. Something *had* happened; her face was white and I was sure there were tears in her eyes. Auntie Gwen didn't look up at all. But she wasn't eating, not really. Uncle Emrys was, I didn't have to look, the scrape of his knife and loud chewing were enough to tell me. I wondered what we were eating. Potatoes and greens, yes. But pinky meat with little bones, more bones than anything. What was it?

Bridget kicked me under the table. I looked up. 'Hurry up – hurry up,' said her eyes. I hurried. Together we collected the plates, washed them and put them back on the shelf. Auntie Gwen was making coffee. Three cups again. I swallowed a sigh, sat back at the table and stared at the surface.

'Take it!' said Auntie Gwen. She was holding out a cup to me! Uncle Emrys went upstairs; I saw Bridget and Auntie Gwen look at one another. Something was wrong.

He came back with a bottle of pale golden liquid, undid his belt and slumped into his chair. He was wearing the socks. Wriggling toes inside them. Staring at them. Now at me. 'Get yourself busy with something, *lady*. Get something to do, and for Christ's sake stop *looking at me*!' He'd started off quiet but ended in a shout; I nodded and hurried upstairs. Something to do . . . something to do . . . I stood by the bed, unable to think past there . . .

Footsteps. I hastily found the painting book. The door opening. Bridget, pale as me. She took her books and led the way back downstairs.

'Shut the bloody door, *lady*!' I'd been hardly through it when he shouted.

'Yes, Uncle Emrys.' The whisper sounded loud too. I sat at the table looking at the painting book. Not much there really, *all* of it would take only a few minutes. I looked up at the gurgling sound from the other end of the table. Uncle Emrys, eyes closed, head back, was drinking from the bottle. I looked away quickly. But he'd seen. He stopped drinking, letting the wet flow down his chin.

Suddenly he laughed. Just sat there and laughed. Auntie Gwen rubbed her neck and made a sign to Bridget. Bridget put down her books and walked carefully out of the room. The yard door *didn't* close behind her.

Auntie Gwen waited on the very edge of her chair. Then swiftly crossed the room. That's when the yard door slammed and the laughing stopped. There was the silence and him staring at two empty chairs. 'Wha . . .? Wha . . .? . . . gone?' I couldn't really understand what he'd said, but those empty chairs were doing something to him. He staggered over to them, touched the empty seats and stood swaying over them; the bottle swung up and he drank noisily, nearly falling backwards. Then he really seemed to see again. A huge hand reached upwards, grabbing for the red-and-green paper loops. 'PAGANS! Bloody PAGANS! It's the burning pits of HELL AND DAMNATION waiting for YOU, boyo – HELL AND DAMNATION! HELL . . . HELL . . . HELL . . .' He was shouting, lurching about clutching the bottle, reaching for the paper loops and missing each time. At last he fell into a chair. 'And HE shall come down from the heavens with fiery *chariots*. Damned . . . damned . . . damned . . . all sinners are damned . . .' I was trembling, too scared even to breathe properly; my fingers still held open the magic painting book, but to move . . . could I move now? . . . The bottle was waving again, he was struggling to get up, struggling as if caught up or fastened to the chair. 'O God, help me – help me, it's the real sinners is damned, not me! Not me!' he was mumbling, his head staring up at the crepe paper. 'PAGANS! PAGANS!' He began to sob, really sob; I'd better go and get Auntie Gwen – the light scrape of my chair had him upright, towering over me, fist banging on the table. Shaking with fear, I backed away, the chair falling noisily behind me. *Where to run?* The words inside me were louder than anything he was shouting, he was coming towards me, I stumbled, fell over the fallen chair; scurrying quickly under the table I crouched there shaking, hearing the dreadful shouting, the beating, beating fists, and suddenly the shattering glass that showered from the table's edge, spilling the golden liquid in spattering drops. He was quite suddenly silent, the grey socks sprinkled with broken glass, glass that seemed to be all around them. I stayed there quite still, wondering why he didn't curse and shout again. Then I saw the red stuff dripping. Redder than the crepe paper. The feet moved slightly. He groaned. Still the blood dropped, mixing with the glass and the socks and the lino. I crawled to the end of the table. The door was there. Auntie was out there somewhere. He groaned again; the glass crackled, I turned to look, saw the bent knees, the swinging arm – HE WAS COMING FOR ME – I leapt for the door, hearing a heavy thud behind me; my fingers rattled uselessly around the lock – a sob of panic – then I'd lifted the latch. A backward glance. I stopped. He was gone. Gone. There was no sound. I crept back to the corner of the table and saw that he was asleep on the floor. But he oughtn't to be. That broken glass was under him, and blood.

I ran out into the yard. Auntie Gwen was waiting in the corner farthest from the door. Bridget was coming from the garden with a man I'd never seen before.

'He's fallen over, there's glass and blood and glass and blood . . .' The sharp slap from Auntie Gwen stopped my words altogether.

'That *kid* was in there?' It was the man who asked.

'No. No, she wasn't. She's been here all the time' – Auntie Gwen held my arm tightly. 'She was waiting with me. Bridget came for you, Evan. I was too afraid to leave him. Fell with the bottle he did, it's too heavy for me he is.'

The man called Evan strode into the kitchen. Bridget and Auntie Gwen waited by the scullery sink.

'It's water – get some water. Cut bad he is – cut bad.'

I ran then. Ran and ran far up the mountain path, panting and puffing to get to the top, I must get up there, quickly, must get away, a long, long way, a long, long time . . .

I sat for a long time at the edge of that flat-topped mountain. There was no other side. Just misty flatness. Low stone walls. Sheep. The mists coming nearer, bringing damp specks – fresh clean specks – like Wash Day. Yes, it *was* Wash Day. Not Christmas. Not really Christmas at all.

Chapter 23 ～～～

'There's laryngitis *she's* got.'

Auntie Gwen took no notice of anything. She was rinsing red patches off my soaking-wet frock; the blue cardigan was neatly folded on my chair.

'Now out of that petticoat. Dew, it's soaked to the skin you are.

If it's playing out' – the petticoat was tugged over my head – 'it's a *coat* you need, see – a *coat*!' She pulled at the vest. My arms felt stiff and useless. Bridget was there holding my nightie. Words moved inside me. My lips moved, but no sound came. I moved towards my cardigan. 'No, not there' – I was being taken to a big wooden chair. Now my legs wouldn't move. More words tried to get thought, to be spoken. There wasn't anything to think, though, only things to see. My cardigan. The cocoa, hot and sweet. Bridget standing by the table watching me, now watching the hands that washed on Wash Day. Only it was night. The blackouts were up. Bridget had done them, last night? Helping hands and a light. The bedroom. The rattling sounds made me start. 'The bucket – you can use it in the night. I'll leave the candle alight; don't touch it, eh . . .'

'You're not asleep yet?' Bridget shook my shoulder. Not asleep . . . words repeating inside my head . . .

''Night, I'll leave the door open, call if you want – oh, you can't call, can you? But I'll leave it open anyway.' I nodded. Something about the door being left open for me touched another something. I wanted it open. All the doors must be open. I lay there awake making sure. Watching the flickering light too. There was a blanket over the window, but it wasn't cold in bed. Could I count? My fingers touched the blanket. One! Yes, another. Two! I *could* think, then, laryngitis did let you do that.

Bridget came to bed. Auntie Gwen stood in the doorway. 'She's all right, bach?'

Bridget nodded. 'Funny, she ain't got a temperature though, and she can't even croak.' Her voice was a whisper into silence.

Then Auntie Gwen: 'Be all right in the morning, you see, bach.' She was gone.

Bridget undressed and got into bed. I edged away from her who'd been kind. Facing the door.

Morning. Getting up, getting dressed. Bridget was gone already. I tidied my bed. Three blankets now.

I went downstairs. The 'Good morning' stayed tight inside me – I tried again. Auntie Gwen looked as if she was thinking about something. Bridget gave me a cup of tea. I sat at the table. I felt worried about something.

A little while later Bridget was taking me back to bed. 'Here's your book.' 'Magic Painting Book' it said on the front.

All day I stayed in the bedroom. The doll was something to look at and I couldn't talk, just like her.

After three days I still couldn't speak. This laryngitis did funny things. But I was getting used to it by now *and* I'd stopped annoying everyone by leaving doors open.

Uncle Emrys was ill too. Still in bed. But somehow I'd learnt not to miss him. Not to care, really. Not that I ever really cared. I'd only felt something else before now but when I tried to think what it had been there was nothing there, just a sort of blank that had got cold in its middle.

Winnie took another sniff at the stocking wrapped around my neck. 'Pooh! 'S'more'n camphor oil on '*er*' – she had turned away to face Jessica.

'What's *up* with '*er*?' asked Connie. Winnie's puzzled look turned itself back to me. I shrugged.

'She's a bit white, in't she?' Joyce's whisper had them all nodding. I nodded too: *they* were pale. It was so cold. We'd sat in the hollow for ages. And when they weren't whispering they were shouting.

Shouting at me the way Jessica had: 'YOU'VE GOT A SORE THROAT, HAVEN'T YOU?' Her head was even showing me how to nod the reply. So my shake of the head had been a bit of a shock. 'WOT'S UP WIV YER?' shouted Jessica. I shrugged; shook my head.

'LET'S SEE IF YER'VE A TONGUE IN THERE?' demanded Winnie. I opened my mouth. ''OW LONG YER 'AD IT?' Winnie was looking again at the stocking. I shook my head. I was fed up with the shouting. And all the bits they suddenly thought I couldn't hear. I pulled off the pixie hood and showed her that I'd got *two ears*. They stared at them as if they'd only just grown. Then Winnie giggled. The others giggled. I nodded, adding the nearest thing to smiling that I could.

The rainy morning had sprinkled the playground with snowflakes and hailstones. Girls were eager to get out there, to see and to feel the real winter. But not me. I had to stay in. Sitting and thinking. Because of the laryngitis which Auntie Gwen knew I had. And now Miss Morton knew it. Anybody could know it. And all because of a word. Words were wonderful things really. They were a bit like balls. The same word could be thrown over and over again and nobody would stop and look at it because there was always someone else to throw it to.

The after-play lesson began. Poetry. 'I wish *I* lived in a caravan,' they were chanting. They didn't sound as if they were wishing anything. For the first time I was glad not to be able to speak. In fact I wished I couldn't hear as well. It was my most unfavourite poem. Fancy wishing to be a dirty earringed gypsy feared by everyone, for ever making paper flowers and pegs and living at the wrong end of a horse.

'More Feeling, girls. Much, much more Feeling.'

I wondered how Miss Daley had got so fond of gypsies, whilst we who'd often *run* from them felt only that we'd good reason for doing so. The *whining* . . . at Mum's front door. The lucky face. And the Curses if paper flowers didn't get bought. Miss Daley with a basket and shawl, dirty face and greasy uncombed hair, threatening or blessing with a toss of brassy earrings . . .

Did these gypsies like poetry? Miss Daley did, she'd moved on to Meg Merrilees. Some of it was all right. But *another* gypsy!

Voices chanted, on and on. This gypsy lived all alone. I supposed even the other gypsies wouldn't put up with her.

Then it was finished and up went the blackboard, peg by peg. And on it a new poem. Miss Daley was saying it had been written by a real live tramp. I wasn't looking forward to it. But I read it. Liked it. Decided to learn it:

What is this life if, full of care, we have no time to stand and
    stare . . .
No time to see, when woods we pass, where squirrels hide their
    nuts in grass . . .

I mouthed the words with the rest; heard the words inside me. A sudden nudge from Winnie – her big grin. My questioning look. And the chanting still going on.

AND ME, ME TOO! Those words were really and truly coming out of *me*!

I'd got a voice again.

Someone would keep putting that book on my case. It wasn't mine and I didn't want it. And besides, if I did, how could anyone paint

140

even a magic painting book without a brush? I'd come to get my hat. The pixie hood was warmest, but I didn't like wearing it unless I was with the Gang. Maybe it was the shadow-shape it made when there was a moon.

There was a man in the kitchen when I went back downstairs. 'Hullo!' he said. I looked at him. Then at Uncle Emrys. At Bridget. But he *was* talking to *me*. I fumbled at the cupboard door.

'She can talk again now,' Bridget told him with a smile. I'd got my coat; was struggling into it.

'You do remember me?' The man sounded as if I ought to. I shook my head.

'No?' He looked like grown-ups do when they don't quite believe you.

'I *don't* . . . I *don't* . . .' – my voice raced out.

'*Dew*, there's the *lady* for you, boyo . . .' The man ignored Uncle Emrys; was still looking at me. But I didn't want him to. He was, I thought, a shepherd, or something to do with grass.

'Oh, there's bad manners . . .' Auntie Gwen jerked her head. I could go now.

The man's voice: 'She *didn't* remember me, you know, Emrys.'

I was over the step. Out. The front door slamming slightly behind me. Just another game, I decided. A new one this time.

As soon as light crept through the window, I gathered up the wet sheet and nightie. Perhaps there'd be less trouble if they were already washed and out of sight. I rubbed and rubbed with the hard soap, not really feeling how icy the water was. Now the rinsing, and I'd better try and use the mangle. Washing didn't dry easily in the winter. Quietly unbolting the door, I crept out into the yard. The old coat that covered the top part of the mangle was stiff and white with frost; trails of steamy breath came out of me as I bent and tugged to get it off. Now the beginning of the sheet was in place; the first tugging pull and the rollers gripped it. I could let go now, just turn and turn that big iron wheel, making the rollers squeeze out the flood of water. Now the nightie, buttons upwards so they wouldn't break. My arm ached, but the water trickled. There – it was finished. Wipe the rollers with the stiff frozen cloth. Cover the mangle with the frosty cloth. Tip the water away. Throw the sheet over the line. Four dolly-pegs to hold it, two for the flannelette nightie. The prop was heavy and frozen to the ground. I heaved and heaved; it creaked – moved slightly – another pull and it was free, sending me staggering on the hard ground. Careful to set it at the right place, I pushed up the line, seeing the stiff-frozen washing hanging like boards. Now take the bucket back indoors. A quick glance at the window. Bridget taking down the blackouts. Voices. Auntie Gwen's laughter. I felt the edge of relief: perhaps she wasn't too angry after all. Bridget looked pleased with herself. Auntie Gwen stood hands-on-hips, waiting. *'Well . . .?'* The sharp question halted me just inside the doorway.

'I . . . I wet the bed, Auntie. I have washed the . . .'

'And it's *very sorry* you are, Auntie Gwen, I'm sure' – her voice had cut over mine like a knife. I nodded, gathering the words together, getting them ready to say.

'You ought to give 'er that thing I told you about . . . *you* know . . . the *cure*,' Bridget said, and bit noisily into the crisp toast, a small trace of smile about her lips as she gave me a sidelong look. Auntie Gwen nodded, motioned me to start my breakfast. She was waiting for something. He came a few minutes later, shirtsleeves flapping, bare feet padding, across the lino to his chair. Uncle Emrys. I heard the grunt as he sat down, but he wasn't able to make me see him.

'She's done it again.' Auntie Gwen was pouring tea.

'Soaked she was! An' I ain't goin' ter keep on sleeping with a Pee-the-bed, never had to do it before – not even in the 'Omes I didn't, beds of our *own* we . . .' Bridget's words stopped in mid-sentence.

'There's upsetting it is for a clean decent girl,' said Auntie. 'It's time we put an end to this, Emrys.' Auntie Gwen had finished with the pot; hands on hips, she stood looking down at him.

'Aye, dirty mochyn it is.' His answer didn't do anything to me, I'd blotted him out long ago.

Bridget pushed away her chair and stood up. *'Well?'* she was merrily asking Auntie Gwen. I stared at the toast in front of me.

'Well, Emrys . . .?' The question was passed to him. He grunted.

Auntie Gwen sighed. Raised her voice to shout at me. 'You've earned it, my lady. Patience is *wasted.*'

Bridget came and stood close to me, dragging my hair so that my face looked into hers. 'You're goin' to have a *Mouse Pie*! See? That's the cure. *Mouse Pie*' – a sharp twist and my head was free.

Uncle Emrys was chuckling. 'Just the thing for a *lady*. I've got some traps.' He heaved himself up . . .

'I'll help . . . let me help . . .' Bridget went with him to the cupboard under the stairs . . .

Auntie Gwen turned smiling away from my horror-stricken face, my whispered 'Please! Oh please . . . don't . . .'

'He's found them! He's found them!' Bridget's muffled calls – then Uncle Emrys shutting the cupboard; the wooden clicking sounds – and the skidding rattle as two mousetraps slid on to the table. One terrified look and I was scurrying for my coat, fighting the scream that wanted to come; holding back the sick feeling deep inside me.

Bridget was laying the table. Three soup bowls; three large spoons. Someone wasn't having dinner. The stew-like smell was a surprise, but we did have stew sometimes if Auntie Gwen's sister had been able to get the bones for it. I took my coat off and put the salt and pepper on the table, busied myself looking for the sauce bottle that was for the grown-ups. Ah, there it was. I turned to put it beside the salt, almost dropping it at the sight of a *flat* plate in my place with a knife and fork.

It didn't mean anything. Nothing, I told myself. But my hand shook as it put the sauce bottle down.

Auntie Gwen was dishing up stew. Bridget hung over the big pot. 'Ooh, dumplings! Can I have two, seeing as . . .'

'Yes. Yes, Bridget – patience!' Auntie Gwen sounded amused.

Bridget took her place in front of the steaming bowl. Slurping sounds from Uncle Emrys; he'd already started. I could even hear him from the scullery.

'Come on, *you*.' Auntie Gwen sounded impatient. I hurried, sat down, and quietly said my Grace.

'You're *quite* ready?'

She *was* cross. I nodded sorry-that-I'd-kept-her-waiting. The splodge of potatoes. Watery cabbage. And . . . I closed my eyes, feeling all the sickness in the world gathering inside me. The pie slid on to my plate with a loud *flop*.

There was complete silence. Everyone was watching me. Me, who'd ignored those nightly cheese-loaded traps and all that Bridget had to say about them. Because it was only a game.

Uncle Emrys spoke. 'You just prayed for it, *lady*. NOW EAT IT.'

I swallowed nothing, staring at the pale pastry. One mouse? No, two traps. The sick feeling needed swallowing. Two then? I turned my face away. Four-and-twenty blackbirds. What a silly thing to think.

'*Get on with it!*' Auntie Gwen shouted angrily.

Bridget stared at me, then at the pie. 'Best get it over with . . .' spooning up her dumpling . . .

I glanced at the pie. Were they just lying there soft and furry? Or were they in pieces? I couldn't bear it any longer. The rush to the shed. Heaving sickness and the dry sobbing ache. That *awful* pie. I'd never eat it, never never never. *And* I'd tell my mum. The tears felt hot on my cheeks. I was shaking with fear huddled in the shed, hiding from them and it.

But someone was coming up the garden. It was Bridget. Laughing. Carrying something. The plate. Oh no! I backed away from the shed; she was coming after me, laughing. Suddenly I pushed at the plate, hearing it flop and smash on the ground. Too terrified to look at the split pastry, I ran. Auntie Gwen's slap across my face stopped the bubbling, boiling sound I was making; now it was just ordinary crying.

Him sitting at the table roaring with laughter and Bridget giggling as she helped to wash up. 'She'll have to have one though, Auntie. She'll have *two*, won't she . . .?

Crunching snow under my feet. Everything white and still in the valley. How light it was! Even though the sky was dark and it was night. A few flakes still fell as if spilt from a careless hand. I watched them drift down like lazy feathers to settle without a sound and become invisible on the waiting whiteness. I'd walked up towards the top end of the valley. Even the colliery noises seemed muffled tonight. But already the white-covered slag heaps had black fresh tips from the buckets to crown them. If only it would snow harder, the race between snow and buckets would be something I could watch. I watched anyway because there was nothing else to do. Even the sheep had huddled down close to the ground, uncaring about the snow on their backs. I watched and wondered about them. Where *did* they belong? And why were they never taken inside out of the bad weather? But they weren't really friendly. How would you get them to go where you wanted them? Oh yes, dogs. Sheepdogs. But there weren't any here, only the horrible back-yard sort that growled and barked at the slightest sound. I crunched on up the road, past the top school and houses, round the bottom of the mountain and past the tips. The old broken chapel didn't look nearly so frightening in its covering of white snow. There ahead the back of a row of houses, thick smoke belching from the chimneypots. I stopped to see *all* the chimneys. This was the highest point of the valley, and I'd been here so long, but this night was the first time I'd really noticed all the smoking pots. Down there in the hollow and up here too – all that black against the white of the mountainsides. All the people inside those houses. Blazing fires. Families. Mums and dads to some. I felt the prickle of tears; stopped looking. Carried on walking in my friendly crunching snow. Was I leaving footprints? I glanced. No, not really, the snow was too hard for me to leave much of a mark.

There just along the pavement was the stool, its thick covering of snow already speckled with falling coal dust. I put out a hand to brush off the snow. It was hard. I couldn't move it. I stood looking at it for a moment, not really putting any words to what I felt about that stool and the only chimneypot in the road that didn't have smoke.

Yes, I'd looked. Looked from a long way off. I turned at the corner for one last look. The stool had a rich look about it, as if the snow was satin.

Chapter 24 ~~~

What was this? Crumpled red-and-silver paper; chocolate pieces. Two pairs of new white socks and a cut-out doll book.

None of it mine.

I picked up the book. It wasn't crumpled. But there underneath lay a white oblong envelope. I picked it up; a coin rolled heavily inside it. A half-crown! I knelt there wondering, hearing the chatter and movement downstairs. No, this wasn't a game. They'd have all been sitting silent, waiting to hear something.

A puzzle, this was. I went to put the money back inside its envelope; felt the little crumple of paper. It had been folded once. The crease-mark of that half-crown showed even when I'd smoothed it out of the crumple. My mum's writing: 'With love from Mum'.

That cut-out doll book. I looked carefully and found a smallish 'Hilda' written on the corner of the back cover.

These things were mine, then. But I'd never seen them before. I sat there for ages trying to find the answer. At last I put everything away, saving only the envelope and money. These I tucked carefully into my gymslip pocket. Then I tore out one of the cut-out dolls' frocks; they had plain backs. Folding it carefully I wrapped it in my hankie and left it on top of my packed clothes just under the lid. I'd need it tomorrow.

The post office was really the front room of an ordinary house. A high counter with a mesh window-thing was where you got stamps. Then there were scales where heavy packets were weighed. After this the counter turned the corner, becoming lower and slanting to show the newspapers and sometimes even a comic. At the back of this counter were faded packets of crepe paper, gummed labels, envelopes, writing-paper, a few grubby-looking birthday cards and some balls of string. On the shelves at the back sat the big high glass jars that once held sweets, but the only sweets in there now were tiger nuts and woody twigs of doctor's-spanish, and that wasn't very often.

I walked past the open door. Nobody'd sent me. But I'd seen two little girls in there waiting, and only one grown-up. I wouldn't get a better chance. I turned and walked in. The girls were waiting at the mesh; the postmistress was ready to serve the lady, though. 'Oh, see what it is they do want first' – the lady turned to read something on the newspapers.

'Please can I 'ave a . . . a . . .' The first girl turned to the second and bigger girl.

'She wants writin'-paper, please Miss.'

'Oh, those . . . Who is it wants writing-pads?'

'It's 'er. She does, please Miss' – the bigger girl pointed to the smaller one.

'Who's it for?' asked the face behind the mesh.

The littler girl whispered something.

'*Eh?* Well, I don't sell them to children. Tell your auntie *that*. And be sure you do.' But the smaller girl was already scampering away.

'Use them to scribble in they do. And paper's difficult enough to get at times like this.' The waiting lady was nodding . . .

The other girls stood before the grille. It would be me soon. I wished and wished I hadn't come; that waiting lady reminded me of a thin hungry spider. I glanced at her and wondered if she'd go before it was my turn to speak words which would be like trying to pass a very difficult examination.

The girl cleared her throat loudly; it stopped the nodding head of the waiting lady; they both stared at her in disapproval.

'Yes?'

'A stamp, please!'

The postmistress looked surprised. 'For post or savings?'

'It's for a letter.'

'Then why didn't you *say* so?' – a ringed hand slid under the mesh.

'I wanna stamp ter send it *orf*, Miss!'

'Well, give it here then!'

The girl hesitated, handed the crisp envelope under the grille. And the stamp money. Rimless glasses hanging on black ribbon were scooped quickly upward and perched on a thin bony nose. The postmistress was reading the envelope. 'No need to wait, child' – taking a stamp and sticking it to the white corner. The waiting lady leant slightly and seemed to be just as satisfied as the postmistress.

'But I wanna *post* it!' The bold girl was actually holding out her hand.

'No need to wait, bach. I'll put it in the post-bag.' The letter vanished inside a sack.

The girl shrugged and turned away. 'Got any sweets, please?' she asked, halfway to the door. They'd been watching her go.

The postmistress smiled as if she was glad. 'No sweets, no comics, and no marbles.' She was already looking at me. Me who had no letter. Because it couldn't be crisp.

'There's next she is!' The waiting lady was pointing at me.

'Well?' The smile behind the mesh was waiting.

'It's . . . it's a stamp, please . . .' The postmistress peered, about to speak. '. . . for a letter,' I added quickly.

Out came the hand under the mesh.

My head shook. 'I haven't *got* the letter.'

'Well, there's a funny . . . a stamp for no letter!' – a tinkling laugh from the face behind the mesh, the ladies were exchanging glances, nods and smiles . . .

The face behind the mesh inclined itself. 'Where is it you do live? I've seen you before.'

'Mrs Jones's,' I mumbled out.

More tinkly laughing from the ladies. 'Jones! Must be all of two or three dozen of them!'

'Auntie Gwen,' I mumbled, wishing I could just die.

'Oh, *that* Jones. Then it's two stamps you do want, *and* the magazine. It's Bridget does usually come . . .' They were looking at me, waiting intently to know the very special reason I must have brought with me.

I tried to look stupid. It was the best I could think of.

'Well . . .' The fingers were busy with stamps. Now she was going round to the magazines. 'There. Two stamps and . . .'

'Please – not . . . er . . . it's . . . well, it's just the stamps today' – and with a courage all its own my hand shot out and *whisked them towards me*. I put the half-crown on the counter.

'But it's *ordered* . . . there's *ordered* it is . . . And a half-crown too, there's seeing about this I'd better be' – they were nodding sort of smiles at nothing to one another . . .

'And how is Mr Jones after his misfortune at Christmas?' The waiting lady bent for my answer.

I stared blankly. What misfortune?

'Better wrap the change up . . .' The postmistress smiled over my head, tearing off a piece of newspaper and counting out the change. It seemed to take her ages. 'Nasty business, that. Not that I heard much about it, mind . . .' The waiting lady moved closer . . .

'Oh indeed, well they do tell me that it's all scars he is . . .'

Clutching the newspaper-wrapped change I raced off down the nearest back alley, shaking off the shudder of suddenly-remembered half-forgotten angry-red scarred arms under the shirtsleeves. It wasn't true, no it wasn't . . .

I slowed to a walk. What was I going to write with? *Not* the pen and the ink in the post office. A pencil-stub borrowed from school? But everybody's auntie addressed the envelope. And *never* in pencil.

The hidden pencil-stub clasped in my hand seemed to grow longer and longer so that everyone *must* see it as I crossed the room.

'Do you need somebody?' Miss Morton's voice. I gulped, shaking my head, and hurried out into the cloakroom. Now down the steps across the playground, running because there wouldn't be

148

much time. Inside the very end lavatory I fumbled inside my blouse for the hankie-wrapped paper, took the folded envelope from next to my skin. My hands were shaking with excitement. There wasn't much time to think about what to say. I smoothed out the torn paper, knelt on the floor using the door to rest on; if I took too long somebody might need keeping out.

'Dear Mum.'

Those first words had been too big; I'd have to write smaller than that.

'I hope you are well and happy.'

Fancy wasting time *and* paper when that wasn't even what I'd had to hide away and write for.

'Please can we come home. Pat and me are both in different homes. We're lonely, come and get us Mum, PLEASE.'

I'd started to cry. And all the paper was used up.

I turned it over and wrote on the picture side. 'Lots of love from your loving daughter Hilda. *Please don't tell no one I wrote.*' I underlined the last bit and made two kisses.

Now the envelope. The pencil needed sucking to make it show up against the crumpling and the grubbiness.

Now the stamp. I stuck it on. Put the letter inside. Footsteps coming close. 'Are you all right, Hilda? Miss Morton sent me.' It sounded like one of the bigger girls. I sealed the letter. 'Oh yes. Yes, thank you. Just coming.' My hands seemed to know what to do. One reached up to pull the chain whilst the other thrust the letter quickly into my knickers.

Now all I had to do was post it.

I passed the red pillar box. I couldn't post my letter in there, the doorstep ladies would see and speak. Anyway, it was still in its secret place and I'd look ever so silly getting it out of there in the middle of a busy street. There were two other letter-boxes, one in the wall up near the top school and the other outside the post office. Which one? I'd seen the postman collecting from the proper ones. But that one in the wall? It was dusty, and ivy hung down all around it, I supposed people *did* use it? Crumbs, my letter might lie there for ever! Even rot away with damp or something. Well, make up your mind. The postman will be coming soon. Upwards then, on to the mountainside. Now sideways and upwards to the hollow, puffing and panting, the ache in my chest growing and growing right through to my back. But I wouldn't stop, not now I wouldn't, it had to be posted *now*. My head felt hot; there was a pounding sound inside it. But there was the hollow. Scrabbling under my gymslip . . . at last the letter was there in my hand. Now to rest, said my tired body. It didn't like being dragged upwards again, the leg pains were fierce; it's downhill now, *downhill*; I have to run, though, I have to run – the postman, you see . . . the stones in the darkening alley scattered under my feet, a slight twist to my ankle – ooh crumbs, a running limp now, but if it stayed there all night someone would be able to see it properly in daylight, might even give it to the postmistress. But there it was, and nobody to see. I slipped my hand deep inside the opening, heard the letter flop down inside. There, it was done. I'd written it *and* posted it. And now Mum would come.

I was waiting across the road when the postman came. Watching that dimmed light, hearing the jangle of keys. A glimpse of the waiting sack, sweeping searching arm. My letter. Already on its way to Mum.

Friday evening. Bridget had got another parcel. She was dancing about, happy with her new material – green this time – whilst tins and packets were being hastily wrapped in paper to be put out of sight. Auntie Gwen was 'so grateful' to Bridget's sister, but Bridget wasn't hearing. '*I'm* goin' to live in Ireland after the war, pity I'm not there already, my sister says she'd have me now but I can't go 'cause of the war, it's not fair, there ain't no war where she is.'

Auntie Gwen sighed. 'There's the way of it, Bridget, and it's selfish I am really, but if you were there, bach, then Uncle Emrys and me . . . well, we'd never have had our Bridget, would we, and there's a difference you do make here, bach, like our very own child you are' – she'd finished wrapping the food; her eyes were on Bridget with the green material.

Bridget smiled, hugged Auntie Gwen and stuck her tongue out at me. '*I'm* lucky, got *two* fam'lies now, no more 'omes for *me* after the war, 'spect they'll need the room for some others I could name . . .'

I knew what she meant. But she didn't know that I'd got a secret of my own. Three days since I'd posted the letter, I wondered if it had got there yet. If it had! – a great happiness filled me – I'd be going home *tomorrow*. Or maybe the day after. Certainly by this time next week.

'What you smilin' at, Four-Eyes!' Bridget had put the cloth away.

'Oh, nothing. Just thinking, that's all.' I quickly went out to the scullery, washing-up, drying-up, carrying things to and fro, hardly noticing anything, the wet towel to hang on the guard . . .

'I'll make some tea, shall I? An' we'll have biscuits an' all' – Bridget's voice found its way into my own happy thoughts; I spread my arms to hang the towel . . . Bridget twirled, laughing merrily: the hot scalding pain was unbelievable, it seared all through me, driving out a cry of startled pain: 'My arm – oh, my arm!' I stood staring at the hot kettle, Bridget's surprised look as she held it away from herself . . .

But the pain was burning into my arm, steam still rising from its bare wetness; then I saw the huge long blister growing and growing from the elbow to wrist; the crying held all my panic. Auntie Gwen, who'd just stood staring, moved suddenly. 'Clumsy fool *you*! There's *daft* to dance with a boiling kettle!' Her hand had taken the kettle. 'Go fetch her-next-door, Bridget.'

'It wasn't me – it wasn't me – I didn't do it, I *didn't*!' My defiance came alive in the pain . . .

'*Shut up!*' Auntie Gwen put the kettle back on the fire; her shouting had me sobbing quietly huddled near the bare wall. She tried to touch me but I pulled away – she'd *hurt*, I *knew* she would. *Nobody* was going to touch me; it hurt enough already.

Her-next-door came in. Glanced at the blister. 'There's nasty. It's hot tea she needs for shock' – her hands didn't reach out for me but her eyes had seen the arm.

'I'll make the tea . . .' Auntie Gwen busied herself.

Bridget sank into a chair at the table. 'Oh Auntie . . . oh Auntie . . .' The lady-next-door put an arm around her. 'What is it, bach?'

Bridget shook her head. The lady coaxed. The crying was sorrowful to hear. 'That *awful* burn . . . ooh, it nearly went on *me*. Always playin' daft things like that she is.'

I couldn't believe it. I *wouldn't* believe it. 'You *liar*! *You* did it! You *did*! You *did*! You *did*!' I was shouting my anguish; the pain mixed with those lies was too much.

But Bridget just cried softer into the lady's apron. Auntie Gwen patted her. 'There, there, bach.'

The apron lady was looking at me. 'It's shock, Gwen, just shock.

It's all right she'll be after seeing the doctor.' I shook my head fearfully . . .

'Bridget won't need a . . .' began Auntie Gwen.

'Not Bridget! *This* one – Hilda, is it . . .? Always so shy and quiet, *must* be shock, Gwen . . .'

Auntie Gwen poured tea. 'You don't know her, Bett, it's not everything I do tell that goes on in *this* house, you know!' Her voice was angry.

The lady called Bett looked surprised. 'There's no offence intended. And I'll take myself off.' She was angry too, but it was a different sort of anger.

'Bett! Bett!' Auntie Gwen called.

'It's no secret that there's cause enough for *you* to hold your tongue, Gwennie Jones!' shouted Bett, and slammed the door behind her.

Auntie Gwen stood white-faced by Bridget. 'She was my *only* friend.'

Bridget shrugged. 'What about '*er*? She called me a liar, she did.'

I knew it was time to go. Time to run somewhere. Anywhere.

Auntie Gwen spoke slowly: 'I'll write a note to the doctor . . .'

Bridget looked angrily up at her. 'You sayin' *I* gotta take her?' The nod must have had something else I didn't see. 'Oh, all right . . . an' I'll be list'nin' to ev'ry *word*, see. *You* just say yes or no. Get it right or . . .' – her eyes fell on the long blister . . .

I nodded eagerly. There wasn't any other way to escape from this pain.

Nothing must touch that arm. I walked up the road with my coat only half on. The throbbing pain was all that I could feel. Bridget was talking about needles and scissors, something in me heard. But I didn't want to hear, so I pretended not to. 'Squealing like a stuck pig you was. Big baby . . .' We were going up the dark pathway. What about *her*? *She'd* cried, and she hadn't even got hurt!

We waited in the green-and-brown waiting-room. It was cold. Nobody spoke. It was the only place in the village where I'd ever seen grown-ups sitting together and not talking.

Pain not only hurts, it makes you tired. I sat on the hard polished chair trying to feel only the tired bit. Bridget flicked the envelope with her fingers. Several loud 'shushes' hissed at her. She sighed. People glared annoyance. Bridget slumped into stillness.

The surgery door opened and a lady came out. The chair nearest the surgery door suddenly became empty. Everyone moved around, including us, and someone else joined those by the wall of the doctor's room. It took ever such a long time to get to that special chair. But all those people kept coming out cured. I wondered how the doctor did it. I hoped he'd do the same for my arm, make it better *now*. I looked at the blister that covered all the outside of my left arm. It hurt a lot, better keep it still. The lady sitting next to me glanced at it, made a slight sipping sound and offered a faint smile. But it was time for her to turn the corner. I moved, careful of letting anything touch the blister. My foot accidentally kicked the lady's bag. 'Sorry,' I whispered, expecting to get told off. But no.

At last out came the kind lady with Veins and bandages under her stockings. Then it was *me*. But it was Bridget who took her seat in the special chair. Still, she took me in with her.

The doctor sat behind a huge high desk and said a loud 'Well?' Bridget handed him the note. I felt myself being looked at from behind and in front. Over in the corner was a tall glass-fronted cupboard full of tubes, scissors, funnels, big spoon-like things and cotton wool. Next to it was a door marked DISPENSARY. I wondered about that.

'Burnt, eh? Let's have a look.' I cringed from the loud voice but held out my arm. 'That's no burn, it's a scald. How'd it happen?'

'She done it messin' about, Doctor' – Bridget wasn't afraid of him. But I was, he was going to a steaming metal tank thing . . . fishing out an enamel bowl . . . then to my horror a long needle with a sort of bottle on the end of it. These he put into the bowl.

'Messing about, were you? Scalded anywhere else?' I shook my head, unable to speak as he broke open the blue packet of lint, fetched bandage and a towel. 'You messing about too, were you?' He was talking to Bridget.

'Oh no, she was all by *herself*. Like Auntie says in the *note*.'

The doctor sighed, pointed for me to sit down. Reached for my arm. I gave it to him. Fearing the scalding water, those scissors, the needle, and . . . and . . . I looked the other way . . .

It wasn't my arm. Not my arm at all. It couldn't hurt, not really. I heard the doctor say something soft but it was *too* soft, I'd gone away and left my arm with him. Later when it was all bandaged up I wiped away the tears. 'Please . . . I'm sorry I cried . . . you didn't hurt and I've only got one-and-six . . .'

He shook his head. 'Tears are part of the cure, child. Now you take this tablet before you go to bed and come and see me in a week.' He'd put the tablet in a piece of paper. Bridget reached for it. But the doctor stuck it in my pocket.

''As she got to pay?' Bridget sounded sullen.

'No. *I'll* see to that part, young lady. And tell your auntie to bring her next time, will you?'

The bed was wet. Slowly my heavy eyelids lifted. The room was pale with early light. I moved quietly, rolling to the left side of the bed . . . the pain that ran through my arm made me groan; I looked at it stupidly, all wrapped up in bandages. Something inside me was still asleep, even though I knew the wet sheet was there it seemed to have no real meaning. But after a while I slipped out of bed. Not because I'd thought about it, it just seemed part of a pattern. The dizzy heavy feeling made me reel. The pain again. I'd fallen against the hard wall, was trying to press myself off . . . must wash the sheet! But somehow something had gone wrong with my head, or was it my legs, thoughts came slowly . . . crawl . . . crawl to the case, my knitted jumper and skirt, nearly-best, lying on top. Fighting the weakness I struggled into my clothes, the heavy feeling inside my head was bearable now. And I *could* crawl. The sheet dragged from the bed easily. My nightie lay on the floor. Crawling out on to the landing. Sitting my way down the stairs. Stumbling along the passage. The kitchen . . . I staggered across it to the scullery, hardly noticing that there was a light there.

A snort. 'The *Lady*! Pissed as a bloody newt! Ha ha ha! Oh ha ha ha!' I leant against the sink, turned on the taps to shut out the laughter that echoed round and round inside my head. But he'd come to the doorway. 'Pissed! Each way! All bloody ways! Oh Christ! Oh Christ! Gwen!' – he'd gone to the other door – 'Gwen! Come and see this, oh for Christ's sake, there's dying for laughing you'll be . . .' – he was laughing, holding his belly – I rubbed soap on the sheet, not wanting to hear or see that wide-open mouth full of rotten teeth, the unwashed skin covered in coal dust from the night shift. But she'd come; so had Bridget. I wished the heavy feeling would go, it seemed to make me unable to stand properly or hold things the right way. But it also helped me not to care about them all laughing in the doorway. Everything seemed to be taking such a long time to do. But things weren't so bad now, the feeling was either going or I was getting used to it. They were all up at the windows watching me mangle, laughing and calling things. I fell up the steps, but it didn't seem to matter as long as I got these things on the line. Over went the sheet. Then the nightie. I'd forgotten the pegs, couldn't bend to the fallen prop, I swayed slightly on the path but held on going down the steps. Where had I left the bucket? It didn't matter. I was so tired.

Inside they sat in grinning silence, a cup of tea at my place steaming and hot. I drank it, pretending not to notice its salty taste. They watched. 'Thank . . . you,' I said, and found the word all separate.

That tablet last night. And the wet bed. Usually I had bad dreams on 'wet' nights. But not last night, just deep deep sleep. Then that funny feeling. It must belong to the tablet.

I was too excited to eat my toast, though I nibbled at half of it. They didn't know about the letter, nor about what would happen today. But I did, and it was still my secret. I thought and thought about it as I polished the windows. Waited in the yard. Watched the cracks wiggling all unmoving up the wall. Yes. I wouldn't go away today. At last Bridget came to the back door. My heart raced, was it . . .? But she was going to the shed. I'd already collected the bucket, so I went inside. He'd gone to bed. Auntie Gwen was straining the potato peelings. 'Here's something to be doing . . .' She plonked the bucket of brown mash on the draining-board. An hour later her anger snatched me away from the sink. 'Lazy good-for-nothing little bitch . . .' She threw herself against the sink and began pounding into the bucket. I didn't really know what to do; my sticky hand and arm held me there like a prisoner.

'Oh, poor Auntie, let *me* help.' It was Bridget. Auntie Gwen sighed. 'There's good you are, bach. And *her* . . . pretending with that arm . . .'

I moved out of the doorway. There was something I could do. Dirty hand or not, I'd pack my things. But really they'd always been packed ever since I'd come here. The few who visited the village had either come on the nine o'clock bus or at dinner time. But I'd wait all day if I had to. As soon as I heard the bucket being taken out to the yard I washed my hand under the running tap. Careful of the painful arm I washed my face too, then into my school coat and out. It was half-past ten. The Gang wouldn't be about yet. But I'd take my mum to see them when she came. Even knock on the doors where they lived, I would. And then I'd say 'Please, I've come to say Cheerio to Connie. And this is my mother.' We'd have Pat with us and not mind being stared at.

I turned into the alley, wandering around till I thought I'd used up an hour. Then back to the bus stop. Hopeful. Sure. Excited as it came around the bend. It stopped. People got off. But not Mum. I didn't wait to see it turn round.

I'd come to church extra-special early. There were no people inside. Not even the candles had been lit. I huddled down on to my knees in the back row and tried to just think about God. There were prayers I could say, words formed by someone else and meant to be said by the whole congregation. But how did anyone pray from *themselves*? *I'd* done those things which we ought not to have done. That letter. The deceit. God knew and I did too. Words moved inside me; I'd only wanted to be where I belonged, with Pat and us together with our Mum, the mother whom we'd been taught to honour. But we loved her and missed her and she never came. The quiet walls of the church must be soaked up with thoughts from people, people who sang and said the prayers with everybody else. But what *did* they think, when and if they themselves had done something wrong? But they were coming now. A boy lighting the candles. The organ softly feeling out a tune. Quiet, hushed, yet faintly echoing footsteps as the worshippers came inside and took their places. The whisper of thin pages turning in prayer books, mingled with lady whisperings and lady nods to each other as hymn books were marked with thin ribbon. Now the girls. Teachers ready to give a warning glance, separate on Sundays yet somehow never different, always *that* glance, and if you were *very* unlucky . . . well, woe betide you on Monday morning.

The service began and Sunday had started to spend itself like money.

A letter for me. Bridget teased, holding it above her head, behind her back, now throwing it up and down. 'Catch!' she called to

Auntie Gwen. But Auntie Gwen too had a letter, her fingers were busy; Bridget flung my letter on to the table. Eagerly I tore it open:

> My dear daughter Hilda,
>   Just a few lines to let you know that I have been to see someone. You will be put in a place together next week. Here is sixpence. Be good girls. I will come and see you one day soon. The raids are getting bad again but we have a good time in the shelters. Must come to a close now,
>   Love from your everloving
>   Mother

The letter mixed me all up inside. Not coming? 'Raids?' The sixpence, where was it? Pat and I together. When? When was next week? Which one? Or was it a time that never came, like Mum herself? I folded the letter. *This* was next week. Today was Monday. A feeling of hope twinkled through me.

'*You!*' Auntie Gwen sounded harsh.

'Yes, Auntie?' My voice trembled; so did the rest of me when she started waving her letter towards me.

'Leave my table. It's going you are, see. *Going.*' She was angry, leaning now across the table, her face level with mine.

'Eh? What? She's . . .' Bridget sounded shocked.

'Read this.' Auntie thrust the letter at her.

'Get up. And pack. D'you hear me? *Pack.* There's not one scrap of *you* to be left under my roof.'

I stood shakily, hardly able to believe what she'd said about me going. When? When? Oh, *when?* – those words wanted to be asked, but I held them back. 'Yes. Yes, Auntie,' I stammered, moving away from that close unsmiling face.

'Mrs Jones to you, *lady*, and don't forget it. *Mrs* Jones, see.'

I nodded. 'Yes, Mrs Jones.'

Bridget planted herself in the doorway. 'Baby! Great piddly Baby! An' your silly ole mother says they've got to be together . . .'er daughters . . . precious things, ain't yer?'

'Indeed she must be – here all these months and never a letter does she get till today. And us' – her voice was rising in anger – 'We – Mr Jones and me – what of *us*, eh? Never a word of thanks, just the dirty little mochyn to slave for . . .'

I pushed past Bridget. Mochyn meant pig. I'd found *that* out.

Bridget's giggling and Mrs Jones's shouting followed me up the stairs. I packed my nightie, took off my school shoes and put them in the case that had never really been unpacked. I was a bit frightened to go back downstairs but there wasn't any use hiding up here either – *they'd* come, come to see what I was doing, to shout, to giggle. Only my school coat and best shoes downstairs. They were silent as I entered the kitchen. But watching. Watching everything I did. Trembly fingers fastening shoes and buttons. Now my hat . . .

Bridget smiled slyly. 'What yer waiting for? Mrs Jones says you've got to *go*, see.'

Mrs Jones turned her head away. 'Tea, Bridget? And tell her to just *go*.'

I cleared my throat. 'Please, Mrs Jones . . . where . . .?'

She didn't answer. Bridget handed the tea, giggling. I was shaking. 'But where?'

Bridget laughed. Auntie Gwen joined her. They stared and laughed and shook their heads. I felt tears starting. The game again, they just had to play that hateful game. But what sort of game sent you out with a case and a doll to nowhere?

They followed me up the passage. Now they'd tell me. *Now.* I waited, facing them.

They were going backwards. 'Who's the *lady*, Bridget?' Mrs Jones peered first at me, then at Bridget.

'What lady? Can't see no one' – Bridget pretended to shield her eyes from invisible sunshine. They bubbled with laughter. My tight throat ached with tears. They weren't going to tell me. It wasn't any use waiting. I opened the door.

'Coo, what's *that* – a shadder on the doorstep?' Bridget's peals of laughter. I picked up the case and my doll.

'It's me. Me and I never lived here, not with you I didn't, 'cause you wouldn't *let* me.' I was choking back sobs and anger and something else; they laughed and laughed as I closed the door. I could even hear them at the end of the path. There they were, faces pressed to the front window. Still playing that awful, awful game.

Chapter 25 ~~~

They'd be out on the doorsteps soon, those ladies for whom the coppers boiled so obediently every Monday morning. I shuddered at the thought of those probing questions for an evacuee with a case. Without thinking I'd turned away from my usual school walk. How to explain over and over again on every doorstep *taking that case to school* I just did not know. By way of back alleys I came at last to the waste ground, deserted and misty-damp. I could run. I could run out of this valley. I could run back down the road past the Co-op. Past the police house. My thoughts stumbled . . . yes, the policeman would be out, I could run on and on if I wanted to, past the big double-bay windowed house where my teachers lived. Follow the bus route. Run all the miles between here and home.

I climbed the iron steps; that big bay-windowed house had made me a prisoner in this valley.

Well then, there was only one place where I could separate that case from its everlasting questions. Brushing back tears I hurried on to the only refuge left: Carrie's back yard. There among the overgrown weeds I looked hopefully upwards for some sign of smoke from the chimney. There wasn't any. A glance around the tangled grass and rusty metal, now a longer look at the thickly coal dust-coated window, blurred eyes slipping to the rotting back doorstep where new tufts of weeds were already springing. No Carrie. I'd known really. So why did this hope always flicker inside me? She was *somewhere*, I could feel her. But it wasn't here, not where she belonged. Oh Carrie, wherever you are . . . But I must hurry. The shed, that fearful rotting shed, the only place to hide my things. I crept nearer, pushing the creaky door gently, meeting the foul smell and gloomy isolation with all the fear that was in me. Quickly I thrust my belongings inside, pulled at the weathered door and ran quickly away.

There, it was done. But why all the running? Why did everything look like waste ground? What about Pat? Yes, we were going to be together, and this was the day. She'd know about it, she must. I'd only got to find her and then I'd know where we were going to live next. I ran past the trailing schoolgirls, past the overalled waiting ladies. Happiness is wonderful, and right now it was mine. Wasn't it? Mine to share and live for the rest of the war with Pat. We'd have a new lady. A new chance. Another beginning. And this time nothing would separate us.

''Ere, you was s'posed t'be turnin' up wiv a *case*' – Winnie was poking her head in and out of lavatory doorways. 'She ain't 'ere.'

'We've got to find her.'

The Gang scattered; quiet corners shouted protest as we dug in amongst carefully played games, shared sweets and whispered secrets.

'Garn, 'oppit!'

'Scram!'

'Oh, it's Them.'

'Leave us be, see.'

'I'll tell Teacher.'

The four corners had been turned over like pebbles on a beach; we met breathless in the middle. 'Well, either she's inside or . . .'

My heart did a flip-flop. 'She's got to be here, got to . . .'

'Come on, it's lines.' We ran.

Miss Daley stood just inside the classroom door. Her hand touched my arm as we were walking through. 'Oh, Hilda – just a moment . . .' I left the line and followed her to the far corner. 'It *is* today you and Pat are moving to Mrs Williams's, isn't it?' I was about to say I didn't know, but she was going on: 'Well, after school this afternoon I'll give you a letter explaining about your sister's illness. She's still coming, of course, but tonsillitis is rather troublesome and it shouldn't be too long before we get the second mattress. However . . . I'll write a letter and explain to your mother.'

I nodded glumly. Pat ill. Me all by myself again. And going to someone who had the same name as lots of other people in the village. How would I ever find the right one?

'Is there something *wrong*?' Miss Daley was bending, looking into my face.

I swallowed. 'Please, Miss Daley, which Mrs Williams is it?'

She frowned. 'Don't you know that already? Hmm . . . there was – or rather there should have been – a letter for Mrs Jones.'

'There was, Miss Daley, it came this morning.'

Miss Daley straightened up. 'And she hasn't told you yet, is that it, Hilda?'

I shook my head. 'She's not going to, Miss Daley . . .' My voice dried up under the frosty gaze.

'Nonsense! You mean she's waiting until this evening. Really, Hilda, this is quite . . .'

'Please . . . please, Miss Daley . . . Oh!' My hand flew to my mouth; I'd interrupted her.

She was sort of frowning all over her face. 'Go on, it's all right.'

I gulped. 'She . . . Mrs Jones . . . just told me to pack and . . . and . . .'

'And what?' She was pacing the floor.

'Leave, Miss Daley . . .' I whispered hoarsely.

'*Leave!* When? Didn't she say anything else?'

'Perhaps she didn't know, Miss Daley – I mean, didn't know where I was going to live.' Miss Daley stopped pacing.

'Oh . . . Quite possible! Yes, that's probably the reason. And . . .' – she smiled; seemed relieved somehow – '. . . with so many people of the same name . . . well, never mind, you are all packed and luckily I do have the address. Er . . . I wasn't really aware that you and Pat *had* been separated, that's what I wanted to tell you. But it's all sorted out now.' A big frosty smile spread over the rest of her face, surprising not only it but me. 'Very well, dear, run along.'

I backed away. 'Dear', she'd called me. Crumbs! And what if I did *run along*? She'd half kill me, that's what.

Teachers are very funny people to understand.

Chapter 26 ~~~

'It's Hilda, is it? Come inside.'

I smiled nervously. My case was taken from me and we went into the kitchen. 'Here she is – this is the eldest one, isn't it?' She'd turned to me. I nodded, still looking at the man holding a little girl on his lap. 'Now you're to call us Auntie and Uncle. This is Sonia. Here, this is where to hang your coat.' I followed Mrs Williams to exactly the same sort of cupboard the Joneses had.

'Thank you, Auntie.'

She smiled. 'We'll go upstairs.' I nodded and followed her along polished lino, up the steep slippery stairs and into the front bedroom. 'There . . . can you put your things in there?'

I smiled again. 'Yes, Auntie.'

She went to the door. 'I'll call when tea's ready. All right?' The door closed, leaving me in exactly the same sort of room I'd left for ever not long ago. But this one had lino *all* over the floor, two beds, two chairs, a small wardrobe and pretty pink curtains. Only one bed had a mattress, though, the other was just bare mesh with folded blankets at the bottom of it. I smiled. This bed would be Pat's.

The new auntie called. I hurried back to the kitchen feeling very shy. The uncle had put the little girl in a highchair; she'd started to cry as soon as I came in. We said Grace before sitting down and everyone ate in silence except for Please and Thank you and sounds of sucking from Sonia, who now had a dummy in her mouth.

After tea the man asked all the questions about home and Mum and Dad; he kept his fingertips together as if he was nearly praying. Auntie was feeding Sonia with something fishy. The kitchen was warm and seemed crowded with the table in the middle of the room and a pram under the window. Auntie washed up and I wiped. They were chapel, she told me. 'No, *not* the Welsh one . . .'

Sonia was crying again. Uncle picked her up. 'She's wet!' he called.

Auntie sighed. 'Oh, just a minute . . . it's one pair I do have here . . .' He was standing in the doorway holding the wailing child.

We finished the washing-up. Sonia was taken and seated on a white enamel chamber, still sucking her dummy and crying whenever she saw me. 'It's the eyeglasses . . .' Auntie said.

Mrs Williams had somehow got Sonia to sleep. I had come home early and they both seemed pleased. I could wash before prayers and that's how it should be. She'd come upstairs to show me how to pull down the blinds – black ones – before lighting the oil lamp. Now to find my nightie . . . I *had* to tell her what was worrying me. 'Please, Mrs Williams . . . I *wet*. And . . . well, there's no rubber sheet in my case, I did have one at Mrs Jones's but . . .' She waved her hand at my words: 'I've got one already, bach.'

I struggled out of my blouse. 'Oh . . .'

'What's the matter with your arm?' She'd seen the bandage.

'It's a scald. I got in the way.'

She tutted. 'Hurry up and undress now. We'll be waiting in the front parlour, there's wash-things ready in the scullery and – oh yes – a po, see . . .' She lifted the bedclothes to show me the china edge. 'I'll be getting you up every night about half-ten. Hurry now, your uncle is waiting.'

I hurried. Making sure that I'd washed all over was easy in the draughty scullery; any wet patches practically froze, so speed was more or less a habit out there.

The front parlour had six straight-backed chairs placed in two rows of three before a table; it looked a bit like a classroom. But on the table lay a big open Bible. Auntie was seated facing the table; she beckoned me beside her. Uncle nearly frightened the life out of me by suddenly rising from his knees; he'd been kneeling behind the table. There was a moment of silence. Then he said, 'Let us pray.' I knelt beside Auntie.

'Our Father . . .' He led us.

Then, just like in church, we got up and sat on the chairs. Now the new uncle preached about the evils of the world: temptations that came disguised as pleasures, looking as pure and God-given as the green apple picked from a tree. We may take the apple – and give it – or we may take the apple and keep it. And only the last bite would expose the worm at the heart, the evil within. The fruit would be flung away, our disgust with it. But what of that we'd already taken inside our bodies? Was it tainted? Did we ask ourselves this? Should we question the fruits taken so lightly? Were we not harbouring part of the shadow where evil had rested, and if we had not, then had we passed it on to others? The evil in life took on splendid shapes, our dazzled eyes never sought beyond. But the eye of God was there, fearful to behold, so sharp it cut into the very soul. Nothing was hidden. Nothing. We hid from ourselves our own desires and lusts. But not from God, not from our Maker; from Him nothing was hidden and on the Day of Judgement, that awful day when we stood trembling before Him, He'd smite us down to everlasting death in hell. Search your hearts. Cast out the wickedness, the rotten core . . .

Trembling, hardly understanding what it was all about, I decided never to eat apples again.

We got down to pray again. I was shivering with cold.

It was finished. Auntie took us to the warm kitchen. 'You did very well tonight, pity Hughie's uncle couldn't hear you, it's taking over from him you'll be soon enough.'

I sipped the half-cup of hot cocoa; went to bed.

'Good night, child' – the new uncle sounded all kind again.

Auntie blew out the light. 'I'll leave the door open for now. God Bless.'

I lay in the darkness wishing Pat was here. Wishing *anyone* was there in that next bed. But perhaps the Eye was looking somewhere else?

Auntie Williams was a very busy lady, always washing and using the flatirons. Sonia hung on to her skirts, sucking the dummy or howling her head off from morning till night. Her little cheeks were rough with salt from her tears. She didn't seem to like anybody and I liked her best when she was fast asleep in the pram.

The Sabbath, as they called Sunday, was the day Auntie took off the overall and left Sonia with an old lady nearby who received two shillings for hearing her cry the two separate hours whilst her mother worshipped and her father learnt about preaching.

Auntie and Uncle would sometimes exchange smiles with me during the up-and-down parts of kneeling, but the sermons themselves were both confusing and frightening. I began to feel that everything around us and all that we did, said, or were was just plain evil, especially when it was the turn of somebody called 'Hughie's-uncle' with his crouching shape peeping over the pulpit peering this way and that, saying in an eerie whisper: 'And Behold . . .! I saw a pale horse! And on its back . . . yes indeed my friends, upon its *back* . . . sat *him* . . . that was named . . . DEATH!' – the word sprang out of fearful hush, the voice raised up now only slightly in front of the body – '. . . and be-hind . . . be-*hind* . . . What was it that came be-*hind* . . .? *Ahh* . . .!' – this bit always made someone jump or drop something. But there he'd be stretched out now, arm raised, pointing to the doorway; the first few times I'd had to force myself not to turn and look – '*Ahh* . . .! . . . And *see* – see be-*hind* . . . *Ahhh* . . .!' – his hand covered his eyes, unable to bear whatever he'd be seeing – '*Ahh* . . .! DEATH and HELL follow with him – and to him is given . . . the Sword! . . . that he may have power to *kill* with the Sword – *and* with Hunger – *and* with Death – *and* with the beasts of the earth . . .'

By this time – and no wonder – he'd be trying to shrink himself back inside his hiding-place, imploring us to 'Pray!' To 'call upon HIM!'

I'd watched that black-suited figure waving the fears towards us. Having released his Relevations, or Revelations, or whatever they were, he'd wipe the sweat from his face and leave *us* to find the courage to do the calling.

Sunday school was taken by a youngish woman and a boy who went bright red any time they happened to look at one another. Miss Phillips always smelled faintly of mothballs. Winnie said it was the green beads round her neck, but Jessica thought it might be her vest. They'd even dared me to ask her, but I wouldn't.

Mr Lloyd had pimples and a big shiny pointed nose; I think he knew the boys called him Conky, but they called everyone *something*.

We sat in two groups: boys with boys and girls with girls. Or that was how it always started off. We girls would be quietly waiting for the boring afternoon to end, when one or more of the boys would be sent to sit with us because he'd misbehaved. That's where Mr Lloyd went wrong. Miss Phillips would go all pink and pull at the hem of her long skirt whilst the wicked boy planted himself behind the farthest-away girls. Then started the torment. Plaits tied to chairs. Spit running from the back of your neck. Undone belts and buttons. Rude noises and swinging, kicking boots.

'Miss – *Miss!* – He's gone and *tied* me . . .'

'Dew, there's fibs she's tellin', Miss . . .'

Miss Phillips would have to go and see. The tied part, of course, would always be already undone, but she bent a little to make sure. 'There's nothing to make such a *fuss* about, Mee-gan,' her thin voice would trill. 'Come, come and sit by me . . . Now where were we? Oh yes, it's you to carry on reading from Verse Six, Miriam.'

The sweetly little-girl voice would stammer away. Another muffled protest. Or from some girls a loud 'Git Orf! Eh Miss, 'e's spittin' on me neck, dirty beast, we'll *get* you outside . . .'

This is where the boys went wrong, you see – they didn't care which girl got the torment, so we ALL had to *get* them. My slipping eyeglasses, snapping chin elastic, pulled hair and kicked shins would all be added up, piled on to whatever all of us had suffered and labelled Retribution. This was something we *had* learnt at Sunday school: the word *and* its meaning. We fought it out at the bottom of the slag heaps, up over the iron bridge and across the waste ground, a running thumping struggling falling-down scrabbling-away war of our own among sheep that were always in the way. But I was glad when this Sabbath sort of Sunday was over. The two services we attended at our own church were the only places we could rest from the Hell fire. The Eye. And listen to the vicar in his white surplice talking, of all things, about Jesus riding his donkey.

'This grass is damp,' I remarked, feeling the coolness being absorbed by my navy-blue knickers.

Winnie threw her china egg up in the air. 'Yeah. Feels nice though, all that runnin' don't 'arf make yer 'ot.' The egg smacked back into the palm of her hand.

'Remember real eggs, Win?' I said lazily.

'Yeah . . .'Ere – lend us yer egg, let's see if I can still play two-balls.' I watched with interest. 'Coo, look – I can still do it, don't 'arf 'urt yer 'ands, though' – she offered me the two eggs.

I shook my head. 'No thanks!'

She chuckled. 'Be a laugh if they turned out to be real, eh?'

I looked at the two eggs and sighed. Winnie spared a glance for the first heat of the relay race. It held no special interest for us because it meant running alone. 'Gettin' 'ard to remember real things like wot we 'ad before the war . . .'

This Sports Day seemed to be giving us courage to speak. 'Things in this valley seem different,' I agreed. 'But it could be the same sort of different things everywhere, couldn't it?'

Winnie stretched herself out on the grass. 'This place', she said meaningfully, 'looks like it's always bin different; it's like there's two Gods, one 'ere and our own wot we left back 'ome.'

I wanted to laugh but didn't dare.

'They ain't got no Picture 'Ouse, 'case they gets tempted,' she went on. 'An' you never catch 'em laughin' or muckin' about. Even the *kids* is like it . . . Even the *sheep* is like it . . . You never catch them slidin' down a slag 'eap . . .'

We both laughed up into the cloudless sky. ''S a lovely colour, ain't it, 'Ild?' Winnie remarked softly.

I gazed up at the beautiful blue ceiling that separated us from heaven. 'It's a holy colour,' I murmured. 'Must be God's favourite . . .' A feeling of awe crept over me as the silence came between us.

'P'raps we shouldn't 'ave it for our fav'rite, then,' said Winnie at last, and she sounded sad.

'It wouldn't be true if we said it wasn't!' I sat up.

Winnie groaned. 'Cor, that word "true", it's one o' the things wot's changed, ain't it?' She turned her head away as she spoke. Her voice had taken on a tremble, as if she was going to cry. I was astonished – Winnie *never* cried.

'Seems like it ain't jest one way or the other no more, if yer see wot I mean, 'Ild.'

I blinked hard. 'Lies aren't always lies,' I heard myself saying in a wobbly sort of voice. I looked at Winnie, needing her to say something – anything. Winnie turned and looked at me, puzzled. My face reddened, but there was something. 'Well . . .' I faltered, 'well, for one thing, if I get a stye on my eye you don't say "Ooh, you look ever so ugly," do you?' Winnie stared. 'And when we see Pansy Cotterham we don't say anything about that big red mark on her face.'

'It'd 'urt 'er *feelin's*,' said Winnie, shocked.

'But it's *true*,' I insisted.

'It ain't *nice*, though!' she countered.

'And who said it *was*?'

She didn't answer and we sat glaring at each other for a long moment of silence. Then: 'You got tears in yer eyes,' she said, softly.

I nodded. 'So have you,' I mumbled.

'Yeah . . .' She grinned. 'Reckon I 'ave . . .' – she rubbed her face on the sleeve of her blouse. 'Come on, let's play cat's-cradle.' And I offered the length of pale-blue wool. We began the intricate weaving of wool around fingers. ''Ere, look – fish in the dish . . .' Winnie held up her work with triumph.

'Oh bother!' I said as my efforts at lady's-mitten went wrong.

'An' none of 'em even talks to anyone wot ain't in their chapel . . .' She sighed. 'Cor, jest see it I can when that there pale 'orse comes an' all the rest of 'is mob . . .' – she was laughing rebelliously –

I couldn't help joining in. 'Oh Win, you *are* funny . . .'

'An' if ole Jesus was ter turn up an' start knockin' jus' when it started . . .' She thumped me on the back. 'No good 'im lookin' fer 'is supper 'ere, mate, not wiv all that Death goin' on, 'e'd 'ave ter break the door in first.' She broke off. 'An' look! I done a mitten without even knowin' how.' We stared at the mitten. But we had to tuck it away in rather a tangle, suddenly summoned for the egg-and-spoon race.

As we walked towards the starting line, Winnie halted. ''Ere, wot about Georgie Washington? '*E* never told any lies!'

I shrugged. 'So he didn't. But he's remembered for what he *didn't* do!'

We had reached the starting line. The china eggs nestled wobbly in their spoon bowls. As soon as one of us dropped her egg, so would the other. We'd seen what happened to those who won together. The first thing they did to them was prove that they hadn't.

Chapter 27 ~~~

Eager eyes were feasting on the brightly coloured pictures in a stick-in scrapbook Joyce had brought. A bowl of fruit. Real oranges! I stared. Oranges had become just a colour in our lives; the fruit itself was almost forgotten. As for bananas – well, they'd become another name for yellow. Not a taste, not a fruit. We saw apples still, green ones for cooking. Even plums appeared sometimes, but the greengrocer sold them only to grown-ups.

I looked at the other pictures in Joyce's scrapbook. Libby's milk on red jelly. Lyons jam roll with a slice cut off. Thick curls of jam in springy-looking sponge. Now a custard-and-jelly trifle. Then a tin of Bartlett pears with halves lying in a glass dish. And down in the corner a single red rose.

''S'nice, innit?' Winnie sounded a bit sad.

'Shall I turn over?' Joyce was letting everyone really feast themselves.

'No! It's that fruit. Let's see it again' – Connie put a gentle finger on the banana.

'Oh come on, we wanter see some *more*.' The page was turned. More food, nearly all sausages or pork pies. But the page next to it! I held my breath. Trees, all in pinky-white blossom. More trees with golden and russet leaves, some floating down to the grass beneath. Snowdrops peeping through snow. Some small yellow flowers without stalks were doing the same in the next picture. Then wild roses tumbling out of a hedge. A picture of Jesus. A field of wheat.

Jesus? My eyes returned to the picture. 'Hey, *that* shouldn't be there.'

Joyce closed her book.

'Oy!' Everyone grumbled at her.

'And why *not*?' – clutching the precious book nearer to her chest.

'Well, all that food and stuff. Anyway, he belongs in a Bible or prayer book.' I tried not to sound as shocked as I felt.

'Well, I ain't got one, an' 'e 'ad ter go *some*where or 'e'd 'ave got lorst.' Joyce was upset but trying not to show it.

'T'ain't *right*, not Jesus in a scrapbook.' Connie sounded a bit like an Infants' teacher.

'Crumbs, she ain't done nuffin' *wrong*. Cor, anyone'd think Jesus never *et*. Come on, Joyce, let's 'ave another look.' Winnie and Joyce settled down together. Connie, Jessica and I stared at one another, wondering how we'd come to leave ourselves out.

'No. No angels,' said Auntie. 'Tell you what I *have* got, bach. And your friend can have them for her scrapbook. *Cherubs.* It's off the Christmas bonbons they did come' – she had gone into the kitchen and under the stairs. She came out carrying a box. Ruffling through various papers and tarnished tinsel, she found the cherubs in the corner. 'There! Pretty little things. I got twelve now' – she was laying out the round fat babies, who all had crossed legs and garlands of flowers round their hips and heads. Tips of little wings showed because their bodies were all turned slightly sideways. They were pretty, but nobody could mistake them for angels. 'There's four, bach – no, it's plenty I do have left' – eight cherubs slid back inside the Christmas tin.

'Thank you, Auntie.'

'Oh it's nothing, bach, there's little enough to please a child at times like this. Oh Dew – that's Sonia.' She hurried upstairs. I scooped up the cherubs and put them in my pocket.

'I wonder if that Syrup of Figs made her sick?' Auntie was studying the rather smelly Sonia.

'Shall I get some water?'

Auntie nodded. 'Dew, these things are sent to try us.' I didn't know if she meant Sonia or the sick that was all down her front and plastered to the curly hair. 'There's thin she's getting too . . .' I waited while Auntie washed and cleaned her little girl, who always seemed so tired these days; it seemed strange not to hear the howling and whimpering, especially as the sores were still there and some on her legs too, but those were from the wet nappies, Auntie had said so. I wondered what Auntie would say about the tiny sores on the inside of my arms: the bit where the elbow bent. It'd been ever so itchy for a few days but now, because I'd scratched, the skin had begun to peel, and it looked as if the same thing was happening to the backs of my legs behind the knees – *they* were itching. I tipped away the dirty water. Auntie would see my sores tonight because of it being bath night. But meantime I had the cherubs and the Gang to meet. We were going to show Joyce about Jesus.

'Bit *rude*, in't they? I mean . . . jest wearin' a bit of flow'rs . . .'

'Shush . . . No peekin'. Everyone wot's got a picture to do with Jesus sticks it in *theirselfs*.'

We settled ourselves in the alley gateway, Joyce in the middle so we could all see the scrapbook. She'd brought a jam jar with flour-and-water paste in it, but it was fingers for brushes. First of all we had to sort out what we'd got. A palm tree oasis in the desert. A cut-out hole to one side of it. 'Wot was in the 'ole?'

Connie looked directly into Winnie's face. 'A *dancin'*-girl.'

Choirboys in scarlet and white round an old-fashioned lantern all decorated with holly. 'Them cherubs can fly up roun' that Christmas tree.'

I began to wonder. 'Not really, Joyce.'

'Me to 'ave first dip.'

Dab.

'No, you can't 'ave the middle.'

Dab.

'Fill that old dancin'-girl 'ole up.'

Dab.

'I want 'em sorta flittin'-aroun' *my* one.'

Dab.

But the dabs grew hesitant after a while. 'Er, well . . . yer gets a shock at *first*.' Swirling cherubs, olive-oil label, desert and

Christmas tree choirboys, dangling grapes that seemed to riot crazily around the picture of Jesus who was standing at a door, knocking.

Nobody said anything. Joyce was still dabbing. We didn't seem to have taught her much after all. She looked pleased, though; decided she'd take the book straight home and come back to play. We watched her go.

'Crumbs!' I said softly. 'She's put the praying hands beside a mangle.'

Auntie dabbed the insides of my elbows with boracic acid. 'There's nasty . . . all the skin peeled off like that. Soon dry it up with this' – the powder settled on to the weepy-looking patches. 'More greens it is for you, bach.'

The rainy evening meant staying indoors, but I'd got to sew some buttons on my blouse and Auntie wanted me to embroider some daisies round the edge of a little duchess set for her sister-in-law Mary who was having a birthday soon.

The evening passed quietly: only Auntie and I to say prayers together, Sonia tucked up fast asleep and Uncle out hearing someone's tomorrow's sermon.

'There's red your eyes do look, Hilda, it's all that sewing. Put it away, bach.'

Auntie inspected the blue-and-white daisies. 'It's quick you are with the needle. Mary will think I bought it.' She folded it carefully. 'So pretty. It's nice things you do learn at school these days.' I smiled, thinking of my first calico pillow-slip. A whole year of French seams and hemming stitch. Nice it was, a needle-work bag. But the worst part of that was over. Embroidering the large flap was the nicest part. There were daisies on that too. My eyes felt sore. I rubbed. Auntie decided I was tired. We'd say prayers, and then I could go to bed. 'Will Pat be coming soon?' I asked as she shook out my clean nightie.

'I expect so, it's only the mattress. Good night, Hilda, God Bless' – the lamp was out and she was gone.

'When 'Ilda gets 'er uvver eye back.' It was a new catch phrase, invented of course by Winnie. Well, it was perfectly true that these days my eyes seemed to be taking it in weekly turns to be covered by the new celluloid eyeshade, flesh-pink on the outside and dark green on the inside. But even before the war it had sometimes been like that. Mum had taken me to the doctor and he'd said I needed Parrish's Food. Then one day we'd been out shopping and Mum and her friend Peg were staring into a velvet-draped window where eyeglasses twinkled and dangled on display. I saw Peg noticing my reflection against the black velvet with my eyeshade and the stye gathering on the other eye *too*, and she turned to Mum and said yes, she needs eyeglasses really, and she meant me. 'Course, she added, it didn't have to be a place like *this*. She was studying the velvet. Mum looked at my eyeshield. The doctor hadn't said anything about eyeglasses. She'd been going to walk on but Peg was saying about 'course you *could* get the Welfare ones from the School Clinic. Wire, they were, lots of other kids wore them. And she said she thought they were free and take me there if I was hers she would.

Mum was the one who stared now and it was Peg who wanted to walk on. But Mum explained to Peg that it wasn't the likes of *her* children who went to the Clinic, that was for nits and impetigo: *that* sort. Her husband – she had his position to think of. So into the posh velvet shop we'd gone there and then, and after I'd sat in the dark and read all the letters on his chart he'd sold Mum this pair of glasses for twenty-five shillings. Yes, they were dear. He'd used the word 'expensive'. But then he'd explained about the rolled-gold bridge, the tortoiseshell frame, and *more* rolled gold to curl around my ears. That had done it. Mum paid over the money and I'd come out of the shop with the glasses. I'd had to have them because I could see too well; the man had explained that this overpowered eyesight led to eyestrain and headaches and, of course, the styes. Peg had been ever so pleased and a bit proud to have a friend who could just spend twenty-five bob like that.

I felt ever so funny walking behind those glasses, and they didn't look nice either but I'd got used to wearing them after all this time – three whole years to be exact. And because the styes still came, Mum often told people I was delicate and that she was building me up with best butter and Scott's Emulsion. It made me different from my sisters – the word, I mean – and it seemed somehow a relief to Mum that I'd been explained.

Chapter 28 ~~~

My arm was getting better; its long scabby scar didn't need a bandage any more. Most of the time it was covered by the sleeve of my blouse. It didn't look very nice and might make some people feel sick. Pat was still away from school and everywhere else, so I supposed her tonsillitis must still be bad and anyway the promised mattress hadn't turned up yet. The bed-wetting had stopped; getting out on to the po every night at Mrs Williams's call seemed to be the answer to that problem. But gradually I was finding it harder and harder to get back to sleep afterwards, so I'd lie there thinking about guardian angels, gentle Jesus and the love of God – anything to blank out that awful Eye that was supposed to be watching. Mr and Mrs Williams were kind enough and somehow I felt as if I'd lived there all the time – well, ever since the Sleweslins anyway. Yes, I liked my new auntie and uncle and the only thing that worried me at all was this fear-of-God feeling they lived in. And the horses, the white one and the red one and that dreadful *pale* one . . . Whatever colour was *pale*? Better stop thinking about them. I'd had a letter from Mum, hoping to find us – Pat and me – well and happy. Auntie was going to buy a packet of writing-paper and envelopes on Saturday. She was kind, even though sometimes her face was all unsmiling like on Sundays. Yes, *especially* on Sundays. And it wasn't anything to do with Sonia; even when Sonia kept on crying Auntie would cuddle and pat and smile down on to the tearful face. But I'd noticed it was a sort of *part* smile she gave, as if she was saving the rest of it for something else. In all the time I lived there she never did use it all.

And me – well, Sonia never did like my glasses; she'd got used to seeing me but her face either turned itself away or stared fretfully around for her mother. She'd got sores on the corners of her mouth, and though Auntie dabbed them with the boracic acid they didn't go away. But if she cried they'd split and bleed so Sonia sort of whimpered instead. 'Just a cold, bach – just a cold,' Auntie told Uncle when he said the sores were spreading. But spreading they were, just the same. We prayed together in the cold front room and Uncle beseeched God to take the impurities – I supposed he meant the cold – from his little child's face. The next few days found me watching to see what would happen. But Sonia's sores stayed where they were and Sonia became even more fretful;

Auntie was often up during the night trying to hush the crying. 'There's more teeth it is, bach, more teeth . . . and there's sore her little bottom is, pity I didn't get the Fuller's Earth, *Dew*, it's in pain she is, hush now, hush, your mam will put it all to rights . . . there now . . . there . . .'

'Unsightly, you must get them bandaged,' Miss Kenny told me rather impatiently. She meant the sticky weeping squarish patches where the skin had peeled from the back of my knees.

'Yes, Miss,' I answered, wondering how you got an auntie to bandage something when she'd already decided they were best left to the marvellous boracic and fresh air. She'd only bandaged my arm because of the marks on the sleeves of my blouses. Oh crumbs, what with a stye and the big scar left from the burn *as well*! Bad enough to be plain. No, downright *ugly*, I told myself. It just didn't seem fair, however I looked at it – everyone else seemed to be growing upwards or outwards while I just stayed exactly as I was. *A dwarf*, that's what I'd be. Not even a nice one.

I turned in at the gateway and remembered that the mattress was arriving today, or supposed to be. My misery lifted a little; slow footsteps changed to running. I tapped at the door.

'It's here – it's come, bach . . .' Auntie held open the front door: the long-awaited mattress lay rolled just inside the front room.

'Oh Auntie, she can come, she can come!' Auntie smiled at my excitement. 'We do have to air it first,' she said, taking me along to the kitchen.

'Air it? Does it take long? Will it be done by tonight?'

She laughed. 'There's excited you are' – she moved the boiling kettle and put the pot of stew in its place. 'It's a serious job is airing, Hilda. But I should say that Friday or Saturday at the latest . . .'

Three days! Three whole days!

She smiled again. 'Pat will be here by the weekend, so don't worry your head about it.'

'Can I tell her? Please Auntie, can I?' I'd followed her to the soapy Wash Day scullery.

'There's no harm in it. But, well, I'll go across and see about it myself' – she saw my disappointment – 'this afternoon, see, bach. Now run upstairs and call Uncle, it's time he was up and ready for his dinner. A good loud knock, mind, or he'll never hear you,' she

174

called as I hastened up the passage. But Uncle was already coming out of his bedroom. Soon Sonia was sitting in the highchair, her crying swallowed up in busy Wash Day dinner-time sounds. 'There's a misery she's been . . . and no comforting her either.' Auntie was spooning out the stew.

Uncle yawned tiredly. 'It's too much of that laxative you're giving her,' he said.

'You stick to your job and I'll be the best one to do mine,' she told him.

He shrugged. 'Aw, there's sorry I am . . . just tired I suppose.' They smiled at each other.

We said Grace and spooned up the stew in the usual silence. I'd ask Auntie about rags for my legs after dinner – no, after I'd washed up would be best really. We all finished together and said our thank you Grace. Auntie was trying to get Sonia to eat, but she just kept howling and turning her head away. 'There's *naughty*,' Auntie scolded, and gave me the untouched dish to add to the washing-up.

'Dada's girl . . . there, there . . . get her some milk. There, Sonia, drink the milk for Dada . . .' I heard him trying to coax, heard Sonia crying louder than ever: *crash!* The mug hit the floor. 'Bad! Bad girl! . . . Dada will smack . . .' Auntie came to fetch a cloth and the chamber pot. 'It's temper, that's what. *Temper*. Getting soft with her you are.' Uncle sounded weary. Auntie didn't say anything. I'd finished washing up. Sonia had at last stopped yelling. Back in the kitchen I sat by the highchair and watched the little girl being sat on the pot. Uncle had made tea and was pouring it out. Auntie had gone now to put a soiled bib and napkin in soak. Should I ask now? No, everyone except me was busy. I sat there feeling the backs of my bent legs sticking together, wondering what Miss Kenny would say if I turned up this afternoon without bandages.

The scrape of Sonia's chamber on lino. I looked. She was crying and walking, dragging herself and the chamber pot to where Auntie was in the scullery. Uncle shook his head, leant back in the chair and closed his eyes. Auntie came back. 'There, there . . . what is it, lovey?' She stooped, placed her hands one each under Sonia's armpits: '*Ups*-a-daisy, there's a . . .' I stared hard, losing the rest of the words, seeing Auntie's arm slide under the bottom towards that . . . that . . . Oh what was it, a long white glistening pipe thing that hung there; the arm nestled the naked bottom, not feeling, not knowing; Sonia's yells seemed far away, so did the words that came out of me. '*Look* – ooh, *look*! What *is* it, what *is* it?'

Uncle snapped his eyes open: 'Eh?'

'My *God*!' He stared, horrified. 'What . . . what . . .?' Auntie was looking to him for a reason and, finding none, she followed his stare: her shriek filled the room; Sonia was held by one arm as Auntie dragged her own bare arm from the long wet glistening macaroni thing that made a faint slap as it swung to one of Sonia's legs. Uncle grabbed the child, flung her face down on to the table. '*Hold* her. For God's sake *hold* her. *I've got to pull it out.*'

Auntie stood as if frozen to the spot: 'I . . . I . . . can't . . . dear God, don't make me . . .'

Uncle reached out and grabbed her arm. 'It's *evil*. EVIL, see. *Feeding* . . . FEEDING . . . *on the very life* of our child.'

Auntie put her hands where he told her, one each side of the waist. Sonia's legs hung down, the slimy evil hanging limply between. I tried not to look, not to hear, there was pain all over me, pain from trying to press myself into the chair, into the very wall of the room. Uncle's hand seized the evil and wrapped it around his enormous hand. Auntie's eyes sought mine – 'Get her *out*. Get her OUT! It's nothing like this we've ever had before, there's no evil in this house that belongs to *us*' – she was crying loudly – Uncle flashed an angry look at me . . . I staggered up . . .

'It's *her* . . . *She* brought it. *She* gave it to our child. Oh dear God . . . oh dear dear God . . . take away this evil' – Auntie's crying followed me as I ran up to the lavatory shed.

I spent the afternoon alone and frightened in my bedroom. Downstairs they were waiting for someone to call. Uncle had stayed away from work and he and Auntie were talking quietly about what had happened.

It was Uncle who'd come to talk to me. He and Auntie had forgiven me, they weren't going to make things worse by saying what it was I'd given to Sonia. Awkward it would be to get anyone to take me in if they got to know about it. And nobody *was* going to know, were they? I shook my head, still staring at the lino; his face when he'd first come in had been too worried, too sad for me to watch any more.

They'd just say that my wetting the bed was too much for

Auntie to cope with. Besides, there were the sores I'd got; Sonia might catch them. No, he wasn't meaning to be unkind, telling the truth *did* hurt sometimes. I stared at the worried face. I didn't wet the bed any more, he must know that. He must, because some nights he'd been coming upstairs as Auntie woke me to sit on the chamber. The word 'chamber' made me shudder as I remembered Sonia's. My gaze had gone back to the lino and now to my twisting fingers. Sonia had had sores when I came. A little tight sob escaped me. 'Pat . . .?' It was all I could manage to say.

Not to worry, they'd arrange about that. If they could. And school too, they'd be sending a note. Just a few days to get over those sores. I could see his boots turning away. Prayer. Fill the hours with prayer. God might find it in His heart to take away my burden. He and Auntie would pray for me too. Better get into bed, there's pale and shivery I looked. A few days in bed, yes, that was the answer, just a few days in bed. The door closed. Great heaving sobs suffocated themselves in the bedclothes. I knelt there pleading God's mercy, remembering that awful silent serpent, and knew that I'd been shut away out of their lives for ever.

Uncle brought up the tray at tea time. But I wasn't hungry. He came again to light the lamp and say the Lord's Prayer with me. When we'd finished he stood up. There was more to be said. I'd go down to the shed when Auntie knocked on my door in the mornings. The visitor had called and was trying to make arrangements. It might take a week, though. Auntie was *still* a bit upset, so I must not bother her with questions. I did understand, didn't I? And – oh yes. There'd be time for me to wash when I got that early knock. The towel. Here it was. And the soap. He reached outside the door for the bundle, laid it awkwardly on the bed. Well, that was all. He had seemed about to say something else, but he couldn't seem to do it. The bundle rolled off the bed and on to the floor. I stared at the green stripes on white. 'Good night, Uncle,' I whispered. There *was* a sound from somewhere inside him, but the door closed on it.

The early-morning knock broke into my bad dream. I got out of bed and said my prayer. Then, still in my nightdress, I took the towel and soap and did as Uncle had told me. Wrapping my coat around me, I went to the shed and came back to find hot water ready in a bowl. I peeped into the kitchen. A cup of tea and a dish of porridge steamed on the table, but there was no one there. I washed quickly and ate the breakfast that had been set by someone's hands in my place. Then back upstairs to the bedroom. I wasn't too surprised to find my bed already made and the chamber emptied. I hung the towel over the back of my chair and put the soap on the seat. The lonely feeling wasn't far away, but when I heard Auntie moving about it went altogether. Perhaps she'd forgive me enough to come and see me later. But I hadn't prayed enough yet. I knelt by the bed and said all the prayers I knew.

It was the sounds from the outside that drew me to the window again. Peeping through the curtains I saw ladies brushing mats, sweeping pavements, scrubbing steps, polishing windowsills. There were no greetings between them and no goodbyes either as front doors closed one by one, leaving a wet patch for the postman to walk over as he delivered letters and pushed his bike up the hill.

There were no letters for us. I wandered away from the window and sat on the edge of the bed. My head ached and the shivery feeling was back again. Uncle was right about being in bed: I got in between the sheets tired and aching – not just my head either, the ache in my tummy was dull and deep. I curled into a ball and wished the bed would hurry up and get warm. Outside the doors must be opening again. I could hear children going to school.

After a time it was all quiet again. A sleepy feeling offered itself; I snuggled down under the covers and went to sleep.

Uncle woke me, the dinner on a tray. 'Please, Uncle, I've got the bellyache.'

It wasn't the sort of thing he was used to being told. His face went all pink. He'd see Auntie about it. I was to eat my dinner and not to forget to say the Grace. I stared at the plate. Brawn, cabbage and potatoes. 'Please, God, don't let me be sick,' I whispered because food wasn't what I wanted, but there was nothing else to do but eat it.

Uncle came for the tray. He'd brought two Aspros, a bottle of Syrup of Figs, a glass of water and a dessert spoon. The Aspros were for now. The Syrup of Figs I had to take after tea. Auntie would knock on the door and leave the tray outside. When I'd finished I was to take the tray downstairs and leave it in the scullery on top of the copper. Then up to the shed and another wash. The lamp would be lighted but tonight I'd have to pray alone, he was going to work. So after prayers I must take a whole spoonful of the Syrup and leave the lamp alight. He was relying on me getting out on to the chamber when he knocked after he'd come in from work.

It was a lot to remember but each word stayed inside my head – it had to because now I seemed to be living on my own. There was a feeling that this first day was the only lesson that was going to be given to me. From now on I'd do things according to the different times of knocking. 'Yes, Uncle,' I said to his sigh and moving-away pit boots.

The Aspros helped. I dozed nearly all the afternoon. The headache had turned muzzy and outside I heard the rain pouring down.

The tea-time knock startled me awake. More pains across my middle bit. It was rhubarb jam on the bread and there was a little cake too. Auntie must like me a little bit. I sipped the hot tea. Mustn't take too long, though. I gathered up the towel and soap, picked up the tray and went downstairs, out through the empty kitchen and scullery and after leaving the tray, up the back steps to the shed. My water was there, hot and steaming in a bowl by the fire. But the smell of disinfectant was coming from another steaming bowl on the copper, one that had my tea things in it. I washed quickly. Better scour the bowl. But Uncle had said to hurry, so I just rinsed it and left it near my tea things. Everything was as Uncle had said it would be when I got back upstairs. And there were two more Aspros beside the water I'd forgotten to take downstairs.

I took the Aspros and the Syrup of Figs and knelt to say my prayers – prayers that were filled with the strong smell of carbolic. I felt a bit sick kneeling there but still kept on asking God's forgiveness. At last, when I'd said everything Uncle would have me say, I pulled back the covers and saw that strips of rag lay on the pillow. Clean rags for my arms and even some for my legs. There was a round box of yellow ointment too. I sat on the edge of the bed, wondering about the burning sick feeling. But it would go. I'd be asleep soon. Smearing the ointment, binding my arms and legs, seemed to take an awful long time; I couldn't get the bindings tight enough and there was no way of fastening them except by tucking the ends into the loose folds. Oh that smell! My head ached, my sore eyes ran with tears. A prickly burning feeling deep down inside me too. At first I thought it must be the soap. That was

179

carbolic. I sniffed at my cold shaky hands. The thin watered smell was there all right. Another sniff down the neck of my nightie. It was there too, slightly stronger. I stopped sniffing, got off the bed and moved the chair with its soap and towel to the farthest side of the room. That would help. It must have been the still-damp soap after all; perhaps I ought to put it in a drawer or something. But Auntie mightn't like her drawers smelling like that. Best get into bed and cover my head up, oh gosh it was aching, all of me seemed full of prickly shivery aches, especially my tummy. But once I'd rolled into a ball under the blankets, the worst of the burning feeling went away. I slept until Uncle's knock.

Two knocks. The first had awakened me, the second had me pushing back the bedclothes. 'Yes, Uncle.' I stood beside the bed, wondering if he'd open the door. But he didn't, his creeping footsteps went towards the back bedroom. I reached under the bed for my chamber, feeling the prickly smell inside me again: the faint slopping sound surprised me. I looked at the dark liquid of unwatered Jeyes Fluid. *Pooh* . . . that was what had been making me feel sick. But I had to wee. And that's when the smell spread warmly upwards, making me cough and cough till my eyes ran tears and the sick prickly feeling burned inside me again. I hastily slid the thing back under the bed as far as I could stretch. Then down, down under the warm covers. Block out the smell. Don't think about why it's there, don't think about anything but sleep. The rags had slipped off sometime and my sticky arms and legs made my tight ball feel all uncomfortable. I'd have to get up and do them again. But not yet, not just yet, there was another pain to nurse in the middle of that ball, my hands clasped over it and pressed. At first it hurt even more but after a little while it must have been all right because it was daylight and I had to obey the knocking.

The day had begun. Things were exactly as they'd been yesterday except I had two Aspros at breakfast time too and the all-day smell to live with. But I didn't seem to care any more. Tired without being sleepy, I lay in bed and listened to the outside lady-scrubbing sounds, children-going-to-school chatter, footsteps and the rattle at our front door. Now the going-away sounds. And me just not caring about any of it.

Uncle brought the dinner tray and a letter from my mum. It had already been opened but there was a sheet of notepaper and a pencil so that I could write to her. I stared at the tray, Uncle waiting for me to do something. Hadn't I slept properly last night? Didn't I want any dinner? What about reading the letter? 'Yes, Uncle.' Now he'd go away. The Grace, he reminded me. And the daily prayers. Important they were. 'Yes, Uncle.' The door closed. He'd gone away.

Stew for dinner – I left most of it. Took the Aspros and used the chamber. The fight against running eyes and Jeyes Fluid drove me under the covers.

But the letter. The letter. I didn't hear Uncle come for the tray but he'd left the letter and the paper and pencil. I sat up and reached for the letter:

My dear daughters,
    Just a few lines to let you know I'm all right. I am glad you are both together by this time. I am sending sixpence each.
Be good girls. My regards to the lady.
                    Your everloving
                    Mother
PS Peg and me works with a lady called Eve and she says her
            Joyce is your friend, small world isn't it.

There were six kisses and a big shuddering sob from me. But the crying didn't even get properly started. I was too tired, my belly hurt, my arms and legs needed wrapping again and there was a letter to answer. I struggled with the rags and then lay on the bed feeling the inside shudders of tears that had all been used up whenever I wanted to weep. At last I started the letter:

My dear Mum,
    Thank you for everything you wrote about. Joyce *is* my
friend. I expect her mum is nice just like she is. Thank you
for the pocket money. I hope you are well and happy.

I stared at what I had writted. A daft silly letter, all jumbled, everything in the wrong places, she'd think I didn't love her any more. Tears splashed down on to the paper. I screwed it up into a tight ball. It was no use, no use, everything had gone wrong again, I wished and wished she could know. But Uncle said he didn't want anyone to know about what I'd done, only them and God and me.

My huddled ball was the only place to escape the smell so I

snuggled into it and lay without really doing anything except dozing off to sleep until the tea-time knock.

I took the tray from the landing and knew that bread and syrup would help to ease the ache, and the hot tea too. Funny, tea time always made me feel a little bit better.

I finished eating and left the room, not forgetting to take the towel and soap. Clean rags waited by the warm water, but I had to go to the shed first. The piney smell of my soaking cup and plate filled the scullery. A paper bag with 'Dirty Rags' written on it stood by the steaming water. I washed, rinsed the bowl and took the rags up to the bedroom. The chamber had been emptied and the air was thick with the new deep layer of Fluid. Two Aspros again, and still the Syrup of Figs. I wondered about that. But they'd have been taken away if my need of them was finished. I filled the spoon and swallowed. Took the Aspros. Did my arms and legs. Wiped at my running eyes. Tried to ignore the prickly fumes and knelt by the window to say my prayers. I'd got plans for that chamber tonight. In the wardrobe, that's where I'd put it, no more stifling sickness that wouldn't come or go. But I'd do it *after* prayers, because really it was quite wrong of me to shut away part of my punishment like that.

I awoke with a start. 'Yes, Uncle – yes.'

'Are you in bed, bach?'

'Yes, just getting out' – thinking he must have been knocking a long time.

'No, don't get out. I want to talk to you. Can you wait or . . .?'

'Yes, it's all right, Uncle, I can wait.'

The door opened. He stood there looking everywhere except at me. His coal-grimed face told me he'd not even had his bath yet. I stared down at the hump made by my knees. It was about the letter. Auntie had found it all screwed up. Upset, she'd been. Shown it to him, she had. And they'd thought it a very nice letter. No need to be upset with the rest of the world. Ironed it, Auntie had, and posted it would be tomorrow. Wasn't I feeling well? Was that it?

I nodded, not daring to tell him of these awful belly pains again. And as for the smell, well, he had left the door open so he wouldn't even guess it was shut in the wardrobe. But guilt is an awful thing; I'd started to cry at the thought of it. 'There, there, bach, don't cry. Aspros . . . And Dew, he was making tea downstairs, I'd like a cup of tea he was sure.' The door closed, I cried gently on.

He came back. 'The shed, Uncle . . .'

He put the tea down by the bed, laid the Aspros beside it, gently took off the top blanket and waited outside while I wrapped myself in it. Still the tears came. But he led the way holding my hand in his. Even a lighted candle-stump when we got to the shed. There's waiting outside he'd be.

When I'd finished he took me all the way back upstairs, watched me drink the tea and swallow the Aspros. 'Good night, bach,' he whispered before closing the door on me. The sudden show of caring hurt more than anything else. I sat up in bed rocking to and fro, letting the tears do as they liked, I was really tired, still hugging the numb dulling pain. Dozing-waking-weeping. Uncle. The tea. The Aspros. Something missing. What was missing? I'd forgotten something. Prayers? No, I'd said them by the window. My eyes roamed tiredly around. The Syrup of Figs! I climbed out of bed. The spoon was sticky; perhaps Auntie had forgotten to wash it. I poured and swallowed, got back into bed and huddled into my ball shape, ever so sleepy. Ever so sad. Ever so tired.

Bellyache woke me before anyone knocked the door; I sat bent over with pain on the edge of the bed. Mustn't use the chamber for that. Mustn't go downstairs yet either. Got to wait for the knocking. I got up and walked up and down the room bent like an old lady – oh dear, why didn't the knock come . . .? I sat on the bed again, staring at the wardrobe, oh crumbs, the chamber was in there, I'd have to get it out. I fumbled with the handle, groaning with my own pain and the reek of the chamber pot that had filled the wardrobe with its germ-killing smell. I'd *have* to leave it open, my coat and everything else would stink of the stuff for ever. I crept away and stuffed the china po far under the bed, feeling already its boring sickness deep inside me.

The knock – I could hardly believe it. 'Yes, Uncle,' I called, and waited just long enough for the footsteps to go away. Towel and soap bundled ready, I hurried down the stairs. My coat inside the cupboard. Now up to the shed.

I sat there for ages and ages. The pain was going, leaving me feeling drained of all strength. At last I stood up, moved away from the scrubbed wood and lowered my nightie. The faint wet slap against the back of my leg just above the knee meant I'd wet my nightie, oh crumbs, what would Auntie say? I sought the hem

183

to look, pulling it up towards me in the dim light. Suddenly my searching hand touched something that wasn't just wet nightie. I glanced. Saw. Smothered the rising shriek that had once belonged to Auntie. It was *there*, that long wet macaroni thing hanging down from *me*! Sick rose up to the back of my throat. I had to pull it out, had to touch it. But *how? How?* I couldn't lie down like Sonia had. I couldn't tell Auntie or Uncle either. Gasping sobs had to be smothered. I dragged a rag off my arm and tied it round my mouth. Sat back on the lavatory and made myself feel that long wet dangling thing – oh, it was *horrible* – I pulled and pulled, only to have it slip through my hand, still dangling and seeming to swing from side to side; everything inside me wanted to scream, to run, to beg for help. But I was evil. And if I didn't pull this thing, it would get back inside me. I forced myself to find it again: a great shuddered horror came with its touch. I knew what had to be done: slowly I wrapped its slippery length around my shrinking hand. I pulled and pulled. Wrapped and wrapped. Pulled and pulled. Wrapped and wrapped. Feeling it coming, feeling its wet coils as they completely covered the pulling hand. So now the other hand, it too had to have the coils around it; great heaving shudders and sobs lost in the ointment-soaked rag; sweat stood out all over my face. And still I sat, not daring to look, just forcing my hands to pull and wrap, pull and wrap that hideous tremendously strong serpent thing, fearing the time when it must finally let go of my heart in which it had lived, terrified it wouldn't do that and was even now making me rip out my own heart, that at any moment my heart would be there in my hands. But still I pulled. Still I wrapped. Pulled and wrapped. Pulled and wrapped. Feeling only the tight coils fitting up over my wrists. At last I felt a wet slap fall down past the arm that was lower down the lav holding the beginnings of the creature. It was *out*. I struggled fiercely to get the coils *off my hands*. No, I didn't look; I *couldn't*. It seemed to take for ever and ever to release myself from it. At last I heard it splatter into the water beneath me. Still I felt my hands and arms, felt and felt and felt again before I could look at them. Now I had to touch the place it had come from. Fear alone made me do it. But there was nothing there now. I took the sheet of torn newspaper and wiped. Jumped off the wooden seat. Ran for dear life away from that which had been inside me. The awful thing that would lie there in wait. Or swim lower down the hill. I washed in the now-cold water. Ran upstairs to the freshly made bed. Knelt for the

184

freshly disinfected chamber and plunged my hands inside, wiping the thick liquid all up my arms, washing my hands in it, wiping it around the place, not caring about the sharp sting nor the browny-stained hands and arms: eagerly I sniffed at the strong-smelling fluid. Took the Aspros and hid myself under the bedclothes. Now I knew why I was different from my sisters. I'd been born with the Evil inside me. Its shadow had shown, making my hair brown, my skin darker, my body smaller. I stood all my life between the two fair pretty girls. Loving them. Sharing with them. And all the time the Evil had been living. And growing. Inside my heart. I cried and cried. Shuddered and hid myself. Was it all gone? Were there more inside there? Could a person like me pray to God?

Chapter 29 ~~~

I didn't waken for the dinner-time knock. Yet somehow I knew that it had come, that Uncle had bent over the bed and gone away again. The daylight sleep was setting me free from the shuddering fears, saving me from having to really remember that it was Saturday, the day when Pat would have been coming. Yet again somewhere in my mind there was a feeling about it. I was glad she hadn't come, glad she didn't have to see or know anything except the bright sunshine outside.

The shaking hand was gentle. I stirred, wishing only that whoever it was would go away and leave me alone.

'It's feverish she looks.' The voice was light and soft. I turned, opening my eyes to see who it was. 'My bag. It's in my bag . . .' Her back was all I could see. She was talking to someone outside on the landing. Those were Uncle's footsteps going downstairs. The lady turned. Blue eyes smiled. 'I'm Mary. Mary Williams, your uncle's sister.' I ought to have guessed really, she looked so much like him. 'You've not been well, have you? Oh, don't worry about me, lovey, just going to take your temperature.'

Uncle was back. A glass of water and her bag. She took them. 'Have you ever had this done before?' – flicking a glass tube up and down so fast that it almost looked like a November Catherine wheel gone wrong. I shook my head. 'Just pop it under your tongue, see. No, don't bite it. Close your mouth.' She took hold of my wrist. 'There's lovely weather it is, pity to be indoors on such a day.' She'd pretended not to notice the brown stains. I stared up at her. Round and jolly-looking, she reminded me of someone nice but I couldn't quite remember who. She put my arm back under the covers, took out the glass thing and looked at it. Shook it. And put it into the glass. 'Well, it's not too bad, bach. Feeling a little headachey and tired, are you?' She smiled at my nod. 'Hungry?' The word itself made me shudder. 'Perhaps a little Oxo, something light. Won't be long.' She went out, closing the door.

The tiredness came again. The beginnings of a dream: Auntie Barbara far away in Portsmouth. A lady called Granny in a long dark frock. She limped, and one day after we'd moved to London the angels had taken her away. Then the war had come and . . . and . . . I was being held up. Funny how those blue eyes reminded me of brown ones, kind and soft. 'You're like my Auntie Barbara,' I whispered between sips.

Mary smiled. 'Just a little more' – the cup pressed, I sipped again. She washed me afterwards, still not saying anything about the change in colour and smell of the water. Now clean sheets, a little pill and the warmth of a stone hot-water bottle at my feet. 'A little sleep now. And don't worry, love, I'll be here when you wake.'

I slept, remembering her face, her touch, the smile.

There was custard at tea time. Specially baked, it was. Mary sat on the edge of the bed and didn't seem to mind when I refused and only drank the tea. A sort of nurse, she was – VAD, it was called – come to visit for a few days' holiday. And there's lucky it was too: all this nice weather . . . She was cleaning the sore patches now. Real white lint and bandage. It didn't really seem true, I felt as if it was just something I was watching. Oh, those daisies. Pretty they were. Perhaps I'd sew them again. Finish it off, like, before she went back to Cardy next week. The bandaging was finished. There's sleepy I looked. Better settle down. She'd come back later. Tell me a story if I liked. It was my turn to smile – and then drift off back to sleep.

Uncle was lighting the lamp when I woke. He smiled. There's better I looked already. Was it bad dreams I'd had last night? Mary would be coming up soon. She came as he spoke, cups of cocoa on a tray. They exchanged smiles, Uncle said Good night and left us.

We sipped cocoa. Mary was trying to understand what had been

186

wrong with me. Auntie had said something about all of us having heavy colds. But I'd got sores as well and she had been a little concerned that . . .

So Mary didn't know, they hadn't told her.

Not been here long, had I? A bit run down, she'd say. How did I get that scar on my arm? Staring at it made me wonder too. What about a nice story? Which sort did I like? Fairies? Yes, she thought I would. Once upon a time, long long ago in a far-off land . . . I listened to the adventure of a little fairy who'd fallen into a pool and lost the magic dust off her wings. It all ended happily, with the fairy marrying the King of Fairyland.

Mary stood up. Bedtime properly now. The shed? I shook my head, trying not to let her see my face. A drink, perhaps? Yes, she'd bring one. I sat hunched on the bed. Better get out and say my prayers. I was only just in time. Uncle tapped and knelt to pray loudly beside me. I stumbled along beside him, wondering if I mattered to God any more.

At last we were finished. Mary was back with a drink of water and the little pill. I drank and swallowed obediently, surprised at her kiss on my cheek. "Night, bach, see you in the morning.' She was gone; the lamp flickered weakly . . . or was it something to do with the heavy feeling inside my head?

Mary wakened me. They'd gone to chapel. Come down by the fire for a little while. Hot sweet tea. A wash. I refused a visit to the shed. Mary had got out the dainty duchess set. There's something I could do. 'It's breaking the Sabbath,' I reminded her.

She shrugged, put it back into the cupboard. 'There's more than sewing does break the Sabbath. It's a war we're fighting. And nobody takes notice of which day is which outside this dump. Lucky me, to have got away . . .' She was smiling, shaking her head. 'It's far too *serious* you are – you know that?' She held me close to her: 'Ooh, there's a stiff little body, it's running and playing you should be. This valley wants opening up, see. Let the world in. Or better still, let some of the people out.'

'Ooh yes, I'd like that. If they'd let us go home again. It was nice then.'

Mary raked at the fire. 'They'll be back soon. I'll do a bottle for you. We'll talk again later.'

187

I went to the kitchen door. She was watching me. 'I'll sew the daisies tomorrow,' I said, and hurried upstairs to my waiting bed.

I slept nearly all the afternoon and woke to find Mary shaking me gently. 'There's a long sleep you've had, bach. Here, I've brought you some cocoa. Uncle and Auntie have just gone off to that chapel of theirs, so if you like to come down by the fire . . .' I climbed out of the blankets. 'Careful, it's still sleepy you are' – Mary steadied my suddenly swaying body. 'Better just sit there and drink this' – she gave me the cup. 'It's more like 'flu you've had, by the looks of things' – a blanket settled around my shoulders.

The cocoa was lovely and it made me feel very much better than I'd been feeling when she'd first awakened me. 'I'm all right now . . .'

Her smile was kindly. 'We'll take your wash-things, shall we? Hope you can manage the stairs.' I followed her, the blanket trailing after me like a robe. What was it about her that was so different? 'Would I like my dinner? In the oven, it was' – she seemed to know already that the answer would be No. 'Well, it's all for fattening the pigs . . .' – she took the plate away and came back carrying a bowl of hot water. I could wash while she made the bed. And not to undo the bandages, mind. The clean nightie was folded over the fireguard. Yes, there was something that made Mary different. It wasn't only that she was kind. I puzzled at it through the rest of the evening, listening and watching as she talked or moved about the room.

'Do you believe in God, Mary?'

'Of course I do! But not the way my brother does. Not any more. No, bach, I got my Scholarship and then when school was behind me, so were the valleys. I was free to choose. But my brother, well, there's no choice for him, the pits and the chapel are his world, see . . .' – she stopped fiddling about; looked a bit sad. 'Sometimes I do wish that it was he who'd got the Scholarship.'

The blinds were down and the lamp had been lit. I should really blow it out now, but I climbed back into bed and decided to do my watching in the light – tonight at least – for as long as the oil lasted.

It was hard not to fall asleep; my head kept nodding down to

my chest, jerking me awake. Those . . . *things*. I had to watch for
them. And pray too. Pray they wouldn't come.

The daisies were finished. Mary was telling me how clever I was.
Liking me. Being almost a friend. I felt sad because she was already
grown-up. She'd be going away soon. Her holiday was nearly
finished. She was glad, too. 'Got myself a nice chap in Cardy. It's
lovely there, bach. Picture-houses, music-halls and dances' – her
voice lowered a little. 'Sometimes I even put on powder and red
up my lips with rouge. Only for the dances, mind. And Tom –
he's my chap – he likes it, he does! Says I look like a city girl' – she
smiled down at her darning, humming a little to herself. She was
so nice.

'Mary?'

She looked up.

'Does it take long to grow up?'

Another smile. 'Depends. Some people only *look* grown-up.
They stop learning and stick to the old ways, see. But to go on and
learn something every day, well, it's what us nurses do, see . . .'
She chuckled. 'Not always the right things, either! But it's wrong
you have to know before you can learn what's right' – she wasn't
smiling now but studying the neat darn in her black stocking.

'Mary? I've got stockings like that but nobody's let me wear
them since we came here. None of us wears them any more.'

Mary sighed. 'Well, it's only Scholarship girls do wear them
here.'

Crumbs, that didn't seem fair, you could be warm only because
of your brains. Mary rolled the stockings into a ball. 'Catch!' – I
missed the ball – but so did Mary! We laughed together. She picked
up her stockings. 'That old Matron makes sure it's like schoolgirls
we do look still . . .'

So even Mary couldn't choose everything. I watched the way
she suddenly became grown-up again as she skewered the darning-
needle back in its home in her sewing-bag.

My sores were healing. The rags could be left off now. And Mary
was going away tomorrow. The news had made me sad at first,
but she'd already started packing her clothes, and on my bed too! I
watched the busy hands – nice hands – folding and smoothing the

things that went into the case. I'd be doing that soon, but not nearly so nicely. Still, if I watched, this was the something I could learn for today.

'I'm going away too, soon,' I told her. 'To live with my sister.'

Mary took my hand in hers. 'There's better things will be then, bach, it's lonely for you here.' She seemed not ever to have noticed that other bed. I stared at it.

'There's *serious* you are again! Is something worrying you?'

'It's just my face,' I told her with a smile.

She laughed. 'Go on with you, it's a child's face. And far too serious it looks sometimes. Almost as if . . . well, as if you were somehow staring out at the world and storing up what you see . . .' She'd turned to her packing again . . .

Didn't other people do it? Didn't they remember yesterday? All the yesterdays? It seemed I'd always been doing it ever since I could talk. And places too. I'd taken pictures with my eyes. It was easy. Just look at something you wanted to keep. Or remember for ever. And there it was, whenever you turned back all the yesterdays.

Chapter 30 ~~~

The rolled-up mattress was tugged and heaved up the stairs. Hope surged inside me – had they changed their minds about sending me away, was Pat really coming here after all? My knitting-needles clicked rapidly as I sat on my own in the front parlour. The pink scarf for my doll grew and grew. Mary had left me the wool and needles, tired of the gloves she'd started to knit for herself. I'd been thinking about the difference there was about Mary and now I thought I knew what it was: she didn't belong to anybody and nobody belonged to her.

Uncle brought my dinner on the tray. 'There's quiet you've been bach. Don't forget the Grace.' He went out, closing the door. I sat up to the table in the front parlour and wondered how I could be anything else but quiet seeing that I was always by myself. I said the Grace loudly, hoping he'd hear me and know that my silence wasn't all my own.

Later on I heard all the moving-about sounds upstairs in my

bedroom. And when Uncle came to collect the tray, a strong disinfectant smell drifted in with him. 'Better come and wash your face, bach.' My coat. Waiting in the kitchen, cleaned and pressed, waiting on a hanger. All that moving about up there had been for me, me whose name was written on the waiting label with a big figure '2' beside it. 'Hurry, bach, we've to be there at two.' Uncle was already pulling on his coat.

Uncle carried my case down the hill. Just as we neared the post office, Mr Sleweslin came out of his door with a case. And Pat, complete with a label, stepped out behind him. I wanted to call, to run, to do something, but Uncle just kept on walking at the same rate and Mr Sleweslin held Pat's hand and kept only slightly ahead. So there we were, on opposite sides of the road going somewhere separately together.

Then Uncle and I had to cross the road. Now we were walking behind Pat and Mr Sleweslin. Then round the corner and up the steps into the Workmen's Hall. Even at the door that had to be held open for us, neither man spoke to the other.

'Over there,' Mr Sleweslin was being told. 'More coming later. No need to wait, Sir.' Mr Sleweslin took Pat and her case to the far corner. Uncle was giving my name. 'Same name? Same place. No need to wait.' We passed Mr Sleweslin on his way out.

'Goodbye, Hilda.' Mr Williams left me near Pat. We stood there staring at the departing men. The man at the door picked up a newspaper.

'Pat!' was all I could say.

She smiled. 'We're goin', then. Look! I gotta *two* on me label.'

'Ooh, so have I. Wonder what it means. Didn't they tell you anything?'

She shook her head. 'Din't even know it was today.'

We looked up at the sound of footsteps and slight squeak of the door. A-lady-in-a-hurry dumped a boy and his bundles. 'Alfred Pitts. Got to catch the bus.' She was gone, slamming the door behind her. The man sent Alfred Pitts to the opposite corner from Pat and me, and picked up his newspaper again.

'You bein' moved?' the boy asked.

'No talking to the girls,' said the voice from behind the paper. I shrugged; the boy went red.

'P'raps we're *all* goin', 'Ild?' Pat's little whisper had the man peering over his newspaper.

The door opened again. Another boy. And then another. Now

voices; a girl's chuckle. Norma Collis stumbled over the step, and behind her was Winnie! "Ild! Cor, you movin' *too*? Changin' me fer a boy they are, 'Ild, say they might as *well*.' Norma was looking at the Jumble Sale notice on the wall; Winnie chuckled: 'Tanner fer a boy . . .' Pat gasped; Winnie shrugged. 'Can't get nuthink fer girls, gives 'em away free . . .'

'Yeah, an' there's more kids comin' from somewhere's-else 's'afternoon,' added Norma.

We hurried to exchange our news – Winnie, of course, having most to say. A new girl had come last week. Talking about fires and bombs in London she was. Everyone had crowded round to hear, and some girls had started to cry. Miss Daley had taken the new girl into the cloakroom. She'd come back with red eyes and wouldn't speak to anyone.

At last the people started coming into the Workmen's Hall. Winnie's auntie was among the first. We watched cold-eyed as she took a Welsh boy from Swansea.

It surprised me when Mr Williams arrived. Two boys for him, but they were Londoners. Tears stung at the backs of my eyes. He'd be kind, I knew. And those boys didn't look as if they'd be afraid of wormy apples.

A small thin lady was trying to decide between Norma and a cheeky-looking girl in the other group. She went off with the two of them.

Now a big lady with a shopping basket, talking to the man, who was shaking his head. Then she wandered towards us. 'Crumbs!' muttered Winnie. I stared at the rolled plaits showing under a dark wine-coloured hat. She was staring back. At me? Pat moved slightly closer – the lady's eyes moved with her. '*That* one. Yes, the little *fair* one.' She smiled. Pat clung on to my arm.

'*You*, little girl. Come here.' Her black-gloved hand was held out, but her voice sounded like the old woman from the ginger-bread house. Now Pat was right behind me.

'Oh, those two. Sisters they are.' The WVS lady had noticed. 'Here's a single,' she said, beckoning Winnie, who seemed suddenly blind and deaf.

The wine hat turned and said something to the helpful lady. Then she came towards us. 'Come on, dear, I'm looking for a little girl just like you.' She was trying to pull Pat out.

'No! No! I ain't yours. It ain't me. I'm not her. It ain't, it *ain't*!' The lady looked surprised but had managed to drag Pat forward, though I still held her firmly by the arm. Our labels said TWO, and TWO it was going to be.

'Pat? There's a pretty name. Now you come along with me, bach.' She was coaxing, pulling gently.

'She *can't*, lady,' I said desperately.

The brown eyes fixed on me. 'Oh, is that so? We'll see about *that*' – she gave an extra tug.

'We're sisters. I promised Mum. It's got *two* on our labels, see . . .' I was desperate to be with Pat.

The man appeared. Pat raised tear-filled eyes. 'I wanna be wiv me sister . . .'

The man looked at her label. 'It's *two together*, all right,' he said flatly.

The lady stared hard at me, looked at Pat, sighed. 'Well, come *on*, then.' And we trailed after her to the table.

'Two it is, then.' The man was busy with his pen.

'Yes, two. But I only wanted one, I'm sure.'

Chapter 31 ~~~

Clutching our two cases, I followed the lady and my sister down the steps and along the road. We turned the corner and I stifled the groan inside me: this blinkin' *hill*, would I never get away from it, anyone would think we belonged to each other, that hill and me. No turnings on it, it just went straight up, suddenly flattened out to pass the chapel and the school, and wound its way around the mean terraced houses past rocky bottoms of mountains and gritty bottoms of slag heaps. Then on and on it went till it suddenly ended by joining up with the downward plunge from our school.

The cases were heavy. A mean-looking curly-horned sheep lowered its head menacingly and trotted towards me. I swung out with one of the cases – bloomin' *thing* – it faltered: *Baa* . . . The lady turned round, made an impatient gesture for me to hurry. She'd felt the first drops of rain. But crumbs, these cases were *heavy*!

We were passing the waste ground now, flatness at last. The twitching of curtains as we passed by the silent blank-eyed houses.

Till finally we stopped, midway between the chapel and the school. Here we were. This was it. I put the cases down with a sigh of relief, surprised that the ache in my trembling arms felt worse. I had an urge to rub them till the pain went away but there wasn't time. We followed the lady into the cleanest, shiniest house I'd ever seen, through the long passage and a dining-room into a warm brass-filled kitchen. A stoutish man smiled at us from his polished wooden chair by the gleaming kitchen range. 'It's *two* we do have, then!'

'Not by choice,' said the lady. She'd taken her shopping basket to the table; the man sighed and polished away at a long silver trombone that he handled with fondness. 'Dew, there's little enough to be had for all the queueing' – the lady was unfastening her coat. 'Well? Is it coats you do wear indoors?' – her head had turned to us; we busied nervous fingers with our buttons. 'There's pegs in the hall. *You!*'

'Yes . . . er . . . shall I go and . . .?' My face was hot under that severe look.

'Auntie Bron! That's who I am!' She turned, making a gesture towards the man. 'And that is Nunky. Now go, and be quick about it.'

'Yes, Auntie Bron,' I whispered and, clutching our coats, hurried back to the passage. Tears were very close as I saw the front door. *She* didn't like me already, it was easy to tell. But the man Nunky looked all right, he had at least smiled.

I went back along the passage, passing Auntie Bron as she took her coat upstairs. 'Sit by there, bach,' said the man. 'Hilda, is it? There's nice names you do have.' I nodded and sat as close to Pat as possible. The pouring rain had darkened the room, but it looked friendly and cosy with just the firelight. Nunky messed about with the trombone, which was now in pieces. I stared at the table-legs, all four of which wore crisp cotton bloomer-shaped covers.

Auntie Bron was back. 'You do have pinafores in there?' – she indicated the cases.

I shook my head, saw the look of annoyance and quickly changed the shake to 'No, Auntie . . . er . . . we don't have any.'

A moment of surprise, then a glance at our cotton frocks and cardigans. 'Hilda! I'll show you where the things are: it's useful a girl of your age should be.' I stood up and was soon finding out where the larder was, the tablecloth, knives and forks, cups, plates, dishes. And just how this new auntie expected them to be set upon her table. She herself carried the food: first of all the breadboard and a fat home-made loaf, now the butter dish, two flaky pies, and a large round sugar-sprinkled apple pie which she placed in the middle of the table, telling me to bring the covered sugar bowl and milk jug. Meanwhile she cut four slices of bread and spread them thinly with margarine. It was me who carried the loaf back to its bin on the floor of the larder.

Nunky packed away his silver trombone in a blue velvet-lined box.

'You may sit by there.' Auntie directed Pat and me to the window side of the table. We sat in front of the empty waiting plates.

'Please, Auntie, do we say Grace?'

She looked sterner than ever. 'Of *course* you do say Grace.' We all sat with bowed heads and folded hands.

'Well . . .?'

She was expecting *me* to do it! I swallowed noisily. 'For what we are about to receive may the Lord make us truly thankful, Amen.'

There was silence. Only Pat moved.

'Is that what you do *usually* say?' Auntie demanded.

'Yes, Auntie.' I was wondering what she'd expected me to say.

I soon found out. The first part had been right, but not the second. '. . . may the Lord make our hearts truly GRATEFUL,' she amended. I whispered it after her.

She smiled. 'That was better! Pat must learn it too.' Nunky sighed. Auntie passed him a pie and gave herself one. A slice of bread and marg was laid on each of our two plates. Now a paste jar was opened and Auntie spread the slices with orangey-brown stuff that certainly wasn't paste. She then cut each slice in two and said we could begin. She watched closely as we ate the first half. 'And how do you like it?'

The truth was, not much, but politeness won the day: 'Very nice, thank you.'

Auntie was pleased. 'You haven't ever tasted that before, have you?' She was quite right, we certainly hadn't, and by now my curiosity could hardly be smothered – it had tasted of a soft mushy rawness, the faint smell was familiar; my eyes searched the remaining half-slice, hoping for a clue. 'It is a very special carrot spread,' explained Auntie, 'recommended by the Minister of Food himself, *very* nourishing and *quite* delicious.' The latter sounded like a demand; we quickly agreed, nodding and enthusiastically biting into the remaining half. There was silence now whilst she finished her pie. The tea was poured and watered down for us two little girls. We were then given a piece of the delicious tart, a tiny thin wedge that seemed to melt on the tongue and then disappear without trace. Tea was over.

I was truly hungry as I folded my hands and said, 'Thank you God for our good food. Please, may I leave the table?' Auntie praised our good manners and told me to fetch the large china washing-up bowl from the larder. On no account was Pat to be allowed to fetch it because she was too small to reach it properly and might well break it.

With tea and the washing-up done, question time began. What was it our father did, Auntie wanted to know? It was me who so proudly told her. It was Mum's turn next. What was it she'd be doing, some kind of war work? I didn't know but I thought she might be working in a factory. Oh really! What had she done before she'd been married? I didn't know. Did we have any brothers and sisters? I could answer *that*, and was thankful there'd be nothing left to answer.

But I was wrong. Our grandparents? Everyone *had* grandparents. Oh, Granny was in heaven, Granddad had married another lady a long time ago. On my mother's side, all this? What about my father's side, just three sisters? Oh, one in Canada, was it? One brother in France, killed; that'd be the last war to be sure. I nodded. Did our parents get along happily together? Was it pub night only of a Saturday? Oh that's right, our father was away at sea. Mother must have had friends, then; she would be off out to enjoy herself sometimes with these friends? All ladies? And there'd be someone to look after us?

I'd nodded, not knowing really what was true, nor what all these questions were for. Grown-ups were very private people; I couldn't think what they did after we'd gone to school or to bed or out to play or even to Sunday school. Visitors went into the front room and that was all we knew really.

Did we get visits from our aunties? Oh yes, Auntie Lou was my favourite. Yes, I thought she did go to work. Auntie Rose came to visit too. Yes, she worked. Sewed furs together. Or no, maybe that was Auntie Lou. Yes, Auntie Rose had a son. I didn't know if he was in the war. He had a young lady. Yes, with short crinkly dark hair. Her name? Oh, Lily. We called her Auntie, though really she was . . . Engaged, were they, this couple? I didn't know, but they did have a tandem and that's what they used to come and visit our dad on. A *tandem*! They went about on it *alone*? I thought it was a bit of an odd question – a tandem needed two, didn't it? Yes, just the two 'cause there was only room for . . . And what did my aunt have to say about *that*? I didn't think she said anything. At this the new auntie looked astonished and sat quietly frowning a little and shaking her head. The stillness of the warm kitchen stole over me; just the ticking of a clock and rain dripping down the windowpane broke the silence. A big sleepy yawn from Pat.

The auntie stirred. It was time for bed. We'd best get ourselves washed at the sink. We couldn't help hesitating; Nunky was reading a paper and we'd never undressed in front of a man before. Auntie, noting our reluctance, quickly helped us off with all but our knickers. Red-faced, we washed very quickly and were escorted to the bedroom. Here was a double bed facing the window with a single bed that was to be ours at the foot of it. There was also a large wardrobe and beside it a polished wooden commode. We'd never seen one of these things before and Auntie obligingly showed me how to lift the lid and remove the china receptacle, which was shaped like a Welsh hat. This, she told me, would be my job each morning: its removal, the emptying and the washing, she emphasised, to be done with great care.

A feeling of pride stole over me. I'd been chosen to look after this valuable article.

Chapter 32 ~~~

The strangeness of the different room had no effect on us that night: we were so tired that anything but sleep had ceased to be important. I could hardly believe a night could pass as quickly as that one did, though, for it seemed that no sooner had our heads touched the pillow than there was a hand shaking my shoulder and a voice telling me it was time to get up.

I sat up in bed, and through bleary sleep-heavy eyes saw that there was someone fast asleep in the big bed, someone who wore a thick brown hairnet.

Pat and I dressed as quietly as we could. Then I remembered my first duty of the day. Kneeling before the commode-thing, I carefully removed the precious china Welsh hat. Clutching it tightly, I crept over the slippery landing and began the most hazardous part of the outward journey: the stairs. I don't know why, but I began to tremble at this point and very nearly let go of it out of sheer fright. The ground floor seemed such a long way down but down there it had to go, and it was me who had to take it. I glanced at the contents: half-full. A moment's hesitation, then I found myself clutching it to my chest with one arm wrapped around and one hand placed firmly underneath the base. Then, taking a deep breath, I moved forward and downward. The descent was quite successful, apart from the liquid slopping down the front of my jumper: it was cold when it got through to the skin but on I went undaunted, walking very slowly and carefully out through the kitchen, over the concrete yard and into the highly polished lavatory. There I rested it gratefully on the wide seat. It was almost with a flourish that I emptied it, and then I felt jubilant, I longed to act like an Eastern water-carrier and place it high on my head to walk gracefully back into the house. But it was the wrong shape, it *could* only look like an upside-down hat, and that would look silly; I sighed and let go of my longing, took a firm two-handed hold on the thing and went slowly back to the kitchen, where Auntie directed me as to how it must be washed. *Here* was the big jar of soda on the floor of the larder, and *there* in the little black kettle was the boiling water – she watched carefully to see that her instructions were carried out, then she handed me a special white towel with the word LAVATORY printed on it in big red capital letters. So, having emptied, washed and dried it, I carried the china hat back to its resting-place, noticing that the covers of the big bed were now thrown back, and all that remained of the sleeper was the brown hairnet hanging limply from one of the bed-knobs.

There wasn't much time to wonder about the hairnet, Auntie was calling already. I hurried back to the kitchen. There's slow I was. 'Hurry, girl, hurry . . .' The impatient arm waved me towards the sink. I washed quickly, then there was breakfast to set, remember to thank the Lord for, and eat. It was Sunday, a special day, and so we had half each of one of those flaky meat pies and a thin slice of bread and marg with the watered tea. More thanks, then on to the washing-up.

The bedmaking came next. Pat and I soon sorted out the small bed and it looked as neat as anything. But there was the big double bed yet and we stood there for a moment wondering just how. Then, taking holds of sheets and blankets, we pulled and tugged this way and that till we thought it was finished. Or was it? "T'ain't right, is it, 'Ild?' Pat stared at the wide expanse of ridges and wrinkles; I shook my head and stood there just looking and trying to work out the best way to go about it when suddenly I heard *her* footsteps coming up the stairs – my heart fell, my arms were somehow quickly full of sheets and blankets; she mustn't see it like this. Her footsteps took her into her own bedroom. I dumped the bedcovers on to the neatly made single bed and, quick as a flash, threw the bottom sheet over the mattress. As if by magic it settled evenly, and when I'd got it all tucked in it remained neat and smooth as untrodden snow. Now Pat was handing me the bolster and pillows, then the top sheet, next a blanket . . . and another . . . hooray, only the bedspread now; I slipped off my shoes and ran nimbly round to the far side of the bed, squeezed myself into the space between it and the wall and tucked in like mad, leaving Pat to smooth our bed to its former neatness. Puffing a bit, and forgetting to put my shoes on, I grabbed at the bedspread and waved it like a sail; it was ballooning down on to the bed as she came in the door. Her eyes missed nothing as she crossed to look at the other bed, then she pulled back the spread I'd just been dealing with to inspect the neatness underneath. My foot was probing around, seeking contact with my discarded shoes. Guilt must have shown on my face; she took a quick look under the bed and there were my shoes: still laced! Pat's white face peeped out from the side of the wardrobe where she'd quickly hidden herself; Auntie, we could see, was very angry – in fact I quite expected to feel the sting of her slap. It didn't come. Then the sound of her voice finally got through to me: something about slovenly habits and learning new ways from decent God-fearing people. She'd thrust the offending shoes at me and I crouched on the floor to put them on, somehow knowing that to sit on a bed would raise all kinds of devils to punish me.

Downstairs again she brushed my hair so hard with the wire brush that I wonder it wasn't removed altogether. This made me want to giggle – a bald girl – it was quite funny really. Then she started tugging it into plaits – the urge to giggle turned almost to a cry of *ouch* – the tiny hairs on my neck must have stood on end, she'd plaited it so tight that it pulled at my neck for the rest of the day. There was no easing it by moving my head, either; that only made it worse.

It was now nine o'clock. Wearing our best dresses, shoes and socks, fawn Burberries and straw summer hats, we stood uncomfortably wondering where we were going.

Then Auntie's youngest sister Gwyneth arrived, wearing a uniform which somehow very quickly seemed to turn into *the* uniform. Off we went then to the Salvation Army. The Salvation Army turned out to be a corrugated-iron hut standing on a piece of waste ground that was much frequented by sheep; one even managed to push its way inside in front of us and bleated mournfully before being ejected. It had left a few currants deposited on the floor and everyone pretended not to notice. We knelt, stood and sat all through the hymns, prayers and Hallelujahs. Then, not knowing why, we were being directed to a long wooden form across the front of the stage. Other people were lined up there already as we knelt wondering what it was all about. Gwyneth called a loud 'Hallelujah' and we both turned round. She was on her knees now, head buried in her hands. After that was over we went back to our seats and the band played loudly while everyone sang about the Blood and the Lamb. Then it was quiet. The Captain came forward and pointed a stick at a girl near the front. This girl stood upon the seat and said loudly, 'God is Love'. Everyone Hallelujahed again several times. Then the girl began to sing a hymn. Everyone, including the band, joined in. Then we had a prayer and it was over. But not for Pat and me, because the Captain was waiting by the door. She placed her hands one on each of us and told us we'd been saved. Then she turned to Gwyneth and asked if were to be the two new Sunbeams. The answer was Yes and everyone smiled, including me; I'd never been called a Sunbeam before, not in all my eleven years.

When we'd said goodbye to the Captain, Gwyneth walked us up the road to the doorway of the church. Before she left she told us that we must return straight home after the service and to be sure that our behaviour was suitably ladylike as required by the Lord's Day. But the service was long and the day was warm and alas we forgot and *ran* happily all the way home being Sunbeams. The running had cheered us up, and when we arrived we were laughing and quite out of breath. We hung up our coats, still chattering, and went into the kitchen. We got our legs smacked hard for unladylike behaviour on the Lord's Day: 'How dare we run and laugh like street sluts?' Well, I didn't know what street sluts were but Auntie obviously did, and they must have been really dreadful creatures judging from the tone of her voice and the expression on her face.

After a respectful silence we apologised for our bad behaviour. Auntie was straining the pale soggy greens and without saying a word she gave us a cup each of cabbage water with salt and pepper added. Somehow without even being told, we just knew that it must be very nourishing. Then came dinner, which for us was a sliver of meat surrounded by lots of fat and a tablespoonful of mashed potatoes and cabbage, followed by a tempting – almost teasing – piece of apple pie.

After carefully washing up the dinner things we prepared our-selves for the two lots of afternoon Sunday school. The Salvation Army was first, and we joined the assortment of children at exactly a quarter to two and listened carefully to a story about General William Booth, who'd begun it all. He'd done this by giving his followers the red-and-black uniforms so that everyone could see they were an army fighting the Devil. The Meeting, as it was called, finished at two-thirty. Pat and I had been the only evacuees there, and I was secretly glad to get away back to the sort of Sunday school I knew about where we had a vicar instead of a Captain and learnt about Jesus, whom I felt we knew slightly better than this General Booth man. But I kept this feeling a secret.

'Wotcha, 'Ild! Cor, I ain't 'arf glad ter see yer!' Winnie's greeting was unusually quiet as she fell into step beside me.

'Winnie! Where were you this morning?' I'd looked and looked all around in church but she hadn't been there to see and Miss Daley who *was* there, had given me a severe look.

'Crumbs, you'll never guess, mate, not in a 'undred years yer won't!' Winnie sounded mournful and very fed-up.

'Well?' I was curious.

'In a bloomin' chapel, that's where Winnie was, mate, an' guess wot, the 'ole bloomin' lot – preachin', singin' *an*' talkin' – was all in Welsh, see, an' this minister or wotever 'e is kep' on an' on an' on an' ev'ry now an' then 'e gets excited an' one of 'em goes "Yeah! *Yeah!*" an' wags 'is 'ead; 'e *likes* it, see – not enough to stop talkin', though. Anyway, jus' 'cos *I* 'ave a go do they like it? *No!* Crumbs, they was tellin' me orf in *English*!'

We were near the church door now, so I whispered, 'Shush,

Win, we've been to the Salvation Army and we were saved. Saved to be Sunbeams.'

Winnie gave me an astonished look. 'You wot?'

'Good afternoon, children.' The vicar was inviting us inside the little special part of the church that was his Sunday school. And there, to our great joy, we saw many of the other evacuees. Yes, we certainly always liked this part of every Sunday the best. I was sorry when it was time to go home at quarter to four. It had been so nice to be there amongst all the familiar church things that we'd almost forgotten all about being evacuees among the mountains of Wales. So we'd asked the vicar to let us sing 'All Things Bright and Beautiful' just once more please.

There was no time for hanging about talking outside; our new aunties all seemed to have said the same sort of thing about expecting us to be back in the house by four o'clock, so we smiled our farewells and hoped to see one another at the evening service. Pat and I walked home together, feeling again the loneliness of separation from things and people we knew. I was beginning to understand that the unfamiliar was usually something I didn't like, something I would in time have to get used to. It was the familiar we clung to and loved, all the things we knew already, all those things that had always been the same and – most important of all – were there with you or around you every day of your life.

But now there was this war and with it had come the terrible loneliness of moving and changing amongst people and places.

We came home from church to find that it wasn't tea time but letter-writing-to-our-mother time. Auntie provided us with a sheet of writing-paper and a pencil each and sat us at opposite ends of the table. There was to be no talking. I sat for a moment wondering just what to write about. Mum didn't even know we were here with this new auntie, and when she did would she ever be able to come and see us? Would she find her way through this mountain-ous land of unpronounceable names? A dreadful feeling of loss began to grow inside me, a feeling that wouldn't go away; instead it shaped itself into a thought. We might lose Mum altogether and never find her again. A lump rose in my throat. It would be too awful to go on thinking about it. I swallowed the choking lump and began my letter – 'Dear Mum' – remembering carefully how the teachers had first taught us that Cheerfulness was the main ingredient. So, sticking to the rules, I covered the first side of the writing-paper and turned it over.

That was when I started to think about Dad – Dad who'd written me only two letters and that had been just before the war began, but neither of them had got a return address so I couldn't write back. He always used green ink. And his lovely slopy handwriting was once described as 'almost copperplate' by one of my teachers. How I wished he'd been able to have that promised homecoming! A leave, he'd called it. My yesterday pages started to turn inside me: the day he'd taken my elder sister and me on the paddle-boat from the Sun Pier all the way to Soufend with music playing all the way there and back; and then there was the Sunday when he took us to Cobham Woods: the primroses carpeted the ground and it was with real love that I'd found what has always since been my favourite flower, the sweet wild violet. It was in a narrow little lane that we'd found the first wild roses, so fragile and varying in colour from palest pink to the colour of a blush. These beautiful flowers and trees I knew now were God's work, and many were the times when I'd wished that I could work for God; I'd never be able to make a tree, of course, or even a rose-petal, but maybe I'd be of some use with acorns or oak-apples.

'Is it finished you are or just daydreaming, girl?' Auntie had come to look over my shoulder; thoughts and words shrivelled up inside me.

Then I was able to say, 'Please Auntie, I've nearly finished' and my pencil fled to and fro across the blank paper in front of me. I could hardly wait to finish because I wasn't feeling Cheerful really, just pretending, and that's how it had been all the way through the letter; the only bit that was true said that I was her everloving daughter Hilda.

I put down my pencil and sat still and quiet whilst Auntie stood reading Pat's letter. She smiled to herself as she placed it, folded, back on to the table and reached for mine. I sat staring down at the cloth and waited for her to fold mine too. But she didn't. Nor did she make any comment as she took both letters into the dining-room.

'You may lay the table now and be quick about it, there's church you've to be for six o'clock' – Pat and I pattered about like trained mice; Auntie stood in the larder and passed the special Sunday food to each of us in turn. The milk jug and sugar bowl, covered with the bead-edged net circles to keep the flies off. A dish of rhubarb jam. The bread, the marg, and a plate of flat round things that looked like neither biscuits nor cakes. Auntie made the tea and Nunky moved his chair nearer the table. Pat and I said Grace and tea began. The rhubarb jam was lovely, and it was greedy of me to wish we'd had more than just one slice of bread. The flat round things were cakes. Welsh cakes. They'd tasted nice but it wasn't until we'd thanked the Lord and started on the washing-up that Auntie had told us what they were. I think it was *then* that I understood that Auntie didn't allow talking at the table – what a good thing it was that we'd been too shy to have allowed ourselves to do it! Mum was the same, though, about table manners; it was only at Auntie Vi's and sometimes with Margaret that we'd all chatted and sometimes laughed around the meal table. And how long ago and far away that all seemed now!

But it was time to leave for church. 'Be sure to go straight to the Meeting afterwards. Auntie Gwyneth will be there waiting for you.' Auntie's parting words were full-stopped by the loud click she made closing the front door behind us.

Neither of us spoke for a quite a long time; it was near the church that Pat finally said what I'd been thinking all day long: 'I don't 'arf wish we wasn't 'ere, 'Ild, it ain't nice, not *anywheres* it ain't' – she was looking up at the steep treeless mountains that even the sheep didn't seem to like as much as they should.

'P'raps we'll get to like it when we've had time to go exploring up this end.' I tried to sound encouraging and found that I really believed it would happen just like that.

Evensong ended, evacuee children scattered quickly. For the grown-ups standing in talk with the vicar the Sunday was at its close, but it seemed that all of us children had one more place of worship to hasten to. At last it was time for us to follow wearily home behind the stiff black-uniformed figure of Gwyneth. Unseen for the moment our attempts at ladylike walking had dwindled to the size of us. It had been so confusing trying to walk like a lady because they all walked differently. And Gwyneth, who'd hardly said a word to us all day, simply marched as if she was leading an invisible army.

She stayed only a few moments to talk with Auntie. Pat and I seated ourselves on the long black sofa and waited. Maybe we could play with our cut-out dolls for a little while before we went to bed? Should I ask . . . or would it be better to wait for Auntie to say we could play a little now . . . I tapped my fingers up and down on my knees . . . Auntie came back into the room; I felt her frown and stopped tapping. The man we called Nunky was missing. Auntie sat herself in his big wooden chair and seemed to be waiting for us to say something. I felt Pat's slight nudge and knew it would have to be me: I smiled with my face; the rest of me felt somehow all wrong about the smile. 'Please, Auntie, can we play with our things for a little while?' There, it was *out*. *Said*. And I felt as if I'd run a a long race.

'*Play* . . .? On *this* day? The *Lord's* Day . . .?' She stood up, looking shocked and angry. 'There's *new ways* you'll be learning, girl. Sunday is a Day of Devotion in thought, word and deed for the Lord. Learn it well. It's only catch you doing otherwise just *once* and for ever sorry you'll be, my girl. It's praying you'll be doing now, praying His *forgiveness*' – she was pointing at the floor; slowly my trembling legs obeyed the pointing finger; I felt Pat sinking to her knees beside me.

'Our Father which art in Heaven . . .' – she prompted me. And kept on until it came to the part that says 'Forgive us our trespasses', and here she stopped. I – and Pat joined me – had to keep repeating that line. That all-important line: 'Forgive us our trespasses.'

Chapter 33 ~~~

Monday morning. I was up and setting about my jobs with a smile. The Welsh hat emptied and washed. The beds made. Table laid for breakfast. And me, washed and tidy, sitting on the sofa whilst Auntie brushed Pat's ringlets and tied on a big green bow. The kettle was steaming on the long black coal-fired range that was Auntie's fire and cooker all at once. A pot of porridge bubbled to one side. Our breakfast. And I, hungry as I'd ever been, felt more than ready for it. But Auntie was taking her time. I turned my gaze on to the table-legs and wondered about those gathered white calico stockings they wore. The sofa didn't have them but it had an all-round frill, so I couldn't be sure really. The mantelpiece had a frill, too, and above it all those brass candlesticks starting small at each end, growing step-by-step tall till they met in the middle and stood towering over the brass alarm clock with its two bells that it wore like twin hats.

But it was time. Time for Grace and breakfast. Porridge with syrup and a slice of bread and marg. Tea, Grace and washing-up. I looked at the clock. Ten past eight. Nearly time for school.

'Hilda!' – from the passage.

'Yes, Auntie . . .?' – I hurried.

She was standing there with a broom. 'It's the mat you do first. Then it's for you to roll it up, see, and brush the floor' – the broom was mine; Auntie was gone. And I hadn't got much idea really – well, we'd played at sweeping-up sometimes when we'd been playing Missuses but it had been much the same as being an elbowy Missus over a pretended back fence when we'd say what naughty or good invisible children we'd got.

I started brushing, this way, then that, sort of downwards and sideways, pulling the dust into a neat heap in front of me.

'Keep the dust in *front* of you, girl, in *front* . . .' – I stared at the dust that *was* in front of me, looked at Auntie: 'Move yourself!' – the broom seemed to move *it*self, only to be knocked from my hands; the strong hand that gripped my arm hurt like anything. 'There's *soft* you are, girl, it's *behind* the broom you do walk, see, *behind* it' – a final shake and I was clutching the broom again, properly it seemed, sweeping forward, ever forward, towards the bottom of the stairs. Now to roll up the long mat. And put it . . . where . . . the yard? That's where I took it, past her . . .? . . . silence. Now the lino. Much easier. A shovel for the dust and it was finished; she came to look. 'Pat! *Pat!* Here, it's the stairs you can be dusting.' Pat bent over the bottom step and rubbed with the yellow duster; Auntie dragged her up . . . 'Is it *two fools* I do have here?' – Pat's frightened face was brimming up for tears – 'It's at the *top* you do start. Go . . .' Pat went wobbling up the stairs, clutching the duster and using it as a mopping hankie. 'Get a bucket of water, there's not all day you do have' – I followed Auntie, wondering what came next. Hot water in a zinc bucket. And a large handful of soda, a scrubbing-brush and the hard yellowy soap that was like dried-up everlasting cheese. I found this out when I tried to raise what Auntie called a lather with which to scrub that front doorstep to keep its snowy whiteness. There was a wood part and beyond that just a concrete step. I started on the wood. 'Wrong. Stupid girl. Furthest away from you, see – wash farthest• away.' I washed out on the concrete, tried to use the scrubbing-brush and soap. 'Wrong *again*. See this stone. This, girl, *this*! Rub. *Rub*! Put some elbow grease into it. Now rinse it. Wipe it. *Drier!* Come *on*, there's *slow* you are!' I wet the wooden part again. Right at last – about the brush and soap. 'To the grain, girl – *to the grain!*' – my round-and-round scrubbing changed to just to-and-fro; I seemed to be doing it for ever. '*Rinse! Wipe!* Wipe *again!* Now get that mat down.' There's late we'd be for school. And hardly enough wits about us even to get there unaided.

At twenty minutes to nine I'd given up all hope of being in time for school. Miss Daley was bad enough if it was only five minutes, but we'd be much later than that. I swallowed a groan as Auntie Bron combed the twirly ringlets and tied the big butterfly bow for the third time. 'There. There's pretty you do look, Pat.' She lifted my sister up to the tiny mirror that hung high above Nunky's chair. 'See?' Pat nodded obediently. 'Get your things, girl.' Auntie was speaking to me. 'There's wool-gathering you are, standing by there.' I hurried to fetch coats and gas masks. 'Mr Davis is very strict about lateness, new or not, my girl. Just you remember it, too.' She was helping Pat into her coat; those curls mustn't be ruffled. But who and what, I wondered, was Mr Davis? Nothing to do with us, because we didn't even know him. I shrugged into my coat and slung the canister over my shoulder; we'd just have to run like anything across that waste ground and hope for the best. Miss Daley might even understand when I explained – if she let me, that is. '. . . to Mr Davis himself, you hear?' – I blinked as a white envelope waved in front of my eyes.

'Er – yes. Yes, Auntie. Mr Davis . . .' – my head was nodding, agreeing, yet not a word of what I'd heard made sense.

We stepped carefully over the doorstep; we each kissed the offered cheek and turned away – the wrong way. 'Hilda! *There's* the school! See it! See it! Stupid girl!' – the fingers clutched at my arm, Auntie bent low so that her voice sang inside my head whilst her other hand dragged at my hand holding the note.

'But Miss Daley . . .' I flung a look of desperate hope over my shoulder, hoping she'd somehow appear behind me; a sharp tug brought me face to face with Auntie.

'Give the note to Mr Davis. Now go, both of you, and be careful that it's like ladies you do walk.'

'Yes, Auntie,' we said, and managed stiff smiles.

207

Walking hand in hand towards the strange world of a different school, we could feel Auntie watching us nearly all the way. At last a small bend . . . ''T'ain't fair, 'Ild, none of our kids come 'ere, it's not for us, is it . . .?'

I was equally hopeful. 'Perhaps Auntie didn't know.'

A few late children gave us far-from-friendly stares as they pushed past us into the cloakroom. 'Dew, it's Uckavees, all nits an' fleas . . .' Pat and I stood there holding the note, waiting until the hymn-singing had finished.

A teacher wearing a button-through smock came into the porch. 'Latecomers! To Miss Powell for the cane' – she was about to go back inside.

'Please, Miss . . .'

She turned. '*No* excuses. It's the same faces every time. Oh!'

I smiled at the surprised look. 'I've a note for Mr Davis.'

'In*deed!*' Her eyes flashed all over us. 'New, are you? I'll find Mr Davis. Hang up your things over there.' Pat gave me a scared look; neither of us spoke.

Mr Davis strode through the doorway, tall, thin and severe-looking; his eyes examined right through us. 'You have a note. For me?' Unable to speak, I offered the envelope, wondering what to say to him when he'd read it. 'Hmm. Yes. I see.' He pressed his lips tightly together. 'Belong with the rest really . . .' – he was speaking softly to himself. 'It's full we are . . .' Hope surged within me. 'But there's two places in Miss Evans's class – eight-year-olds . . .' He looked hopefully at Pat, who shrank from his sight behind me.

'Please sir, we don't mind going back to Miss Daley.' I tried to sound helpful.

'Wait there.' He went back into the classroom. Now a beckoning hand. 'Miss Evans will have you till we sort something out. This way.' He held the door further open. A blur of faces turned to stare. Pat clung to my arm.

'Sit there' – the teacher waved to a desk at the front. We squeezed in beside each other and joined in the morning's recital of times tables. Then on to simple arithmetic. And then the inevitable playtime. Pat and I followed the rest out into the playground. The first thing to be thankful for was that the boys had gone the other way. They, it seemed, played separately. But the girls! They crowded around us as soon as we got out of the door, and there at the top of the steps began the questions.

Sisters were we? Twins? A nod and shake answered that.

Both in Miss Evans's class. One of us must be simple.

'We're not!'

Slums from up London way. Dirty mochyns.

Now I was angry. 'Welsh pigs!'

A sort of shocked silence surrounded me. Only me. Somehow Pat was on the outside. '*What*dyer say, Mochyn?'

I refused to answer. They began to push and shove. A teacher appeared from behind me somewhere. 'Ah, meeting the new girls, that's very thoughtful. But I'm sure she'd like to have a little more room.' The girls melted away. Pat crept closer to me.

At last it was time to go back inside the school. I ignored the shuffling kicks and digs along the corridor, thankful to reach Miss Evans's class once again. It was Reading Lesson. As we listened to the halting sentences and stumbled words I knew why I'd been called a dunce. This class seemed full of them. Pat read very well, and I skimmed quickly through my page. Miss Evans said I had a nice speaking voice and we passed into Composition, I chose 'A Day in the Country' and wrote about that lovely time we'd spent at Mayfield.

We were sorry when dinner time came. First of all we had to run from the bigger girls; and secondly, Auntie had seen us running and smacked our legs for it.

Miss Evans, we'd found, was very nice. So were the other girls in our class; we ignored the boys. It was only the bigger girls who were being hateful and not all of them either, but it took us a long time to find out because the nicer girls kept to themselves and let newcomers get on with it till they had decided whether or not to accept them. But we, being Evacuees, were a different kettle of fish, so no group ever really made us a part of it.

Our school work kept us at the top of the class but we'd done it all before; it seemed strange to whip through embroidered chairbacks with Dutch boys and girls in bright-coloured wools whilst forty pairs of less able hands took ages and ages over one single stem-stitch outline, often having to undo it and start again.

But there were other things to learn. I'd mastered the sweeping and scrubbing each morning and bedmaking was no longer a puzzle either, so by Friday I felt the only problem was getting through playtimes and in and out of school, but even that wasn't so bad now; they'd called us everything and done all the sly pushing and shoving till they themselves tired of it.

Auntie was strict and we were getting used to that too. There was something to look forward to, though. Next week we'd start to learn how to be Sunbeams.

Chapter 34 ~~~

It was Tuesday evening when Auntie produced the jerseys. Second-hand, they were, but Mrs Edwards was as clean as a new pin so the jerseys, outgrown by her sons, were as good as new. I stared stupidly as Pat's head emerged through the high neck of the smaller one. Crumbs! A flaming golden sun and a bright-blue scroll with all about the Blood and the Lamb. Now Auntie was urging me to hurry into the slackness of the larger jersey whilst she adorned Pat's curls with red ribbons. Her glance at me was enough to tell me I'd failed to transform myself; she tugged at my skirt and Evan Edwards's jersey but it was no use – the neck still flopped and the sleeves still hung loosely down, the cuffs covering my hands and the bright-blue scroll all jumbly. There's awkward I was. She shook me. 'Now stand this way. Head up. Chin in.' I tried. She sighed. At last she rolled the sleeves, threaded elastic through the neck, and that was it. Gwyneth was at the door and it was time for our first-ever Sunbeam lesson.

The Captain was a great tall wide lady, and she'd rise up from the piano like the big black sail of a ship. Then I'd hear all about her excellent self-control as she grasped me by the back of my jersey and forcibly had me trying to march gaily, smile brightly, sing and wave my tambourine with zest, and all at the same time. Pat managed quite well right from the start; though too shy to sing she was able to smile and wave her tambourine joyfully; as for me, I just didn't seem able to do anything right. It wasn't for the want of trying – I wanted to please the Captain, and above all Auntie – it was just that I seemed to find it difficult to keep my balance on the wobbly form and smile broadly whilst singing 'Jesus wants me for a Sunbeam', and then there was that wretched tambourine; banging it and waving it around was one thing but those coloured ribbons flying in all directions seemed to blot out our faces anyway and when it came time to really be a Sunbeam, well, unless people knew just what we were supposed to be singing it could have been 'Any Old Iron' for all they knew, for the band would always start blaring away at the same time, with us racing one another underneath it to the end. I found it all rather like having a lot of little pieces which I never could fit together right. I began to realise that sometimes it is not the easiest thing in the world to be a Sunbeam.

'What did you call him Owl's-Eyes for?' We were walking back to school.

Pat shrugged. ''Cause it's wot they *look* like.'

'Now look here! His blinking sister and her gang *got* me at dinner time.'

'Yeah, she said she would. So I runned 'ome.' Pat's voice had a shudder in it.

My anger rose inside me. 'You mean you *knew*?'

She nodded.

'But you could have *told* me.' I felt shocked; I'd slowed almost to a stop.

'Nah, they was there, see. An' *you* was comin'. An' 'sides, Owl's-Eyes was tellin' 'em you was me big sister.'

'You mean they saw you?'

She nodded.

'And they didn't *do* anything to you?'

'Nah, it was you they wanted to 'it, see, Ild. An' there was a lottuvem. So I jus' came 'ome.'

I stared at her. She walked on. I was still trying to sort it all out. The prods. The punches. The stinging double-slaps. My glasses swinging tear-dripped from one ear. And I didn't even *know* this . . . this 'Owl's-Eyes' . . . and they *knew* I didn't. And her – my own sister – deliberately not looking or else pleading with her eyes whilst I was getting smacked for being late to dinner, *and* being a cry-baby.

I hurried. Caught up with her.

She sighed. 'Wasn't anythink *I* could do.'

'If you hadn't called him that silly name . . .'

She shrugged.

'*Well!*' My anger made the demand.

''E kep' on *starin'* at me. An' 'is eyes was big an' roun' an' all sorta . . . well, *Owl's-Eyes*. So I said it.'

She seemed to think everything was all right now.

'What *is* his name?'

'Dunno.'

'And don't care!' I yelled into her startled face. 'Well, you just *find out*! And don't think you needn't bother, because next time it's you they'll get, so there.'

Her face went red. 'That ain't wot they was sayin'. It's *you* wot they don't like.'

Her quiet words had told me the truth. 'But I haven't *done* anything!' My protest was quiet and seeking at the same time.

'Yer talks posh, some of 'em says. Copies the teachers. An' yer wears nice frocks wot girls in eyeglasses shouldn't 'ave. 'Sides, yer gets sores on yer eyes.'

We turned in at the school gate, Pat now walking shyly ahead of me: me who felt as if I'd just had another stinging slap. The afternoon story, 'Amelia Ann Stiggins', fell on my deaf ears. I sewed furiously at a cushion cover and discovered that apart from Winnie and the Gang now beyond my reach I hadn't a friend in the world. Nobody liked me. Or wanted me. Not even those silly Sunbeams. As far as everybody was concerned I was just a raincloud. But I *had* had friends – real ones, even. But that was before the war. Doreen Jeffries was my favourite then and a girl named Olive who wore silky frilled frocks and had Parties on her birthdays. My cheeks felt hot as I remembered *my* promised Party. Mum telling me to ask Olive, and her wearing that satin frock to school all ready to come to my Party. We'd run all the way home, to find the door locked and Mum out. I'd peeped in the window. The bare table that wasn't ready for a Party had stood before the dying fire and Olive had seen it and gone away. Mum came home later. Party? Wot party? She must fill the coal bucket. Renee was minding us tonight. My heart had got its first faint crack then. And Olive never spoke to me again.

All day at each service I'd felt the stares of others, seen the sedate lady hats draw closer together as the ladies drew each other's attention to Pat and me. And why? These jerseys, that was why. Not that I was absolutely sure, but looking around at the neatly summer-frocked girls, I'd at some moment become uncomfortable about how my sister and I were dressed.

We knelt to pray. It was near the end of the service.

The squeak of hinges and evening sunshine spilled into the church. Prentice-the-Plate had opened the door. Now the soft slow shuffle up the aisle; we were going out now; the slight touch on my shoulder halted me; I stepped obediently to one side and pulled Pat to stand with me. The congregation filed out slowly, a few words here and a handshake there. I glanced out into the street: Gwyneth in the uniform idled, looking impatiently towards the doorway. The vicar and Mr Prentice, last to leave, were still in the doorway. Now Mr Prentice's sweaty face was about to be mopped on a spotless handkerchief; he seemed to be saying an awful lot in a hurried whisper.

'Ah yes, quite . . . er . . .' The vicar glanced at me.

'Please, Sir, we have to go,' I blurted.

'The child seems eager to be gone . . .' It was Mr Prentice speaking.

The vicar sighed loudly. 'I want to have a little talk with you afterwards.'

'Oh please, Father, there's someone waiting.'

He nodded Mr Prentice to go inside and stood looking at me sternly. 'That isn't the way to behave, child; where is the respect for your elders?'

I hung my head. He waited for my answer.

'Please, Sir, there's one waiting outside and she'll be ever so cross because there's the Meeting . . .'

I glanced up. His head was shaking. 'And which faith were you baptised into?'

I swallowed. 'The church, Sir – least we always went to church once, before the war that is.'

'Then your first duty is to your faith, is it not?'

'Yes, Sir,' I answered softly, thinking about all the first duties and all the faiths I owed since I'd come here.

'Then have the courage to stand firm by it.' His order was an order – I quaked inside; just the thought of all those aunties and me standing firm by *anything* was enough to turn my bones to jelly.

'It's these garments . . . I hardly think them suitable for the church' – he was looking at the big yellow wobbly sun on my middle. 'You will please ask your auntie – or whatever – to see that when attending church you are more suitably dressed.'

I felt myself going white at the simple thought of it. No words came, though, and my blank eyes rested on the vicar's long black tunic.

'Very well now, child, that is all. You may go. Good night and God's Blessing go with you.'

I watched him turn away; Pat seized my arm. 'Ooh 'Ild . . .'

'Come on, oh stop crying, we'll tell Gwyneth it's about – oh, a new prayer to learn or something' – we hurried to the black-and-red-uniformed figure.

'There's late. Tell your Auntie Bron I will. No respect for your elders, that's the truth of it, no respect . . .' – it seemed to go on all the way to the meeting-house door; her glance as we heard the blaring from inside was like daggers. Pat and I joined the waiting Sunbeams collecting the tambourines from the band room, a large cupboard really. Yes, Gwyneth would tell, and I knew somehow that what the vicar had said about courage and all that wouldn't help with the jersey part. I'd just have to think of something. Maybe I could smuggle a blouse out. There must be *some* way. I followed the last row of Sunbeams on to the wobbly platform. Waving yellow, red and blue ribbons. The blaring band. Smiling faces, mouths shaping the chosen hymn: 'We are but little children weak'.

There was a silence whilst Auntie closed the door and stood herself in front of the fireplace. A silly feeling stabbed at me as her eyes glared. I shuddered, still standing on one leg, seemingly unable to take the other one out of that high sink.

'You were last out of that church.' Auntie's voice was sharp; accusing.

'Yes, Auntie.' I felt silly standing there in just my knickers with one foot in a sink.

'Was it something to do with your behaviour?' Our eyes met; mine fell away . . .

'No, Auntie.' I took the unwashed foot out of the sink. I wanted to cry because she could see my ribs and the way my legs shook.

'Gwyneth says . . .' Her words went on and on and all I could think was how awful it was to be told off without clothes on.

Footsteps coming along the passage; I turned as Nunky came in. 'Cover yourself. Dew, there's a simpleton she is and no mistake.' I scrambled into the comfort of my nightie as the window moved noisily downwards.

Nunky glanced at me, shook his head slightly and sat heavily in his chair. 'A storm tonight, Bron, from the looks of that sky.'

Auntie sighed aloud. 'Fetch the Book.' I hurried away, eager to forget the questions and, most of all, my cowardly way of answering them. Faith? I wasn't brave enough to bear it. Though perhaps with clothes on . . . ? My hands held the Bible. Dear God, I'm a coward. Ooh God, even the vicar wears that long black thing! Forgive me, but I needed my clothes too. The darkening passage swallowed the silent prayer.

'After that, Hilda' – Auntie was putting on her dark-blue coat – 'a small bucket in the coal hole over to the tip. No slag, mind.'

A knock at the front door. Auntie picked up her handbag and basket. 'I'll expect to see it before it's emptied, mind.' She bent and kissed Pat. 'Coming, Mam, coming!' she called, and turned to the door.

There was a long silence after it had shut. 'She's gorn . . .' Pat sounded relieved.

I hastily started our next job: cleaning the cutlery. 'We ain't goin' ter play, then?' Pat sounded a little bit hopeful.

''Course we are!' I answered with a smile.

Pat's face lit up. 'Yer mean it?'

I nodded, hastily polishing a knife. 'They'll all be there just waiting for us; come on, Pat, hurry up!'

Winnie and I dug side by side into the steep side of the slag heap; little nuts of coal rained into our baskets. 'Cor, 's'ot, innit?' Winnie wiped a grimy hand over her flushed face; I grinned as the streaky marks suddenly appeared. 'Your face! Better wipe it.'

'Ta, 'Ild' – my offered hankie was accepted. She rubbed at the grubby streaks whilst I pulled up my skirt and sat my navy-blue knickers on the slag, glad of the excuse for a rest.

'Wotcha gonna do, then? 'Bout them jerseys?'

''Spect I should've told her. Only . . . well, I'm too frightened to. And now it's too late . . .' My voice trailed off.

Winnie flopped down beside me. Our fingers began the idle

picking. "'E ain't got no right tellin' yer orf in the first place. Not that I blame 'im, mind, them jerseys is really 'orrible.'

A short silence fell between us. I stood up. Little irritating bits of dust had found their way inside my socks.

"'Ere, jest 'ark at 'er' – Winnie gave a chuckle as we listened to Joyce farther down the slope chanting her way through the Creed. 'Yer 'as ter wear all white when it's done ter yer . . . Bet she sews paper bows on!' We couldn't help the giggles . . .

The morning was filled with warmth and bright sunshine. It was so warm that Auntie put out the green crepe frocks and straw hats for the day. It wasn't until tea time that she reminded us to change into the thick red jerseys for our performance as Sunbeams. It wasn't any use pleading about the heat. The sun had fled across the sky, leaving a cool evening and goose-pimply arms behind it. 'Perhaps we'd better take our macks?' I ventured as Auntie ushered us out of the front door.

'There's no need, it's warm enough you'll be.' Her voice was sharp, yet she kept it low enough to be within the bounds of the Lord's Day of self-discipline.

Pat and I walked smartly along the road like two red jam pots. When we turned the corner I slowed almost to a stop. 'We've got to be a bit late, Pat,' I explained to her puzzled face. We entered the dim porchway as the congregation stood to sing the first hymn. 'Quick, do as I do' – my arms slipped inside the jersey; now a quick twist – and arms back inside the sleeves . . .

Pat stared in amazement; she peered round my shoulder . . .

'Of course it's there!' I told her. 'So the vicar won't have to see it, see?' I was helping her twist inside her jersey too.

Something was bothering Pat. 'But we gotta come *out*, 'Ild!'

I pushed the inner door. 'We're going in the back row, see – and coming out *fast and first*, see?' She nodded doubtfully; I pushed the door wider. We slipped in quickly and squeezed our back-to-front jerseys tight against the back of the seat. The vicar prayed on undisturbed by the flaming suns. And whilst everyone was joining in the last prayer, Pat and I crept softly backwards to the dim porch behind us. It was a funny feeling really, it almost made you wonder whether you were coming or going.

Chapter 35 ~~~

On Tuesdays and Fridays Auntie Bron mixed her bread dough. This she did in the morning so that by dinner time it would be what she called 'proved'. This meant it sort of doubled itself and swelled up in the oblong loaf tins where it lay covered with a cloth. After dinner it was another of my tasks to carry these covered uncooked loaves to the bakehouse, where I'd collect them directly after school. There were always three of them and unfortunately I had only two arms; Auntie tried various ways to bend and wrap them around these tins but in the end even she had to see that three into two wouldn't go, not even for her, so with much sighing and grumbling about my awkwardness and stupidity she had been forced to allow Pat's arms to enclose the third tin, reminding me that should anything happen to it on the way to the bakehouse, I'd be held responsible. We kept our grumbles until we were out of her sight. I glanced at Pat. 'It's all right for you, you've only got one.' My voice sounded cross like Auntie's; already my arms were aching.

''T'ain't my fault' – holding the white-wrapped tin snugly in front of her. No, it wasn't her fault. But she had two arms, she had ringlets, she was pretty . . . Nice too, I thought carefully. Crumbs, though, if *I'd* dared hang my head when a grown-up expected an answer . . . but then my eyes didn't go swimmy-blue and lovely with brimming tears, just horribly red and sore-looking.

I pushed open the rough wooden door with my foot. The smell of freshly baked bread made me feel as if we were the Bisto Kids arriving. The baker showed us where to put the tins and how to write the name on each of the long sides with a piece of chalk. Then he hurried to one of his huge wall ovens and flung the black iron door wide. I watched marvelling as he picked up a long-handled wooden spade-like thing and slid it under the hot fresh loaves, easing them in twos or threes out on to the wide wooden table so quickly that in no time at all that great oven was emptied and clanged shut. All those lovely crisp loaves lay in neat rows; his glance at our astonished faces brought a smile. 'Never seen it done, bach?' We shook our heads. He smiled broadly. 'Come again, then' – loaves were already skidding down the second table.

I pulled the wooden door closed – and was instantly gripped

from behind and swung round. 'Oh, Win!' I gasped, wondering how she'd managed to just be there like that.

'On a messidge . . . Saw yer goin' in' – she was pleased with her surprise. We were all laughing and chattering, wandering to the sparkling water, bending over our neglected fairy pool. A few stolen minutes was all we had together. But from now on we'd meet on bread days.

We were sedately passing Auntie's front door on our way to the school. Did the curtains twitch?

Mr Davis had written that next term I'd be going up to the Scholarship Class, and would be required to do an hour's home-work each evening. I'd thought Auntie'd be pleased, although I myself was scared silly. But she wasn't. '*She's* not going to be sat wasting my time night after night. There's few enough places for our own kind as it is' – her voice spoke to Nunky, but I could feel her eyes making darts in my back as my hands lowered the washing-up bowl on to the pantry shelf. Crumbs, it wasn't *my* fault, *I* didn't ask for one of their precious Places. But it wasn't children who did the choosing, this was what Auntie didn't seem to understand. There'd be a sort of blankness about the room whenever I came in, and if she spoke at all it was to Nunky or Pat.

Pat was such a sweet child. 'It's almost as if she really belongs,' Auntie would say as she brushed the shining hair or buttoned a blouse. And Nunky would offer a faint smile at Pat's reddening face. It seemed true, too, because they'd always be in a little group up near the big chair, just as if Auntie was deliberately making it true by arranging it that way. Sometimes it made me feel I wasn't in the room at all. Pat hated it, especially when Auntie asked her how she'd like to really be their little girl. I'd been outside in the lavatory and had come in to see Pat being hugged tightly. It was only later, when we were in bed, that Pat whispered about it.

'Crumbs, what did you say?' I asked in astonishment.

She began to cry. 'I was frightened, 'Ild . . . so I said Yes. She'd 'a bin a bit angry if . . .' but I'd stuffed her head under the blankets: 'Shut up, she'll *hear* you . . .'

But the muffled sobs went on: 'I *'ad* ter say it, I *'ad* ter . . .'

'Shush, it's all right, she didn't mean it, you'll see.' My hand patted her back, my voice made soothing quiet sounds, but my mind was full of the awfulness of what had happened. I wondered what *my* answer would have been and knew only too well how hard it would have been to say No to a grown-up. But nobody asked me anything. Anyway, we already belonged to someone; we'd got a mum and a dad and a home of our own. Pat had gone to sleep. Oh well, I told myself, it probably isn't a real worry anyway, I already had one of those: what to do about my homework next term. Because I didn't own a single piece of week to fit it into.

It was holiday time and Auntie allowed us out to play in the afternoons, although skipping, running and playing hopscotch were forbidden. It became quite easy to forget one or the other of these, and Winnie soon found a way for me to play hopscotch: she lent me her shoe each time it was my turn. But for now we'd had enough of hopscotch and lay sprawled on the dusty grass. Winnie stopped chasing the badly split tennis ball and shoved it into her pocket. 'Get up, you lazy lot! Let's go an' look for some shade.'

It was nice where the shade was, only scraggy hedges and steep mountainside and no more village, all quiet with a narrow ribbon of road that curved and twisted to goodness knows where. Then the long thin alleyway from where we could see the vases of flowers, concrete crosses and clumps of long overgrown grass. We'd been here before. We stared at the corner heap of old wire-and-moss shapes with dying and dead flowers dripping miserably down. Joyce stared the most. 'I'm *goin'*!' she decided.

'Oh no you ain't! 'Cause you're bigger'n *us*, see. Don't yer want any 'air ribbons?'

It was the first we'd heard of hair ribbons.

'We're gonna 'ave 'em afore someone else gets 'em.' And now we could see them, glints of ribbon woven in among the heap. There were rain-washed cards too. We squeezed our way after Winnie through the bent bit of railings and, stumbling over a couple of overgrown mounds, set to work on the heap. The strange quiet seemed to soak up the excitement and leave our fingers hurrying with a sense of urgency. The red bow had rust marks on it but I stuffed it up my knicker-leg. Now a white one. Then a yellow. Yet Joyce, the Paper Lady herself, wouldn't take even one. Jessica showed me her three ribbons. Mauve. Yellow. And a darker mauve. And it was Jessica who took over the problem of washing the ribbons; she even promised to try and iron them, but we'd have to wait till Ironing Day.

We played on the steep mountainsides, vain in our new hair ribbons, even if they did have slight rust marks on them. Winnie had found a cardboard box that had somehow escaped the salvage sack, and on it we slid recklessly down the bumpy slopes. Well, recklessly enough; we'd taken care about *where*, and we'd first got rid of the loose stones.

At half-past four we crept in the back door and found the silent house our own. We took the ribbons off and tucked them back in their hiding-places at the back of the drawer filled with our winter liberty bodices, replacing them with the old ones. But after we'd laid the table there was nothing to do but wait for Gwyneth, who was expected at tea time. So out came our treasures and we tied them on again. The scarlet bow suited Pat, and my pink one adorned shoulder-length hair that I'd combed free of plaits. I tied the ribbon round my head and took off my glasses. 'Ooh, you look much nicer, 'Ild!' Pat's look was admiring.

'So do you,' I told her.

''Ave a look, 'Ild,' she urged, glancing up at the mirror. But I shook my head, and lucky for me, because I now heard Gwyneth coming through the house and stuck my glasses back on, dragging the bow off at the same time. There wasn't anything I could do about the plaits, though.

Gwyneth gave me a long hard look – my hand flashed upwards to drag back the flowing hair. 'No! Leave it be.' She turned to cut the bread. Pat and I stared at each other wonderingly. 'It's *one* slice you do have?'

'Er, yes! Yes please!'

'It's ready, then.' She indicated the table and busied herself making a pot of tea. She seemed not to notice anything more than the inside of her handbag. But after we'd finished putting the tea things away: 'There's thick hair you do have.' Her voice was directed at me. I nodded and tried a smile. Was thick hair something nice? She stood up, her hand touching it. 'It shines. Pity to keep it in plaits, don't you think?'

I shrugged. 'Stays out of the way,' I added, quickly realising it was rude not to answer.

'Those glasses don't suit you. Take them off.' Reluctantly my hands removed the glasses. Gwyneth stood back, looking at my face. 'There's better you do look now. See! Look! I'll show you' –

220

Pat gulped loudly beside me as Gwyneth reached up for the mirror. She held it up in front of me.

Too nervous to really look, I nodded. 'Yes, it does look better,' I mumbled. Crumbs, Auntie might come in any minute!

Gwyneth propped the mirror against her handbag, which she'd placed on the table. We watched her studying her reflection, a frown here, a smile there, turning her head this way and that. 'Do you think I have nice skin?' Her eyes fixed on me and went back to the mirror.

'Er, yes. Very nice,' I told her loudly, wondering if she'd ever noticed the line of dark hair that grew along her upper lip. And why didn't she hurry up and put that silly mirror away?

'It's nice for a girl to have nice skin. And thick shiny hair.' She seemed to be talking to herself, so I stayed quiet. 'Most girls do get spots. Nasty things, too' – she was looking at me again.

'Yes, I know.'

My whispered answer brought a smile to her face. 'Come here,' she said quietly. I fidgeted, wondering whether I ought to tell her about Auntie and the mirror. 'Oh, come *on*, girl!' Her tone was sharper. I went and stood beside her. 'Sit there and look at your skin.' She rose from Nunky's chair.

I backed away. 'Oh, but . . .'

Her hand round my arm guided me. 'There's no harm. And see how different you do look now, more grown-up like.' I peeped nervously into the mirror. 'Here, I'll just comb your hair a bit and you'll see.' Gwyneth combed, I stared. Yes, I did look different, but it was a long time since I'd really seen my face anyway.

I smiled, began to get up; Gwyneth gently pushed me down again. 'Wait, I'm just going to the lav. We'll try something different when I come back.'

I sat on the very edge of the chair. A glance at Pat and, seeing her smile, another peep into the mirror. If only my eyes weren't so big and my neck so skinny. Was my mouth too wide? I stared harder. And harder still. And the door opened. I looked up expecting to see Gwyneth, but it was Auntie herself who stood there. An angry gasp and she was across the room, snatching away the mirror and shoving me out of the big chair. 'Oh Bron, there's back you are! And how was the old lady?' Gwyneth came smiling into the room.

'She's . . . she's . . . not-so-well . . .' The mirror still swung slightly and Auntie's anger must have been plain to see, but

Gwyneth chatted away, something about going home to put the boys' bath water on. And gathering her bag, she started to edge out of the room.

'Thank you, Gwyn . . .' Auntie's voice was tight with anger, but she went up the passage and talked quietly to her sister before the front door slammed and her feet pounded up the stairs. The sounds from the room above told us that Auntie was putting her coat away with much more noise than usual. We even heard the slam of her wardrobe door. Then she hurried back down the stairs. 'Get ready for bed. *Both* of you.' Her angry face just poked round the door, then she hastened up the passage and we heard the front door slam. Trembling all over, I stared at Pat, and she at me.

'Ooh, 'Ild, she's 'narf angry' – Pat's tears were already brimming.

'Better hurry up and do what she said.' And we began to undress. Pat got the nighties and I got the wash water. Quick as a flash we plunged into our wash and donned the nighties, fearful of Auntie returning to find something else wrong. But we sat on the end of that sofa for ages before she finally came back, bringing Gwyneth with her.

'Pat!' Auntie was pointing to the floor beside her. 'Come here. *You!* Stand by there' – her finger indicated the sink. Gwyneth sat by the fire looking faintly surprised but not very interested, especially in me.

'Who got that *mirror* down?' Auntie glared at me. I looked at Gwyneth, expecting her to speak. '*You* did!' Auntie had answered for me.

'No, Auntie, I didn't, really I didn't' – my trembling voice was hardly above a whisper; all my body was shaking with excited fear.

'*Liar*. Now it's the *truth* I'll hear. Who took that mirror down off the wall?'

I shook my head. 'No, it wasn't me, Auntie.' I tried to tear my eyes away from hers, to look at Gwyneth, Gwyneth who would surely own up. But she just looked right through me.

'Well? Who *was* it, then? Old Nick?' – the angry voice dared me to deny again. I shook my head. You couldn't tell tales on people, especially on grown-ups.

'So! We'll start at the beginning, shall we? Gwyneth says – and she's *here*, remember – that you were already *admiring your hair*.

Loose, it was, and no eyeglasses either. The mirror was just being put back on the wall.'

There was a long pause. It was true, my hair was loose. But the mirror bit – that wasn't right.

'I didn't touch the mirror, Auntie.' Her sudden slap across my face stopped the trembling at once. I cried, loud choking gulps. 'My plaits *were* undone. But not the rest, not the rest. Ask Pat.' Pat's head nodded.

'Is *my* sister a liar, then?' Auntie hadn't seen the nods; her slaps slammed my head from side to side.

Gwyneth said nothing. But then to her sister: 'I'd better go, Bron. You can lock from a thief but not from a liar.'

I flung Gwyneth a pleading look. 'Please! You know. Tell her. Tell Auntie.'

'By all means,' she said in a bored kind of way. 'She had that mirror. Talking about nice skin she was. And staring at her hair; *you* came in and caught her, Bron. It's wicked, that's what, wicked, and I won't listen to another word. Ask her about *the pink ribbon*, why don't you? She's got it somewhere.'

Auntie didn't see Gwyneth out. A fresh new question came: 'The *ribbon*, where is it?' I took it from my folded knickers. Another slap. 'Liar. Thief. This isn't yours.' I shook my head, sobbing all the while, hearing Pat's sobs too as the ribbon burned in the fire. 'Get to bed at once. *Go.* Get out of my sight. And remember, this is not the end of the matter, there's punishment to come, a liar is the worst of all things. Now remove yourself. You *too*' – she pushed Pat roughly towards me. Together we sobbed our way up to bed. Dreading the coming of morning.

Morning. Auntie calling me from sleep to dull weary wakefulness. Trouble was the first thought that came. I dressed quickly, helping Pat, who seemed ready to cry at the slightest thing. Now the search for my usual dark-green hair ribbons – a quick hasty business because Auntie was waiting somewhere down there. But there were no ribbons . . . a feeling of panic swept over me; they'd been there last night . . . Pat was looking under the bed; she came up shaking her head. Neither of us spoke. I'd have to go down there with the china Welsh hat and loose flowing hair. Fearfully I crept downstairs, hugging the slopping article. 'Good morning, Auntie,' I quavered to a silent, unmoving face. She didn't answer but that in itself wasn't unusual; what *was* unusual was that she was looking at me, watching everything I did, *and* my hair. Oh dear God, I thought in the safety of the lav. My hair! Where *had* I put those ribbons? Surely Auntie would say something about the lack of them when I went back inside? But she didn't. All through breakfast I felt her eyes on my shaking hands, felt my hair falling foward as I bent slightly to eat the porridge. Oh why was she so quiet, why didn't she say something? All I wanted was to get it over with, take my punishment now and know that it was over. Auntie stayed quiet and watchful as we went about our usual jobs: my arms ached with scouring, my face and neck were damp with sweat as my hair kept falling forward making me hot, making me pause to brush it back with a damp hand. And somewhere behind me she was watching . . . watching . . . Perhaps this was the punishment; my hopes rose with the thought – in that case it was nearly over and I'd learnt that vanity such as mine had no place with scrubbing and polishing. But it wasn't nearly over at all – Auntie kept us hard at work all the morning, never speaking a word, not even when she led me roughly to the washtub with the steaming soaking dusters and cleaning rags. The soap and rubbing-board were there and I got busy, knowing she was just the other side of the window, watching. At last she came out, bent to inspect the cloths I'd rubbed and placed in the bowl, and with a sharp slap across my arm she expressed her contempt of my efforts at washing – all the lot were tipped back into the tub, more bleach was poured in and her sharp prod acted like a winding-key: in went my hands, found a duster, soaped it, now rub-rub-rub-rub up-and-down on the zinc board. More soap. More rubbing. My hair, that had to be shaken back every few minutes.

Pat came and whispered just the single word: 'Dinner'. I went inside, saw Nunky's look of faint surprise flash from me to Auntie. 'Say Grace!' and we all bowed our heads. My hands were red and stinging from the heat of the water and all that bleach. A glance around the table showed Nunky's hands, pinky-white with coal-rimmed fingernails and faint bluish marks; Auntie's, plump and nearly-white with shiny oval fingernails; Pat's, tiny, pinker than Auntie's. And mine, glowing painfully red like my cheeks that were curtained by hair.

At last it was over; Nunky went inside his paper and the last of the washing-up had been put away. I sought Auntie's face and knew that it was back to the tub for me. Those dusters just wouldn't lose their stains; three times Auntie had tipped them back and twice she'd added hot water. I rubbed and rubbed. Then I heard Nunky's faint 'Cheerio' and knew Auntie was seeing him off to work. It must be half-past one, I thought dully. But Auntie was back. The dusters were suddenly considered clean enough to rinse and hang on the line against the high wooden fence. Now to empty the tub. Sweep the yard. And then I went into the kitchen. Pat was missing. Auntie was waiting with crossed arms. 'Sit there.' She nodded at Nunky's chair.

I gulped and, not daring to speak, slid myself between it and the table it had to be drawn close to. Propped in front of me was the mirror. A small sound forced itself out of me. I didn't want to sit there.

A stinging slap on my arm; Auntie towered over my shaking body. 'Take off those glasses' – her hand snatched them away. 'Now you be as vain as you like, girl. Just as you were yesterday. Only we're making a little change today, see. *I'm* here, and if you dare to take your eyes off that mirror I'll make you wish you hadn't. So sit there, you vain little hussy, and know I'm watching you every moment.' Her hand dragged my head to face my reflection. Then she placed my hands on the table, flat, palms down.

I stared at myself. Lips trembling, eyes red with unshed tears and my hair hanging limp and damp on either side of thin pale cheeks. The table moved slightly as Auntie sat herself at the other end of it. Not that I dared look, my eyes were fastened on the mirror just big enough to frame a head, close enough for me to take up *all* its space. No sound from Auntie, just the tick of the clock and me staring at me.

After a while the white cheeks became pink, my mouth too had long stopped trembling, and I saw that I was a very ordinary little girl. No spots or marks of any sort, and nothing much to look at. My eyebrows . . . long dark brown hairy lines that curved, not thick like Gwyneth's, no hair on my lip either; now if I had those hairs I could count them. My nose was ordinary enough, not big, not small. Perhaps if I could see my ears? But I couldn't move those carefully placed hands.

Well, my mind was saying, you *are* plain, you haven't a single interesting thing on your face to look at – no long lashes like Pat or twinkling blue eyes like Winnie's. My eyes? I looked. Grey? No, flecks in there; what colour were those flecks? Yellow? Oh, more gold-ish than that. And the grey – *was* it turning blue? Now the flecks looked grey, with only a few bits of gold. But surely the blue was going . . . slate grey taking its place . . . greeny flecks . . . I didn't like it at all, my head jerked itself; Auntie banged the table and then jumped up and slapped my face because I'd looked at her instead of *me*!

. . . *me*! with tear-filled eyes, red finger-marks across my cheek, a twisted trying-not-to-cry mouth, a glimpse of even white teeth, a tear rolling down one side of my face – now another raced it on the marked side but I knew it was no use; tears didn't cross out marks, not really they didn't; I watched the mark – those were the shapes of Auntie's fingers; they sloped downwards to my mouth, or maybe it was my neck, I could see the top part of it – my eyes went back to the mark: not such an ordinary little girl *now*, was I? I brushed the thought away and saw again my face as a whole thing, the front part of an ordinary girl, she was me, I was her, the ticking clock grew louder, coals moved down inside the range, the ordinary girl stared on and on . . . suddenly she was different, that face in there was different. I lowered my eyes to the lips. Lips that were smooth-closed. In repose? Don't look, I told myself and found the marble cheek, it had to be marble, those pink marks had made it so. But the other cheek – why wasn't that made of the same marble? Was it wax? Eyes met eyes – me and mine – sad, sad eyes – a moment's fleeting hurt . . .

Hullo!

Why hullo? We're not strangers. Or even friends. We belong. You are a reflection of me. Who? Me of it or it of me? The eyes refused to let go now, the whole face was theirs to see: that flat unliving carving in marble, or was it a statue of stone? I didn't like it, whatever it was, but still the eyes held, drawing and dragging me into that cold empty thing; pain ran up my arms as all of me seemed to turn into something unbending, unmoving, resisting that pull; only the beat of my heart thudded inside me, still those eyes stared, strange eyes, ticktock, blank like twin marbles. The changes were gradual; my racing panic contained itself somewhere on the edge of this blank empty stranger and me, hair swung wildly to cover the face, a face that mocked, a face that pleaded, the slaps rained, melting the stranger away leaving a sobbing picture of me, but even through the sobs I hated to look at those eyes. They'd frightened me, mocked at me, called to me, but the calling was to something not there, not me . . .

I felt something slapping at me, heard the deep sobs, felt my head shaking, my hands covering my face from that awful thing that stared. But Auntie was strong, my hands were behind my back, held fast by her: '*Look*, I tell you. *Look* . . .'

Her other hand dragged at my hair but I couldn't meet that face again, I *couldn't*, I struggled, pleaded and pleaded again: 'Yes I am a liar, yes oh yes I did take the mirror . . . I did . . . I did . . . I did . . .'

'I knew it!' she shouted. 'You little slut, lie to me, would you?' Her slaps were harder but she'd dragged me away from that awful empty face that had stared back at me. Suddenly her fury ended. 'Come here' – she was beckoning me to an ordinary chair, she was holding the scissors. I sat with a towel draped around my shoulders and heard the snip-snap around my head. Long hanks of hair fell on to the newspaper, hair that had been part of me. But I didn't care; something inside me had already gone away. I could feel the coldness of the scissors high up at the back of my neck. Now hair fell down across my eyes.

'Put these on and then get ready for bed. No tea for you, girl.' I fumbled with my glasses. Saw that it was after half-past five. I'd been sitting at that table for over three hours, seeing nothing but me. Then Auntie had cut my hair as punishment for being vain.

I crept upstairs and into bed, feeling the shortness of my hair and a fringe that stopped near the tops of my glasses. Auntie had wanted me to look at my punishment. It had taken every ounce of my strength to stifle the scream as she offered the mirror. 'Don't like it now I've cut off your vanity, do you?'

Vanity? What, my hair? Didn't she know what the mirror did?

Chapter 36 ~~~

This holiday the vicar was mostly busy with his garden. So whilst he dug for Victory, we did without lantern slides. The greyish squares were knitted to singsongs conducted by the vicar's wife. Pat sat quietly beside me. Now and then she'd lay down her knitting and wet the tips of her fingers. Then she'd pit-pat the wet tips across her forehead – first one hand, then the other – before taking up her knitting and doing a few more rows. I lost track of whatever it was we were singing, curious about this new habit of Pat's. She'd done it several times today. There it was again – dab-dab, pit-pat – and two long wet streaks across her forehead.

I leaned towards her. 'Headache?'

She glanced up, frowning. '*Eh?*' The wet strips were drying into faintly dirty streaks.

I produced my hankie, offered it. 'You got a *headache*?' I was right close to her ear.

'I *ain't*!' Her eyes flashed back scorn at me.

'Well, wipe your face. It's dirty.'

''Ere, leave me *be*' – she brushed my hand away.

'But it's *dirty*.'

''T'ain't, so *there*' – she was already licking her fingers again, staring at me in surprise. I pretended to interest myself in a dropped stitch.

Pit-pat. The sounds were soft. Nobody else seemed to hear them. And Pat was knitting again. I glanced at the two wet trails. Crumbs, Auntie'd blame me anyway. Headache or dirty face, it made no difference, somehow it would have to be my fault. I seemed to sprout faults faster than anyone I'd ever known.

On the way home I cleaned Pat's face, forbidding her to touch it again until we were at least under Auntie's eagle eyes. Let *her* see it happen, and then she'd know it wasn't anything to do with me.

But Auntie didn't seem to notice it. I watched it happen several times during the evening, once even while Pat was sitting on her lap. Surely she must see her hands move, hear that wet pit-pat sound? I waited for her to say something about it. Waited and waited in the quiet kitchen.

At last it was time to wash. Now she'd see those marks. Auntie had often helped Pat to wash just lately, and did tonight. But again nothing happened. I puzzled about it. Winnie had seen it as well as me, so it wasn't something I'd invented. And Auntie was so sharp-eyed she even saw things you hadn't done yet.

Her sudden prod filled my eye with stinging soap. 'Hurry yourself, girl, there's not all night you do have to stand mooning over a bowl.'

'Sorry, Auntie.' But the hairbrush was swishing up and down through Pat's hair whilst Auntie talked quietly about the lovely flowered satin she'd bought to have made into a special frock for a certain special little girl – blue it was with little pink rosebuds, there's pretty it was, even Mam had thought so.

From the time the front door shut Pat had been doing a lot of crying into her pillow. I'd just about given up trying to guess what the really-their-little-girl bit might mean. Pat's sudden burst of speech brought a halt to her tears: 'It's true, see – true, she's gonna try an' 'dopt me from Mum.'

That wasn't Pat talk. I sat up. 'She can't. There's *me*, remember, and she wouldn't adopt me for anything.'

Pat tugged at my nightie, I lay down beside her. ''Ild . . . you know when she cut orf yer 'air . . .' I nodded. 'Well, I 'ad ter stay up at the Gran's 'ouse, see, an' there was lots to eat, not like we got 'ere. They was all there, 'Ild, an' that's when I 'eard 'em.'

'Heard what?' I felt suddenly afraid.

'That Gran, she finks our mum don't want us no more 'cause of somefink wot's changed back 'ome.'

'What? What's changed?'

'I didn't 'ear all of it but you're gonna be a maid in a big 'ouse soon as yer fourteen. Then they can keep me, see, keep me for ever an' I'll never see yer any more. Ooh 'Ild, yer won't lettem, will yer? Yer won't?' She lay there crying quietly.

I felt cold all over. Those letters I wrote to Mum – she *mustn't* think they were true. And what was it that had changed at home? My thoughts whirled around. Surely Pat had got it all wrong? We had to be asked by someone. Didn't we? Who? Well, whoever it was I'd say No when they asked me. I'd get a good hiding, but I'd still say No and keep on saying it.

But what if they didn't ask me? What if it was only Pat, Pat all by herself being asked? She'd be too frightened to say anything but Yes, and that would be even more frightening than saying No. Poor old Pat, no wonder she was scared, she wasn't daft enough to believe they'd have me too, not even if I wanted to stay. No, they'd got plans already for me. A maid in a big house. No big house around here . . .

I'd never been afraid to go to school before in my life. It was always something that had to be done, and mostly it was nice. A new class meant leaving one teacher whom you'd got used to for a new one who might or might not be as nice or as strict as the last one. But this first day had me shrinking and shaking like a jelly inside my crisp blouse and navy-blue gymslip. Other children seemed quieter too, especially those who passed, like me, through the open door of Miss Jones's Scholarship Class. Of Miss Jones there was no sign. Just rows of empty waiting desks. And the blackboard and easel leaning against a cupboard and *her* desk high up on a sort of platform. Quiet murmurs of uncertainty passed around me, bolder children moved forward, sweeping me with them. I looked for a friendly face, realised that boys were doing most of the moving and pushing. Now came the girls. Nerys Griffiths, Megan Evans, one or two others whose names I wasn't sure of. They moved past me and seated themselves side by side, friend with friend. A bell rang in the cloakroom. It was time! My eyes sought a vacant place as a further press of children arrived. Ah, *there*, way up in the corner, farthest from the high window, farthest from that high-up desk too . . . I hurried and seated myself hastily beside another girl with the same idea. Just then the door opened and in came a small slender woman. Her dark-green frock was thick wool material. The tied-back black curly hair made the back of her look like a schoolgirl. But I knew about teachers' clothes and so, it seemed, did all the others. A silence fell over the room as this girl-woman walked towards the high platform, mounted it and waited. We rose to our feet. 'Good *morning*, Miss Jones', about half the class chanted.

She inclined her head, then sat down to call the Register. After this was done she herself stood and looked at us. 'In future you will answer "Present, Miss" when I call the Register. Is that understood?'

'Yes, Miss,' we chorused to the nearly-smiling face.

'Now I see that you have all made yourselves comfortable.' Her smile was broader. 'The boys, now . . .' – she looked at the solid group sitting under the windows. 'Quite happy, are you? Friends with friends? *You two!* Thomas and Pugh – come out. Megan Evans, go and sit by Thomas. Pugh will sit by Olwen.' Looks of dismay from the girls and red faces from the boys as they changed places. Soon the whole class was on the move. *None* of us had chosen right.

'Hilda Hollingsworth?' I put up a shaky hand. 'Come here. And *Hughes!* You will take the corner.' 'Here' was a desk right in front of hers. *And* she'd sat me by a boy, but at least he was clean and tidy. I didn't like the front desk, though. But someone had to sit there and Miss Jones had decided who.

She didn't seem the tartar she was said to be; so far her voice had been pleasant. Faintly amused. Yet it held a note of Authority. Now the Groups were being explained. The two columns on the left were considered to be the Top Group. I shuddered. I was in it! There were two middle groups and one bottom group. The blackboard and easel were set up. Exercise books were given out. Clean orange pen-holders and new pen-nibs came with freshly filled inkwells.

The first lesson began in absolute silence: Arithmetic. Only the squeak of chalk interrupted our busy thoughts. Miss Jones filled the board and told us to begin. At first the sums seemed easy. I hurried along, proud of the neatness of my first page, seeing in my mind's eye all those red ticks and perhaps even ten-out-of-ten at the end of the exercise. But alas, the sums got more and more difficult. I looked at number eight again. 'Tommy has seven marbles.' That's what I'd written. Somehow it didn't look like a sum at all. From there on I became more and more scared. Perhaps I ought to do that marbles one again? I looked at Miss Jones, who was doing something to papers on her desk. Did she allow corrections and alterations . . . ? Suddenly our eyes met – I bent quickly over my book, aware that I'd got her attention and that I didn't want it. I struggled on till the bell went for break. 'Pens down! Use your blotting-paper carefully. Books closed. Sit up; arms folded.' Other classes were already filling the corridor. Miss Jones directed one person from the back of each column to collect the books. When this was done, we were told to stand. 'No talking. Olwen, lead out please.' We left the classroom in single file. Silent. Subdued by the watching eyes of Miss Jones.

We'd never spent such a quiet, controlled day as this, our first with Miss Jones. Yet she wasn't a bit frightening. Just didn't talk much. Expected us to answer only what was on the blackboard. A strange way of teaching but there it was, I wouldn't be so scared tomorrow nor would anyone else.

Next morning Miss Jones called the Register, joined with us in Morning Assembly and then took her place in front of the class. I was faintly surprised that she hadn't gone straight to the blackboard. It had always been Arithmetic after Prayers. The sudden fury that erupted from her was therefore completely unexpected. Never had I seen anyone so small become as big as Miss Jones. Our Arithmetic was the most Out-*rage*-ous Dis-*grace*-ful De-*plor*-able thing she'd ever en-*count*ered. Were we all feeble-minded? Had NONE of us – not even ONE of us – grasped the basic principles of times tables, simple *this, that* and *other?* . . . I stopped listening; it was too awful. She paced the class, throwing down Arithmetic books in front of red-faced boys and girls who dared not look up at her scathing comments. Suddenly she was beside me: my book flapped angrily on to my desk. 'And just *how* do you know Tommy has seven marbles, may I ask? Some sort of *mystery*, is it?' – she was gone before I could take enough breath to begin to answer.

At last she stood before the shamed class and told us that we were the worst crop of her whole teaching career. But *she* was a teacher. And teach us she *would*. We'd begin with Arithmetic and go on and on with it. All day. And every day. Starting like Infants. 'Open your books.'

I looked at my first page. 'Tommy has seven marbles.' It had a red tick and the red writing beside it said *I want to know how you arrived at this answer*! I'd got seven out of ten as a total mark. For me this would normally have been *good*, but Miss Jones didn't think so.

We spent a whole week doing Arithmetic. My biggest fault was that I could arrive at an answer in my head but didn't know *how*; hence no workings to be seen. Miss Jones had me by the blackboard time and time again and whilst she held the chalk I'd arrive at my answer. But as soon as the chalk came into *my* fingers the workings became a tangled maze from which I couldn't escape. This was something that never came right. Try as I might, it was easier to work it out inside me.

Miss Jones's power and knowledge seemed almost as great as God's. Her voice could paralyse every heartbeat in the classroom. Lumps of chalk, and sometimes even the blackboard rubber itself, would be hurled at a whisper. And it was nothing for her to signal to me at the front to *move slightly* so that her keys could fly fast, jangling the inattentive boy whose desk they landed on. Sometimes fingers or heads got in the way, and that meant a red-faced boy out at the front of the class for not even being attentive enough to dodge, let alone nearly stopping Miss Jones from calmly going on talking.

As Miss Jones said, she was a teacher. And how she could teach! How anyone could not want to listen and drink up every word I never knew, for Miss Jones possessed some kind of magic that transported you out of time and space. Hunting with Hiawatha we'd be, living with old Nkomis in front of the deep dark forest. Or maybe in the hot dustiness of the summer city, watching the lucky carter handling his ice. Led by Miss Jones we'd go; sapphire berg and emerald floe . . .

My fear of Miss Jones fell away in just the second week of term. My respect for her grew and grew. Never had I seen anyone make things spring out of print and live. Yet it made not one shred of difference to Miss Jones. Arithmetic: that was to her the all-important thing that won Scholarships.

The Welsh lessons, too, had something to do with this mysterious word Scholarship. I found them difficult at first; there didn't really seem to be any rules. We repeated sounds after Miss Jones and watched the pointer move from word to word on the blackboard. I could make no sense at all of the spelling; I learnt to concentrate first on the sound, remember where it *was* she had written that sound, *which* little patch of blackboard was its home. And so I became ready for my turn at reading Welsh. But we moved beyond that. Printed sheets of paper were given out. 'Dictation', Miss Jones called it, and we were to get ourselves ready for it. After we'd supposedly read and understood the paper, it would be gathered up and Dictation would begin. At first it was awful, bringing the wrath of Miss Jones upon our bowed heads. But then I found a way to do it by studying the paper; I'd sort of click it into my mind like a photograph and then write as fast as I possibly could. It worked. My marks rose and rose until I was considered the best in the class. Though what it was all about I still didn't know.

Meanwhile my homework was getting me into all sorts of trouble. Now and again Auntie would let me spend perhaps half an hour on it, but this soon tried her patience and I'd have to stop. This meant facing Miss Jones with blank pages, her dark eyes holding the question . . . ? I gave my usual answer: 'Please Miss

Jones, I didn't have time.' The waver in my voice was something to do with shaking knees.

'Very well. Go and sit down.' This from Miss Jones! I staggered to my desk, wondering why I kept on being so lucky.

Then Miss Jones made me Class Monitor. I did my homework at playtime whilst she took care of the preparations as she'd always done. Every day she found some extra time for me. Drill, sewing, singing, reading – all these were times for me to work on the precious homework. And somehow it didn't seem strange at all to be sewing a cap and overall whilst following Miss Jones over the icebergs. I'd have followed Miss Jones *anywhere*.

Chapter 37 ~~~

I'm sure that all School Nurses were identical. This one had the same scrubbed pinky hands and white stiff-looking hair that stuck out of her high starched cap. The smooth scrubbed face was severe and showed no sign of the discomfort her tight white collar must have caused. She rustled around me, looking for nits and bad teeth. Then I was sent into the next classroom. Screens had been put up in a corner near the fireplace and a man's voice was coming out: 'Come in, come in . . .'

I'd found him now.

'Name? Age? Card?' I handed him the big white card. He stood up and stared at me. 'Turn round, bend down, touch your toes, lie up here, any aches-and-pains? How did your hands get like that?' His fingers were probing my arms and legs. 'Always get like it, do they?' He was writing on the card. 'I see. Go and get dressed, send in the next girl, would you?' – and as I hurried out a girl with sores got up off the Nurse's form. 'Come in, come in . . .'

Hastily I put on my petticoat, blouse and gymslip, pulled on my socks and tied my shoes in neat bows. Back again in the classroom, sewing needles moved carefully along white calico hems ten stitches to the inch; Miss Jones was reading to the class. She smiled as I sat at my desk, moving her small feet carefully to the side of my seat. She often perched herself on my desk these days, leaving her high-platformed place of Authority vacant and lonely-looking.

I liked her closeness and soon lost myself in the story as my eyes pictured it in the big crackling fire that warmed the room.

Mr Davis came in and whispered something to Miss Jones. She beckoned me to come out. 'Just wait outside my office, will you?' said Mr Davis. Crumbs, what had I done? My feet took me slowly to his office. The girl with sores was there, but she was mostly painted mauve now.

But Mr Davis soon had us smiling. He explained that we'd done nothing wrong; that we were there because the doctor had left special instructions that we were to have a little extra treat: a special sandwich and a large spoonful of cod-liver-oil-and-malt every day. And this treat would begin on Monday.

'Ooh, thank you, Sir,' we bleated, grinning from ear to ear.

He sort of smiled, shook his head slightly, and sighed. 'Very well. Now off you go, and *do* remember to tell your mothers or aunties, won't you?'

I saw the mauve-painted girl again at playtime. There was a crowd of girls at the top of the steps and she was dabbing her eyes near the bottom. But it was none of my business. Miss Jones was waiting for her Monitor to come back. There was some Arithmetic to finish off.

'Excuse me? . . . Excuse me? . . .' I tried to get through the huddle and suddenly they were all around me, prodding, poking and punching. 'Nits-an'-fleas – nits-an'-fleas' – the chanting had started; so had the hair-pulling; I struggled to free myself: 'I haven't . . . I haven't . . .'

'Nits-an'-fleas!' – I staggered; then from the back of the crowd someone shouted '*Fight!*' It wasn't anything of the sort but it had a name now; eager girls pressed closer, thumping and hitting and laughing: 'Cry-baby! Cry-baby! Nits-an'-fleas!' all mixing up with the excited cries of '*Fight!*' from the back. I gave up the struggle to get to the door; now it was I who was trying to get down the steps away from those hateful girls who laughed and jeered whilst they punched me from one to the other.

The sudden shrill of the whistle brought instant silence. A teacher. Ending the playtime. A seond shrill. Face averted, I ran to my line, fresh tears – of relief – pouring down my face. I saw the mauve-painted girl stick her tongue out at me, but I never found out why.

We were going into school. I brushed away my tears and sat with bowed head at my desk. Those telltale red eyes mustn't be seen by Miss Jones.

That evening, when school was finished for the day, she called me to her desk. Shamefaced, I waited for her to tell me off. But she just quietly packed our exercise books into her shiny brown case, asking if I'd like to walk part of the way to the bus stop with her? My eager nod made her smile. And all misery just fell away as I remembered we had to pass the very house I lived in. And once she'd even remarked on the shiny knocker and beautifully scrubbed doorstep. Well, after that, who could help but put one's heart and soul into the cleaning of these things that Miss Jones passed twice a day? That evening I carefully carried her case and was soon chatting easily about my dad and the lovely violets that were nearly always so hard to find, adding that there just didn't seem to be any in this valley. Taking her case from me because we were opposite Auntie's house, she smiled and told me to keep looking for the violets whenever I had a spare moment. She was quite sure that one day I'd find them again.

The front door was open and Auntie was glaring at me as I crossed the road. It was obvious that she was very cross about something, and when she'd shut the door of the kitchen she delivered a stinging slap to my cheek. Just what did I think I was doing, hanging around telling all sorts of lies to the teachers? I couldn't answer. There'd been no lies. Another slap and a push – I fell, hitting my head against the sofa. She dragged me off the floor and shook me for falling over on purpose. Now she was telling me to get changed and take the bucket to the slag heap.

That night the bucket and I were practically alone out there. It seemed to take a very long time to get it even half-full. My head was aching and I felt very homesick. It was then that the thought of running away first occurred to me. But then there was Pat. I was deep in thought when Pat came running, saying that Auntie said to come home at once. She helped me carry the bucket and off we went. I'd missed tea, meaning the slice of bread and marg with the nourishing carrot spread that both Auntie and Nunky, through what must have been very firm self-control, kept solely for us growing girls.

Carrying the bucket, we went round to the back of the house in order to leave no traces of dust in the front passage. Auntie was in the yard back there, still cross. The bucket was inspected. Only half-full. Angrily she turned and pulled me into the house. Nunky was sitting by the fire, reading from his newspaper. Her voice rose up in the quiet room: 'This dirty little slut. Craftily tried to empty the coal bucket without being seen. Talk about sly. Just look at the state of her!' Aware of the clinging coal dust, I turned my face away in shame. The blow nearly knocked my head off, the room spun, was swirling around me: suddenly I was swept off my feet across her lap and punished for being ignorant – how dare this crafty little slut refuse to listen to decent God-fearing people? In future I'd be watched and handled very firmly indeed; all her kindness had been wasted on me.

The sandwiches which had been recommended by the doctor were quite lovely, brown bread and butter with dates or dried apple-rings or Bovril and cress. Usually it was one sandwich a day, but sometimes there'd be two and always the lovely thick sticky stuff that came twisting its way out of the big brown jar on to Mr Davis's teaspoon. I am sorry to say I forgot to tell Auntie about any of these things, or else I hadn't the chance to, or hadn't dared; I expect it was a bit of each really. So the first Auntie knew about the sandwiches was that I'd already had them. She was furious and announced her intention of going to the school about these charity sandwiches, adding that not only God knew but the whole village knew that she'd always kept a very good table. I was certainly not going to drag her good name through the filth and mud. Just *who* did I think I was? Well, she'd tell me: a bloody ugly little *misfit*, that's what!

Misfit? The word struck me harder than any blow, I wasn't listening any more; the voice just seemed to go on and on whilst I hung on to this single word, recognising it to be the truth.

The sting of her slap across my face snatched me back to the harsh reality of her voice, her world, her kitchen. Did I realise that she and her husband were slogging and slaving for the likes of our mothers, who were doing nothing more than getting out and about having a good time with *Yanks*? She was shaking me now. But that word 'Yanks . . .' What did it mean? Something to do with the war, maybe? *Another* slap, much harder than the first – she was shouting about my lies and deceitful ways as she dragged me over to the sofa. I knew what was going to happen next; desperately I called, 'Oh please Auntie, please, I . . .'

My words ceased; it was too late to explain now, up went my skirt and down came my knickers. 'How dare you speak without being spoken to!'

Bewildered and smarting, I wondered who she *had* been speaking to.

The next morning at school I said a polite 'No thank you' to the 'charity' sandwiches offered by Miss Jones. It was playtime and everyone had by now left the classroom.

'Why not?' asked Miss Jones, replacing the cloth over the plate.

'Please Miss, I'm not hungry,' croaked my lying voice. I stared at the floor, feeling my face going all red.

'Oh really?' came Miss Jones's quiet voice. I fumbled with my girdle, wishing that the ground would just open up and swallow me.

She spoke again, still very quietly: 'Is that the true reason, Hilda?' Her kindness was far worse than all the beatings. My throat seemed to have a great lump inside it.

'Please Miss,' I stammered, still not looking at her, 'it spoils my dinner.' At this moment I could raise up my eyes and nearly look at her.

She smiled a little. 'I see.' She paused, then: 'Did you manage to finish your homework last night?'

Down went my head again. 'No, Miss.' I wanted to cry. Auntie was always calling me a liar, and although I'd never lied to her she just kept on saying it until I didn't care any more. Yet here I was, lying to the one person who mattered.

'You may sit down and begin your homework, Hilda,' came the quiet voice.

'Thank you, Miss Jones.' I sat down at my desk. The door shut with a sharp click. Miss Jones was gone.

Just before we went home to tea, the headmaster sent for me. This time I didn't need to search my mind for a reason. There were at least two very good ones: either lying to Miss Jones or else my neglected homework that always had to be finished during play-time. Trembling, I walked as slowly as possible. It would be the first time I'd ever had the cane. At last I stood before the pale green door – my fingers tapped its cold surface. 'Come in,' called the headmaster. Unwillingly I turned the icy door-knob. He was standing near the window overlooking the playing field. He didn't look at all fierce as he asked me to sit down. 'Ah, Hilda, isn't it?' He sat himself in his swivel chair.

'Yes, Sir.' My voice was overloud in this quiet place.

He smiled: my face flamed. 'Well, first of all, let me assure you of one thing.' He paused, picked up a sheet of paper, continued: 'You are not here to be punished.' My relief came in a great sigh. 'However, I do want to talk to you about the sandwiches.' I tensed again. 'Your auntie has been to see me this morning. You knew she was coming?'

My eyes fell on the sight of my rough, cracked hands. What to do with them? 'Yes, Sir,' I mumbled. 'It was my fault, Sir. I forgot to tell her about them. The sandwiches, I mean, Sir.'

He stood up and walked to the window. Quickly I slid my hands under my bottom. He turned. 'Well, my dear, it's unfortunate when we "forget" things; it usually leads us into all kinds of bother.' He raised his eyebrows questioningly; I could only nod. He went on: 'Now I want you to understand that the situation has been sorted out. I had a long chat with your auntie and she has agreed that you will continue to have all the things the doctor recommended.'

I nodded and murmured, 'Thank you, Sir.'

He came round the desk now and I forced myself to stand up, keeping my hands out of sight.

'Well, Hilda, if you have any problems at all in the future, just remember that your teachers and I are here to help wherever we can.' I searched his face, wondering how he could suppose that I had any problems at school with wonderful Miss Jones to take care of everything. He smiled. 'Is there anything you would like to ask me whilst you are here?'

I shook my head. 'No, Sir, and thank you, Sir, for talking to Auntie, I mean.'

He walked to the door and opened it. 'Very well, now go along to the staff room and eat that sandwich before you rejoin the class.'

I slipped quickly out of the office and into the corridor. No wonder Auntie hadn't spoken to me at dinner time. She'd understood everything and was simply waiting for the headmaster to tell me about it. Gosh, how I'd worried, and all for nothing! The staff room was empty, so I stood by the sink and ate the date sandwich, remembering to wash and wipe up the plate before leaving.

After school I ran all the way home. It had all been a misunderstanding. If I really, really and truly was to please Auntie . . . I'd work and work for her . . .

Well, I had to do that anyway. The thought sobered me. But, I reasoned, if I smiled all the time, well, it must surely make all the difference in the world!

Auntie wasn't looking to see my smile when I went into the kitchen. She was upstairs, and her voice was sharp as she called me to bring the polish and dusters up there at once. My smile faded; the edge of misery made itself felt for a moment. Then, remembering my vow, I gathered her requirements and, fixing the smile firmly on my face, hurried up the stair. She was making up a bed in the small room, and, without a glance she told me to polish the floor. Still smiling, I said, 'Yes, Auntie', and began at once. The lino was sort of bumpy – little bumps all over – and it was hard work trying to get a shine on it. However, bumps or no bumps I was really going to work hard on it. I polished till my arms ached and had just finished the last bit when Auntie called me to come down for tea.

The table was laid out all ready and waiting. Nunky was in his chair and Auntie was cutting the bread. I washed my hands at the kitchen sink and then took my place at the table. Gosh, I was hungry; really looking forward to my slice of bread and carrot spread. Folding my hands, I said the usual Grace about being grateful, and grateful I was too that the misunderstanding about the school sandwich was all over at last.

Then Auntie passed us our plates, as she always did. But something was different tonight. On my plate was just half a slice of bread.

Christmas. At school we sang carols and Miss Jones hung up paper chains. Everyone seemed excited and happy at the coming holiday. I dreaded it. Holidays had become things to be endured since Miss Jones had become our teacher. And I was upset too because Miss Jones had told us all that she'd be acting in a play in the next village every evening for a whole week. She was only playing the part of a maid, but that didn't matter to us. I'd run home and asked Auntie if she'd allow me to go with some of the other girls to see this play. But the answer had been a sharp slap. How dare I even think about entering such a wicked place as a Playhouse? Even if it *was* a church hall. Here she was trying to bring us up decent and God-fearing, only to have a teacher, of all people, leading us the other way. No good would come of such a person – indeed, she'd suspected it all along.

I stopped listening; even I could tell that Auntie hated Miss Jones, hated her simply because I'd carried her case. Because I was in her class. Because I liked her.

So it wasn't only the play. Slowly I put Miss Jones back together again.

School finished and Christmas began. No paper chains hung from Auntie's ceiling. And when Pat and I spoke of Father Christmas we got a long lecture on Greed and Expecting-always-to-be-given-things. Christmas was a time of rejoicing in the birth of our Saviour. And we'd be doing that. And only that. Father Christmas indeed! There's hard times the valleys had always known but Truth was there, not like the big cities where the likes of us were lied to.

But Mum sent us a new frock each and a tin of toffees. And Auntie let us wear the frocks on Christmas Day.

Pat and I decided to have last year's Christmas presents all over again. I crept along to the boxroom and fetched the baby dolls and now-too-small slippers and cut-out doll books. Gwyneth would be ages coming to bed and by then I could take it all back. Pat sat up in the dim light, prepared to make-believe with me. We pretended to be surprised at opening boxes that didn't exist, till Pat grew sleepy and I crept the presents back to the boxroom. 'Ooh, it was lovely last year,' I reminded her – in a whisper, of course. 'Auntie Vi letting us play and play. And all those mince pies. And the Christmas stockings . . .' I'd been careful to leave out the sad bit about waiting for Mum at the window.

'*Eh?* We wasn't *at* Auntie Vi's last year, 'Ild.' Pat seemed to be fully awake.

''Course we were. Don't you remember . . . the slippers?'

'Nah. We wasn't even tergether last Christmas. You was at the Joneses an' I was on me *own*. At the . . . the Sleweslins'. An' it rained an' rained . . .' She was sitting up staring at me.

'No, Pat, it wasn't like that at all. Don't you remember waiting for Mum to come? And "The Laughing Policeman"?'

She was silent. Thinking it all out.

'I *ain't* wrong, 'Ild. Them things was before we come 'ere. An' you *was* at the Joneses 'cause I brought yer fings over there, see.' She lay down, satisfied that now everything had been put right.

'But *Pat!*'

She turned to face me. 'You was ill afterwards, an' all,' she retorted.

That sentence made something tremble inside me. But I still didn't quite believe her. Had it been Christmas when I was ill? Somewhere a faint reminder of a yard with cracks in the wall. I felt afraid of something. Had there been cracks at Auntie Vi's? No, there hadn't, and besides there'd been three of us: Roberta, Pat and me. I pushed the thoughts away. Auntie Vi and her lovely roast pork. How long ago? The Joneses. Just a faint stirring of some horrid game they played with a girl from the Homes. Bridget. Yes, Bridget, who'd gone home or gone somewhere else a long time ago. But Christmas? Much as I tried, I just couldn't remember Christmas. Yet just thinking about it made me feel all funny because I knew I'd lost it. Lost a whole Christmas. Forgotten it had ever been.

Chapter 38 ~~~

For some reason or other Auntie'd put a large plait of dough across the top of one of the two loaves I was to take for baking. I was to take special care not to squash it.

A motorcar honked its horn somewhere, and we didn't often see motorcars. A sheep grazing nearby started to run. I tried to get out of its way, but too late: it scrambled past, knocking one of the unbaked loaves from under my arm. But it seemed undamaged. 'Lucky there ain't no sheep currants 'ere,' said Pat. Morgan-the-Bread, in his tall hat and white overall, took the loaves and asked what name. I gave Auntie's name and he chalked it on both sides of each tin, handing me the cloths that had covered them. I took one last glance at the tins. 'Oh wait!' Something was wrong. 'Oh dear, it's gone . . . it's gone . . .'

'What's gone?' asked the baker.

'The plait. Auntie's plait.'

It wasn't outside either. Pat started to cry.

'Now, now, bach, don't take it so bad. Look you, I'll make a plait and put it on' – the big clean hands were already twisting and placing it.

Pat stayed with Auntie when it came time to collect the baked bread. Morgan-the-Bread was busy with his huge ovens, but he'd been as good as his word. There stood the loaf, complete with a golden plait. The tall white hat nodded to my thanks and Cheerio.

Auntie took the tins and put them in the larder. On the sofa sat a very old man with white hair. He smiled, so I smiled back. Auntie took the old man's arm and they went along the passage and out of the front door.

'Who's that?' I whispered to Pat.

''E's called Uncle Dan,' said Pat.

'Can't be a real uncle, though.' Crumbs, I thought, an uncle doesn't just happen whilst you're out at the baker's!

''E is real. 'E's 'ers, not ours' – she licked her fingers and wiped them across her forehead.

'How do you know?'

Pat tossed her curls. 'Not tellin'!'

'You don't know, that's why.'

'She said so.'

'Oh!'

There was a moment of silence.

'Wot's "deaf"?'

'God takes you up to heaven.'

'Not "deaf"! Deaf!'

'Deaf! Oh, when you can't hear things. Why?'

Pat closed her mouth firmly and shook her head. 'It's a secret.'

'What is? Being deaf?'

'No, silly, no, not that – not bein' deaf isn't a secret.'

I put on a bored sort of big-sister look.

'I'll tell yer if yer want me to.'

I stared at the window.

'Well, 'e can't talk neither!'

'Can't talk!' I'd never known anyone who couldn't talk. 'Why not?'

''E ain't got no teef.'

'Well, he looks kind.'

''E's goin' ter sleep 'ere, too. I 'eard Auntie say so.'

So that explained the little room with the bumpy lino being polished. Pat was licking her fingers again. She wiped the wet fingers over her forehead.

'Stop it! Your face is always dirty. Come on over here and wipe it on the flannel.'

She came and wiped both cheeks, ignoring the rest of her face. I rubbed at the marks for her. 'We'd better lay another place at the table, then.'

Pat squirmed away. 'Ooh no, 'Ild – it 'urts. 'E won't be 'ere. 'E's going to the granny an' on'y jus' sleep 'ere.'

'How do you know all that?'

'I was in the lav when Auntie was tellin' the lady next door. She said there wasn't no room to sleep at the gran's. She said 'e was so quiet you wouldn't know 'e was in the 'ouse.' She paused. 'I'm goin' to watch where 'e 'ides.'

I sighed. 'Never mind about *you*, just say about him.'

'Well, she said 'e wouldn't 'arm a fly.'

I sat and wondered whether maybe sometimes Uncle Dan would let us write things-to-say to him. But Pat was ending the pause. '. . . this fly is a nice little fly, she crep' up on it an' shut it in a paste jar because it is a nice little fly. The nice little fly 'ates it in the paste jar an' she feeds it on carrot spread an' . . .'

'Shush!' Words fled and Pat's curtain of shyness was back. Auntie's step could be heard in the passage.

If it hadn't been for the extra chamber pot to empty each morning I'd hardly have known that the old man called Uncle Dan slept in the next room. He was always very quiet when he came to bed each night, and he got up after we'd gone to school in the morning. He'd been with us a couple of days – well, nights – and I'd forgotten all about the loaf with the plait. Then came Thursday tea time and Auntie had her friend to tea. Pat and I had to lay up the table in the dining-room, using the best cloth and second-best china. Auntie gave me a little dish of home-made rhubarb jam and some Welsh cakes to put on the table. Then she went into the larder for the bread. She turned it out of the tin and of course my heart was turning over with it. But now came a new shock. The lost plait had never been lost in the first place. There it was, baked on to the *bottom* of the loaf. I *did* feel silly. Expecting all kinds of trouble, I stood there waiting. Ready to confess. Auntie looked puzzled. She turned the loaf over. Yes *two* plaits! Like a sort of double upside-down birthday cake. But to my astonishment Auntie just shrugged and proceeded to slice the telltale loaf. I sent a swift prayer up to the Lord, thanking Him for sending Auntie's friend to tea today.

When we were all seated round the table I noticed that the friend was still wearing her hat; she must have forgotten to take it off. Ought I to offer to hang it up for her? I looked to Auntie for guidance. None was forthcoming. 'Say Grace, Hilda,' came the lightened voice, sweet as a silver bell. The friend smiled and folded her hands. I obeyed the probing steel of Auntie's eyes. Pat and I knew that we mustn't, of course, speak. But nobody had ever said anything about listening.

'Do you take sugar, Dilys?' enquired Auntie, offering the sugar bowl.

'Just a tiny bit, Bron, and very little milk' – taking a liberal helping of both. She leant forward and swooped on the dish of jam. 'Well, I must say, Bron, you seem to have two very well-behaved little girls here. What's the little one's name?' She thrust her face towards Pat, who coloured up all over her face and neck as though words were ink and she so much fresh blotting-paper.

Auntie stroked Pat's lush ringlets. 'This is our Patricia' – darting a quick glance at me. 'You'd never believe they were sisters, would you, Dilys?'

Dilys, reaching for the teapot, sort of put an astonished look together. 'No indeed!' She plonked the pot down. 'One so fair and the other so dark . . .'

'And so with their souls,' said Auntie.

Dilys's eyes widened; her head nodded gravely. 'You'll have your work cut out then, Bron.' Both women were now staring at me as if looking for the mark of Cain. I fumbled with my cup.

'Ooh!' gasped Dilys. 'What awful hands! You can tell a lot from hands, you know, Bron. Why, the doctor was telling me only last week' – she looked away from me – 'that he knew about Owen's heart complaint just by looking at his hands!'

Auntie was most interested. 'You must know a great deal about that sort of thing, working for the doctor. You know I did hear that Mrs Parry . . .'

Pat and I cleared the table whilst Auntie and her friend sat talking on the sofa. As we washed up, bits of conversation drifted through the partly open dining-room door. Auntie's voice said, 'No, the mother doesn't write much. Flighty, if you were to ask me!'

Dilys murmured something; I couldn't quite catch what it was. Then Auntie was speaking again: '. . . want to keep it quiet awhile yet, though.'

Dilys's voice was this time quite clear. 'Adoption!' I stood frozen, midway between the sink and the larder.

'The little one is quite worth saving. A sweet child, don't you think, Dilys?'

Pat crept away from the sink; grabbed at my arms. 'It's me! It's me!'

'No, it's *not* – low and firm. 'Now let go of my arm, we have to put this lot away.' She began to cry quietly. 'Pat!' I whispered urgently, 'Don't cry. She'll come out and then . . . oh well, what's the use? . . .' I knew nothing I could say.

'Don't let 'er, 'Ild, you won't, will yer? Honest, I don't like it 'ere . . .' Her voice was getting louder. *Too* loud.

'Hush, Pat. Auntie will hear you. Listen, you go out to the lav and I'll come out when this is all done. Off you go – quick, she's coming!' – Pat unlatched the back door and was in the yard when Auntie came into the kitchen.

'Well?' she demanded. 'What have you been doing to little Pat?'

'Nothing, Auntie,' I faltered. 'I think she's got stomach-ache.'

Auntie bent down and hissed in my ear: 'Get this lot cleared away, you little slut.' She stood up, breathing normally again. 'Poor little Pat. Tell her to come into the dining-room when she comes in.'

'Yes, Auntie. Shall I go and tell her now?' Auntie shot me a suspicious look, then nodded abruptly and went back to her friend.

Pat was huddled on the floor of the toilet. Her face was dirty with grimy finger-marks and tears. 'Oh, 'Ild! I don't wanna be 'dopted.'

I knelt down beside her. 'Listen, Pat . . .' She sobbed quietly. '*Listen to me.*' I was wiping her face with my hankie. 'I told Auntie you'd got tummy-ache.'

'So I 'ave, *now*,' wailed Pat.

'Oh, Pat, stop it, you'll get me into trouble. Please listen. I'll write to Mum.'

She stopped crying. ''*Ow?*' she demanded.

Gosh, for the moment I hadn't thought of that old difficulty.

Auntie read our weekly letters to make sure there were no what-she-called-mistakes in them. And where would I get writing-paper, and envelopes, and . . . and everything?

'I'll find a way,' I said. The promise slipped out so easily, and now it had been said. 'You be a good girl now. Promise?' Her face was now quite clean, though her eyes were a bit red. She gave a little nod. 'Run along, then. Don't forget. If Auntie asks, it's tummy-ache.' I was almost pleading. All too often Pat had forgotten her part in things like this and I'd been slapped and punished for it.

When I returned to the kitchen Pat had already made her peace with Auntie. The hairbrush was missing from its hook, that's how I knew. Auntie always brushed Pat's hair when she was happy.

I put away all the dishes and got out my homework. The murmur of voices didn't interrupt me at all – at least not at first. Then I heard Dilys-the-friend say, 'Poor old Dan, it's nice to see him about again though, Bron!' I don't know what Auntie said, but Dilys continued, 'How good you are, Bron! It must wear you out, your sister *and* old Dan both sleeping here. Whatever do you do about the washing?' A murmur of voices. 'Oh, they don't eat here, then, why, indeed to goodness, how does your old mother cope!'

Auntie sounded a bit on the defensive as she answered this. 'The two girls are excused war work to see to that, Dilys, but you knew that, didn't you!'

Dilys, unruffled, replied, 'Oh, I just wondered, Bron. And talking of the war, have you been to Swansea lately?'

Auntie said something I didn't catch. I bent my head quickly over the homework as she stepped into the kitchen. 'Put that rubbish away,' she said coldly. And called over her shoulder in a lightened voice: 'Come out here, Dilys, the fire is lovely now.'

Dilys came, holding Pat's hand. 'Sit by there,' said Auntie, indicating the long black sofa.

But Dilys was bending over the table. 'What's this then, Bron? Homework?' I sighed inwardly.

'Yes indeed, Dilys, she's rather behind the rest at school, bit backward, you know. Put it away at once, Hilda. Come, Dilys, sit by there . . . That's better.' She inclined her head at me. 'Likes to show off, that one does.'

Red-faced, I gathered up the books and took them upstairs. Gosh, I wasn't backward – why did she make out I was? And that

Dilys-the-friend was a proper busybody. Fancy wearing her hat at the tea table! And all that sugar she'd taken! Now I remembered. I'd seen her polishing the brass plate outside the doctor's house. She'd been wearing a hat then as well.

Auntie's voice flashed up the stair. 'Come down here at once, you sulky girl.' Wearily I collected my scattered thoughts and went back to the warm, cosy, hateful kitchen. The friend was perched on the edge of the sofa daintily sipping tea, the little finger stuck out like a signpost.

'That's better,' said Auntie. 'Really, these evacuees . . . How some of them have been dragged up – no manners at all!' She turned to me. 'Tell Auntie Dilys you're sorry now.'

I stood there inwardly quaking, wondering what to be sorry about. 'I'm sorry, Auntie Dilys.' The words came automatically.

Auntie Dilys took another sip. 'Sullen as the day is long, Bron,' she said, putting down her cup. 'However do you put up with it? I'd get rid of her if I were you.'

I heartily agreed with that bit – if only she would! But there was Pat. I wondered if Mum knew, when she called out 'Look after Pat', how hard a job it would be. I couldn't even have said what it was, really, that was happening to my little sister.

Chapter 39 ~~~

We awoke in the early morning to a Sunday with no sun. I did all the usual things without even having to think about them and without troubling Auntie with my gaze. I sensed that Auntie was cutting bread. She hadn't answered my 'Good morning, Auntie', but I didn't mind – not now I didn't, now that I'd sorted it all out. I'd been doing the same thing wrong over and over again. Looking into her face. Looking and pleading and even appealing each time she spoke or moved. I kept on making her see me, me that didn't fit – no wonder she got angry, I was always searching her face for approval. There was no need to keep on repeating this mistake; in future I'd do all the jobs and anything else she wanted, but the right way this time. I'd remember that Auntie's face was hers.

At the breakfast table I was very conscious of Auntie staring at me. The feeling that something was different grew and grew inside me. Quite suddenly Auntie got up and dragged me from my chair. 'You little bitch!' The blow landed somehow on the back of my head. 'I've been watching you! Yes, I've been watching you!' Slaps and punches rained down on me; I cried, but even my crying seemed different. 'Who do you think you *are*? That's what I want to know. *Well* . . . ?' She was holding me by my hair, her demand floated around me, there wasn't anything in me that made an answer . . .

'WELL . . . ?' she was screaming.

'I don't know, Auntie. *Really*. Please, I don't know' – my desperation had forced its way out, I was very frightened by my own answer – it was true, I didn't know.

Auntie was furious. 'Play games with *me*? I'll show you, my girl.' I was across her lap. The blows were almost unendurable, my voice cracked on a scream. Suddenly she threw me to the floor and I saw with awful eyes that she'd been hitting me with Nunky's wide leather miner's belt. I crouched there trembling. Auntie stood holding the belt and I could see her shaking. The sound of Pat crying seemed to be coming from a long way off. I felt sick but didn't dare move. My eyes were fixed on the belt. 'Get up.' I got up. My head seemed to be spinning. 'Wash your face.' Dry sobs shook me. 'Shut up.' I stood by the sink aching and smarting and seemingly unable to control the occasional sob that shook my entire body. 'Now get on with your work and just remember, there's more where that came from.' She hung the belt over the back of Nunky's chair. 'Don't you worry, Pat, you're not a bad girl, come and let me brush your hair, dear.' Pat sat at the table as if paralysed. Auntie went smiling to her and lifted her up into her strong arms. 'Poor little Pat. There, there, don't cry, lovey.' Then she carried Pat along the passage. The front door slammed. Auntie was taking Pat to the gran's house a few doors away.

I bathed my aching head with the cold flannel. The sobbing had become occasional body-shudders now. Slowly I cleared away the breakfast things. As I picked up Auntie's cup, bewilderment flooded me. She didn't *like* me not looking at her face. She *hated* me for it. I put the cup into the washing-up bowl. The pain in my back and legs was there because I hadn't looked for her approval. I'd been me, that's all, that me that she'd always been able to see. I reached for the tea towel. Perhaps it was my face that Auntie

249

wanted to see. Of course. Well, she could see my face, I'd turn it towards her as freely as always. But I remembered a saying my mum used:

You can look without seeing.

'Wot's on yer mind, mate?' asked Winnie.

'Well, er . . . it's . . . er . . .'

'It's wot?'

'Well . . .' I sighed. 'P'raps I'd better tell you about yesterday. But . . .' I realised suddenly that I didn't want to talk about it.

'You don't 'ave ter tell me if yer don't want to.' Winnie bent swiftly to the bucket and started removing the flat stones hiding the coal underneath.

Then quite suddenly the story of the day's disaster tumbled out. Winnie frowned, looked at the rest of the Gang and said seriously, 'Y'all gotta swear on yer mothers' lives that this is secret.'

'I swear it,' we each mumbled with bowed heads.

'All right, that's enough, don't drop orf!'

We started to giggle. 'Can't see wot's so funny,' said Winnie crossly. 'Are yer gonna listen or not?'

A murmur of 'Sorry' rose up the mountainside towards the leader's place at the top of the circle.

'I couldn't get any real paper, Win,' said Joyce.

All eyes fastened on her. 'Why not?' demanded our leader.

'There wasn't none.' Joyce was very red-faced now; she didn't like being stared at.

'Wot about you?' Winnie looked towards Connie, who shrugged her shoulders. 'Saw my auntie use the last piece. She's gone to buy some more,' she added quickly. 'P'raps if we waited till next week . . .'

Everyone groaned. 'Same ole yarn' – there was silence as Winnie gazed off into the distance. I didn't know whether to speak or not. Then Winnie demanded, 'Didn't anyone manage ter get even one scrappy ole bit o' paper, then?' She sounded a bit upset now. 'Cor, you lot call yourselfs a Gang?' Nobody said anything, so she went on: 'We gotta look after each other.' We all nodded, knowing that nodding wasn't good enough.

I swallowed before speaking. 'Winnie, I've got a bit of pencil and the inside bit of a fag packet. I'm going to write on the packet and ask my mum to come and take us home. All I need is a stamp . . .'

Winnie examined the fag-packet middle. ''S like a postcard really, innit?' she decided.

I nodded. 'We could all write on fag packets as long as they've got stamps on them . . .' I saw hope light up in the faces around me.

Winnie was delighted. 'Cor, yeah, we can all get at them old salvage sacks . . .'

Later, when I let myself in at the back door, Auntie was upstairs. Pat was already washed and sitting on the sofa, staring at the hairbrush. Waiting. I followed her gaze, wondering vaguely in how many ways my little sister's side of the hairbrush was really so very much better than mine.

Winnie and I crouched down behind the bakehouse. ''Urry up, 'Ild, there's a post at 'alf-two.'

I licked the pencil-stub. What should I write? 'Dear Mum, please come and get us, the letters aren't true, please come soon, Hilda.'

Winnie read it through. 'Why don't you say you was 'it wiv a belt?'

I flushed. 'I can't – not now, anyway – look, there's no room.'

She handed me back the rough-edged card. 'You'll be goin' 'ome soon, 'Ild' – her voice seemed to tremble, then she sort of shook herself. 'I better run an' post it; give it 'ere' – she ran off along the back alleyways.

I went along to where we were gradually building a new fairy pool. Pat had collected several suitable stones. ''Ave you done it?' she whispered.

I nodded. She smiled. 'We'll be goin' soon, won't we?'

'Yes, Pat. Soon.' I bent down. 'But we have this little job to do first. We can't leave the fairies with no pool can we?' She shook her head and we set to work.

Winnie came back. 'It's gone!' She crouched down beside us. 'An' we ain't got long 'ere, neither. It's nearly one o'clock.'

The three of us set to work happily, sowing fresh daisy and dandelion heads to float on the water that we'd sealed off from the fast-moving stream. A few little toadstools grew nearby; Pat and I were quite certain that fairies did live there, and also that sometimes they used the flower-heads for little hats. I don't know what

Winnie was certain about, but whatever it was, she too seemed to feel little need to speak.

A week passed. There'd been no letter. Each day I'd been expecting that Mum would arrive, especially when it got round to Saturday. She didn't, though, and the days dragged round to Tuesday again.

'She isn't comin', *is* she?' Pat was staring into the newly finished fairy pool. Winnie nudged me with her elbow.

''Course she is, Pat. It's the war that's making things go slow.' I tried to believe it.

'P'raps it got lost,' said Pat.

'How could it?' I said firmly, not wanting to recognise the secret fear inside me.

'Mighta done, though . . .' said Winnie thoughtfully.

'It had a stamp on it!'

'Yeah, but ole Griffiths-the-Post mighta seen it as 'e shoved the letters in 'is bag,' reasoned Winnie. ''E mighta even chucked it out as rubbish' – her conclusion seemed to astonish her: 'Crumbs . . . !'

Pat went pale and started licking her fingers. 'We won't 'arf get in trouble,' she said, near to tears. 'Auntie won't 'arf 'it you, 'Ild; ooh, I *ham* frightened' – the fingers flicked over her forehead, leaving the streaky marks.

'Wipe your face, Pat.' I gave her my damp hankie.

'Wotcha gonna do?' asked Winnie, worriedly.

'Nothing. Just wait, I suppose.' I hadn't much faith in my own words. If Griffiths-the-Post had found the card, it wouldn't take him long to find *me* – me, the only Hilda in the village. I felt very sick as a new thought occurred. He wouldn't actually be looking for me, it'd be Auntie he'd tell . . . I felt sweat break out on my back.

'S'pose yer right, we'll 'ave ter wait an' see,' came Winnie's careful faraway voice, and I knew that she'd been thinking the same as me.

The days slowly passed into the second and even a third week and I accepted the only reasonable explanation: it had got lost. We decided to try again: 'Dear Mum, we are unhappy, please come and get us, H and P.' I read it out to Winnie, who said it was an improvement on the first one. Pat just nodded. We posted it and the excitement was aroused again within us. Surely our mum would be here on Saturday.

Again the excitement gave way to disappointment and in turn again to apprehension as the days slipped by into the second week.

'We gonna try *again*?' Pat watched me picking on the tip.

'Might . . .' I said wearily. 'Can't yet, though: no money for a stamp.'

It was five or six weeks since we'd heard from our mum and I was very worried. Winnie had found out from her uncle what 'Yanks' were: '. . . soljers an' that from America. They 'ave chewin' gum an' lotser money an' they never go nowhere 'cept in taxis, an' . . .'

But I'd lost interest. Our mum wouldn't let us have chewing gum because it could twist round your heart and kill you, so if these Yanks chewed gum my mum wouldn't like them anyway.

'I got a thrup'ny joey,' Pat was saying plaintively at my elbow. 'You can 'ave it for a stamp.'

There was no need for words. Winnie took the tiny silver coin and slipped it down inside her shoe. We all knew the drill now. Tuesday would come and I'd write on the card: 'Dear Mum, please.'

We'd just despatched the seventh card when Uncle Dan, the old man who'd come to stay with us, was taken ill. Auntie kept me busy polishing and cleaning. My trips to the tip were stopped altogether, I didn't laugh with the Gang any more, I just didn't have time to laugh. As for homework, what little time there ever had been for it shrank to nothing at all. My hands had split again and the cracks were very painful. Miss Jones put some cream on them one day at school and wrapped them in pieces of clean rag but I had to take it all off at dinner time and couldn't get it on properly again in the afternoon. Miss Jones didn't say anything, though, and I hoped she hadn't noticed.

''*Ere*, somethin' for yer' – and Winnie'd dig in her pocket and fish out maybe half of a somewhat battered boiled potato for me to eat in the school lavs. She never asked nowadays whether I'd heard from my mum. She, like me, had accepted the daily disappointment, always ending with the thought: 'Maybe it'll be tomorrow.'

After we'd gone to bed one Thursday night I heard the door-knocker rattle. I sat up in bed, sure that at last our mum had come to take us home. I heard Auntie speaking as she came up the stair.

Excitement darted through me. I must wake Pat. We were going home. I'd tell her . . .

Auntie paused on the landing. 'In here,' she said, so nicely. I hugged myself. 'Thank you,' said a man's voice, and the door stayed firmly shut.

Not my mum! I couldn't believe it. But *something* believed it – the tears splashed on to my arms, hot tears that had been there waiting all this long time. 'Oh, Mum, Mum, why don't you come?' I cried into the pillow. The cold starched whiteness absorbed the words and the tears and remained exactly the same.

By tea time on Saturday I'd given up hoping that our mum would be coming. It was as much as I could do to hold back the tears. Auntie Dilys, who'd been minding us all afternoon, was sipping her tea noisily. She'd smacked my legs no end of times for having untidy hair, talking too loud, moving too slow, being clumsy, looking sullen and lots of things I couldn't remember. It had been a rotten day, I decided to myself. Dilys poured herself another cup of tea and for an instant my eyes rested on the curious dull-grey hat. It reminded me of a snail-shell. I stared down at my empty plate.

'You finished?'

'Yes thank you, Auntie Dilys,' we chorused.

'Say Grace, then,' she said between sips.

We washed up and Pat helped me to put everything away. 'I don't like her,' Pat whispered as I wiped the larder shelf.

'What are you doing in there?' Auntie Dilys appeared in the doorway.

'I've finished now, Auntie Dilys,' I said quickly.

'And not a minute too soon. Indeed, here comes your Auntie Bron.'

Auntie Bron poured herself a cup of tea and took off her shoes. 'Come into the dining-room, Dilys,' she said. They went, closing the door firmly behind them.

Pat moved closer to me on the long sofa. 'Why did we 'ave our bath at dinner time?' she asked in a whisper.

'I don't know,' I whispered back, remembering that I'd thought it strange too at the time.

'Is our mum gonna come soon?' Pat was tugging at my arm. My heart sank and I could only nod a reply.

The door opened. 'Say "Thank you" to Auntie Dilys,' commanded Auntie.

We stood up. 'Thank you, Auntie Dilys,' we intoned without looking at her. She didn't answer with words; she might have smiled, but I wasn't looking. The front door shut with a sharp click; she was gone.

Auntie poked the fire. 'Get the polish, girl. That front passage looks disgraceful.'

I got the polish and dusters.

'Sit by there, Pat' – Auntie indicated the fireside end of the sofa. 'You! Come with me!'

I followed her up the passage. She paused at the parlour door. 'In here' – she stood aside for me to enter. The light coming through the tightly closed curtains gave the room a peculiar transparent-greenish drowning look. Clutching the polishing things, I moved towards the window, thinking to open the curtains; Auntie must have forgotten. Suddenly my body stopped moving, I stood absolutely frozen to the spot. A long shiny box glinting with brass lay across rough trestles in the middle of the room. I don't know how long I stood there trying desperately not to see the lacy frills and greenish waxy hands; terror slowly seeped into me as my eyes sought, yet tried not to see, the huge grotesque doll with covered face; the polish tin fell from my hands and rolled crazily around the floor; a shriek of horror escaped my rigid lips. I scrambled backwards for the door. It was shut. My hands scrabbled with the door-knob; panic seized me; in vain I tried to turn away from the box; no sound came from my screaming mouth. The door suddenly swung open, knocking me forward and downward, the lino rushed up to meet me – I lay trembling on the floor. Then hands were pulling at me, dragging me upward – my eyes slid sideways, terror filled every part of me, a greenish hand was clutching at my arm, the other one was smacking my face, I tried to escape the hands but they were pulling me into the passage; from a long way off I heard Auntie's voice; then quite suddenly realised that she was here, they were her hands; I tried to speak but no words came. She hit me a stinging blow across the face. 'You will do it!' she shouted, the words echoed around inside me, Auntie had let go of me and gone away – I could hear her opening and closing drawers in the dining-room.

'*You will do it!*' – suddenly appearing again; taking hold of my arm, she thrust me back into that awful room. The door slammed as I threw myself towards it; my hand found the knob just as Auntie on the other side turned the key in the lock.

'Please, please, Auntie!' I sobbed through the door. 'Please, please, don't lock me in.'

There was no answer.

'Pat – *Pat*!' I cried loudly. 'Oh Pat, please make Auntie let me out!'

Auntie's footsteps approached the door; I could hear Pat crying nearby. 'Pat! Oh, *Pat*!' I sobbed, leaning against the cold painted wood.

Auntie was shouting at Pat now: 'Naughty, ungrateful little girl that your sister is' – the key turned in the closed door, opening the lock.

'She's cryin' for me,' came Pat's tearful voice.

'*Very well* . . .' said Auntie, and pushed her through the hastily opened door: she came straight into my arms and we stood crying together as the key turned, locking us in. 'Now get that floor polished,' came Auntie's voice. 'I'll give you just twenty minutes, Hilda my girl!' She paused. 'Are you listening?'

'Yes, Auntie' – my voice was like a whisper.

'You'd *better* be. And mind you mark my words well: it'll be the belt across your backside if that floor isn't done.'

Pat was clutching my arm, seeking to bury her face in my jumper. 'Yes, Auntie,' my voice wavered. She went away. A fresh flood of tears poured down my face: I didn't want Pat to see the box. After a little while I got her to kneel on the floor with me, but as she did so her head turned inevitably towards the trestles: I felt the shudder that passed through her. '*Don't look any more*,' I whispered urgently. 'You *mustn't* look. *Promise* me.' She turned a white, shocked face to look at me. 'You mustn't *get up off your knees*, Pat. You *mustn't*,' I begged, and didn't know if she could hear me. 'Pat! *Pat!*' – I gently shook her shoulders – a thin wail spread itself around the room. 'Shush . . . shush, Pat, please, please don't do it.'

The wailing stopped and she burst into tears. 'I'm frightened, 'Ild! Please let me out, *please*!'

Her crying was getting louder; I put my hand over her mouth. '*Shut up*, Pat. Just don't *look*, that's all. Now you stay there, I've got to polish the floor.' The words, once uttered, brought me face to face with my fear.

'Don't leave me!' cried Pat, clinging on to my arm.

'All right, keep beside me but don't look at anything 'cept the floor,' I said, more for myself than for Pat. Then together we crawled within reach of the tin of polish. I stretched my trembling fingers and avoided touching the rough trestle: a sob rose in my throat as we crawled hastily into the far corner. The smell of polish suddenly filled the room and our minds. Together we crawled around, rubbing and shining at the floor; never once did we dare to raise our eyes off that floor, not even to look at each other, so great was our fear.

At last the floor was finished. We crawled to the corner nearest the door and waited for Auntie to come and let us out. The sound of the key turning made us both jump. 'Out!' ordered Auntie. We stumbled eagerly into the passage, ignoring our aching legs. 'Get washed,' she said, pushing us towards the kitchen. Nunky didn't look up from his newspaper, not even when Pat was suddenly sick. 'Take her outside,' Auntie snapped at me. 'It's all your doing anyway, you little slut.'

Pat and I stood shaking in the darkness of the lav. When she'd finished being sick we went back and had our wash. Then we had to recite the Twenty-third Psalm. Our voices stumbled as we said the bit that goes, 'Yea, though I walk through the Valley of the Shadow of Death'. It had taken on a terrible new meaning, and I was relieved when we got to the Amen.

After we had chanted our 'Good night' to Nunky, Auntie took us upstairs and into the little bedroom that had been used by Uncle Dan. I shivered between the icy sheets. ''Ild . . .' Pat whispered after a while, 'where's Uncle Dan gorn? It's 'is bed, in't it?' she added.

'Shut up! *Shut up!*' I told her, trying to hold back my fear. Pat started to cry. 'What's the matter now?' I felt a bit sorry that I'd been angry.

'I'm scared.' She sobbed. 'Scared of that big coffee-box downstairs . . .'

The next morning proved different from any other. Instead of attending the usual Sunday religious meetings, we'd been told to stay in the kitchen where, I'd heard Auntie tell Dilys, '. . . she can be of some use for a change.' Dilys-the-friend had cooed agreement. She meant it, too. As soon as we'd washed up the breakfast things she'd given me the potatoes to peel, the carrots to scrape,

257

and the cabbage to chop. I was fast; I'd had to learn to be; yet still I couldn't seem to do anything fast enough, my legs were smarting from the frequent slaps.

'A lazy good-for-nothing girl,' she'd told Pat. 'I'll have to run about laying the dining-table myself at this rate!'

The door-knocker rattled. She hurried along the passage. Pat hovered just inside the dining-room. A kettle boiled and I hurried to remove it. Auntie Dilys came briskly back into the kitchen. 'Where's that kettle?' – her hand was on it before I could answer.

Pat came in, saying to Auntie Dilys, 'Please, Auntie said would you make tea . . . er' – she paused, frowning – 'oh yes, for gentleman payin' for 'is specs.'

'His *what*!' Dilys stared.

''Is specs.'

Auntie Dilys patted the fair ringlets. 'Dear innocent child,' she sighed.

The door-knocker rattled again. She was gone. I peeled the last potato and dropped it into its saucepan. 'Make yourself useful!' Auntie Dilys, darting in again, poked at me with her long fingers. 'The visitors will need refreshment.'

I poured water into the teapot.

'She says ready now, Dilys.' Nunky's long face appeared and disappeared at the door . . .

Dilys muttered as she poured hot water on to the 'Camp' coffee. She gave the jug a stir and stood it in the hearth. 'Get those cups and saucers.' I got them. 'Spread them out, you foolish girl!' I spread them out. 'Hurry yourself, we haven't got all damned day' – the straw hat was rather askew, the hair wispy and damp on the perspiring forehead; the boiling tea hissed its way through the hot spout. 'Fill that pot.' I obeyed. 'Make more coffee.' The door was opening and shutting, dirty cups and saucers arrived endlessly, there were teapots to be filled, coffee to be made, and Auntie Dilys, who seemed sandwiched between rage in the kitchen and sweetness in the dining-room, to be got out of the way of.

At last the flow of liquid and dirty china ceased. Auntie Dilys took Pat with her to lay the dining-room table. I finished the washing-up, only to get embroiled in the serving-up. The precious cabbage water was drained away down the sink by the uncaring sharp-tongued Dilys. 'Get those tureens from the oven.' She was holding the oven-cloth. I waited. She slapped me for disobedience and reached into the oven for the tureens. 'Ouch!' – she rubbed her burnt fingers. 'God give me strength!' she muttered, rolling her eyes heavenwards. The door-knocker rattled. '*Yessy Grist!*' she exclaimed – or at least that's what it sounded like.

Auntie Bron poked her head round the kitchen door. 'The Captain's here, Dilys. Are you nearly ready?'

Dilys gave a sweet smile. 'Why of course, Bron, I'm just this minute coming.' Auntie Bron went away. 'Get the gravy boat,' snapped Auntie Dilys. She sucked at her burnt fingers, gave me a look. 'I'll deal with you later, my lady . . .' She picked up the meat-dish and headed for the dining-room. Behind her Pat wrinkled her nose and stuck out her tongue.

The kitchen door shot open. Auntie Dilys plonked two plates on the table. Our dinner had been served. We took advantage of the limited supervision and scraped the fat meat and cabbage stumps into our hankies.

We'd hardly finished dinner when the stream of washing-up began all over again. Auntie Dilys lined up the teapots and jugs. I moved automatically from the sink to the stove and back to the table. My hands were red and the cracks were bleeding slightly. 'Don't you dare get blood on those cups.'

'Yes, Auntie Dilys.'

'Terrible hands for a girl.'

'Yes, Auntie Dilys.'

'It's a brazen girl who isn't ashamed of hands like that.'

'Yes, Auntie Dilys.'

'Mind what you're doing with that pot!'

'Yes, Auntie Dilys.'

The door swung open. Nunky came into the kitchen. 'The Captain's ready now, Dilys.'

'Oh, I'm ready and waiting,' the sweet singsong voice trilled forth. Without turning away from the sink I knew that the hat was being attended to. Then came the rustle of the starched overall being removed. 'Fold it up and put it by there' – she aimed the words at my back . . .

'Yes, Auntie Dilys.'

The door closed. They were gone. I folded the overall and went back to washing the cups.

''Ild . . .' said Pat.

'What is it?'

She licked her fingers. 'You won't be 'noyed, will yer?'

I dried my hands. 'No, I suppose not.'

She crept closer to me. 'Bend down, then.'

I bent.

'Is that thing gone away, 'Ild?'

The sound of grown-ups singing made her spring away from me like a startled bird. We stood listening. 'Abide with me, fast falls the eventide . . .' I sat down on the sofa. 'Come over here, Pat. Now what were you on about?'

She sat beside me. 'That thing . . . *you* know . . .' she whispered. I knew all right. 'Tell me!' She tugged at my arm.

'I think it's gone,' I answered hopefully.

She licked her fingers.

'Don't *do* that,' I said crossly. 'Here, give me your hankie.'

She fumbled. 'Ooh . . . ooh look . . . it's got all that ole stuff in it . . .'

I stared at the congealed fat. 'We'd better get rid of it. I'll put it down the lav.' I stood up.

'You hain't leavin' me . . . ?' Pat ducked out of the back door. It was just beginning to rain; dark clouds hung low over the mountains. We hurried back indoors.

'God's not 'arf angry,' said Pat.

'Don't be daft,' I told her. 'It's only rain!'

She licked her fingers. 'An' 'ow do you know?'

I rubbed at her streaky forehead. 'Never mind, keep still, will you?'

There was more singing now, and somebody coughed quite badly. A little while later Auntie Dilys came bustling back to the teapots. The door-knocker rattled. 'There's no Peace!' Auntie Dilys told the ceiling. She thrust herself back into the print overall. She sighed. 'And no gratitude either!' she suddenly snapped. 'Get those pots filled, you shiftless article!'

'Yes, Auntie Dilys.' I took hold of the kettle and poured, accepting that we were back to normal now.

The last visitor left, calling loudly, 'No stars . . .'

Auntie Dilys simpered and called out, 'And good night to you too, Trevor Roberts.' I carried the last pile of clean china into the larder.

Auntie Bron came into the kitchen carrying our nightdresses. 'Why aren't you washed?' Her gaze rested on my hands, then slid away. 'Get washed and hurry up. It's almost seven o'clock,' she added for Auntie Dilys's benefit.

'There's slow she is, Bron . . .' the singsong voice began.

Nunky poked his head round the door. 'Mam's left her bag, Bron. I'd better take it along, don't you think?'

Auntie Bron nodded. Nunky withdrew.

'There's kindness for you, Bron,' fawned Dilys-the-friend. 'The patience of St David himself,' she ventured. Auntie Bron's impatient fingers reached for the hairbrush. Dilys touched Pat's hair. 'Lovely . . .' she murmured.

Auntie Bron moved Pat ever so slightly. 'Yes,' was all she said.

'What loving care and patience you must have put into that child, Bron.'

Auntie Bron smiled. 'Do make another pot of tea, Dilys,' she said in her very friendly voice.

Dilys, smiling to herself, elbowed me away from the sink. I stood in the corner and put on the long white nightie. Auntie hung up the brush. 'I'm too tired to listen to any more prayers tonight.' She stood up, smoothing the front of her uniform. 'We'll just take them in to say good night, shall we?' Dilys put the lid on the teapot. 'Come along,' said Auntie, and we followed her out into the passage.

I felt a prickle of doubt. The passage was in darkness. *There was no one there to say good night to.*

The prickle turned into a stab as Auntie opened the parlour door and reached for the switch . . . There's no one there . . . there's no one there . . . the thought had kept repeating itself all along the passage. The darkness vanished as the long gleaming box sprang into being. I backed away. 'No! *No!* Oh no, *please!*' Auntie Bron was pulling my arm.

''S 'orrible, lemme go!' cried the struggling Pat, but Dilys held her firmly.

'Please Auntie, oh please don't,' I begged, still pulling backwards. She gave a sudden jerk and I was pressing up against the shiny wood . . . I spun my head away . . .

'Put me down . . . put me down . . . is 'orrible . . . is 'orrible, put me down, lemme go!' Pat was crying and struggling in the arms of Dilys-the-friend.

'Pick her up, Bron,' said the singsong voice.

'No . . . no . . . no!' I reeled away from the memory of the green waxy hands.

'Up you come.' Auntie Bron swung me under her arm; my legs

kicked but found no resistance, I wouldn't look, my head was turning this way and that . . . Auntie Bron grabbed a handful of hair and I was staring down at the doll's face, the bonnet was frilled and tied under the chin in a bow, the hands crossed over the chest held a small posy of flowers. Not a doll – it's not a doll – fear flashed through my head, something inside it twisted and cringed.

'Kiss Uncle Dan good night.'

Realisation brought the once-familiar face sharply into focus. He was real! *Real!* I struggled.

'Kiss him,' ordered Auntie Bron. I shut my eyes on the yellowy face with the sunken mouth, tried not to accept the dark stubble on its chin . . .

Not its chin, my mind shrieked, his chin, *Uncle Dan's* chin! My captor tugged at my hair, the unwilling eyes had to see. She lowered me nearer the figure lying so still in the white nightie; I tore my eyes away, they sought desperately for another place to look, the frilled lacy edging around the coffin . . . the hands . . . the bonnet . . .

'Kiss Uncle Dan.' Exhausted, I pressed my unwilling mouth to his forehead; a scream strangled in my throat frozen there by the cold, the bitter unexpected coldness.

Auntie stood me on the floor. Dry sobs racked my body as my struggling sister jerked violently sideways in the grasping arms. The clatter of a falling saucer burst upon the room and a piece of peeled onion, spinning like a top, slid wildly across the floor.

Then Pat too was lowered, sobbing loudly, to wish Uncle Dan a good night.

Chapter 40 ～～～

The wet pit-pat of my sister's journeying fingers sounded over-loud in the stillness of the dining-room, and Auntie's slight frown of annoyance came and went as if she hadn't really noticed the reason for it. The three of us stood around the red-plush-covered table upon which lay eight silver sixpences and the little green pot that was usually kept locked in the bow-fronted china cabinet, the doors of which were now hanging open.

'Well?' said Auntie in her new quiet whisper. I swallowed hard before answering in a thin wavering voice: 'Please Auntie, I didn't take it. I didn't.'

Her hand thumped down on to the table. '*Liar!*'

I stared miserably at the coins. Eight when there should be nine. Nine sixpences in a little green pot. A pot that I must have seen hundreds of times, but I'd never handled it or guessed its secret. How could I when it was always locked away? This thought strengthened me. 'Please Auntie, I didn't know there was any money in it and it's locked up so how . . . ?'

'Liar. Liar. *Liar*.' The strange quiet tone made me shudder. 'A thief, that's what you are. A thief.'

A feeling of indignation swept away all caution. I'd got used to being called all sorts of things and Auntie called me a liar so often that it didn't much matter any more. But a thief! No, I wouldn't be called a thief. 'I'm not a thief,' I said loudly, almost angrily.

She stood ever so still, a look of disbelief curving her mouth into a sort of sneer. '*What* did you say?'

My indignation began to shrink away, I felt my face whitening under her mocking eyes, the desire to run fought to be uppermost in my mind.

'Go on . . . "Thief!" Say it. Say it!' she coaxed as she came round the table towards me.

'Please . . . please, I'm not a thief,' I said, and was amazed at the sure tone of my voice.

Auntie snatched at my arms and twisted them up behind me; a fearful sobbing started inside me. 'Thief. Thief' – she flung me against the table. 'Do you know what happens to thieves . . . ?' She smiled into the whisper. I stood against the table, wondering if this was a nightmare. Auntie was angry but she was whispering and she was smiling and I – *I had never been so frightened in all my life*.

'. . . well, I'll tell you.' She seized one of my hands and held it on the table. 'They just *cut off their hands. See!*' – her free hand chopped down across my wrist, the room swirled, the sound of Pat screaming seemed to break into and unlock what I was now certain must be a terribly bad nightmare. I opened my eyes.

'I 'ates yer, I 'ates yer,' sobbed my struggling sister as Auntie forced her into the darkening kitchen. The sound of a sharp slap changed the screams into pitiful crying.

'*Stop* it. Stop it at *once*!' Auntie sounded as if she was . . .

pleading? I got up off the floor. From the doorway I could see Auntie rocking to and fro on the kitchen sofa with Pat still struggling in her arms. Something inside me almost wished I *had* taken the sixpence so that I could give it back and make everything all right.

I felt desperation grow again. Wishing couldn't make anything right. But if only I had a sixpence! My eyes filled with tears as I stared into the kitchen's warm, rosy glow. 'Auntie . . .' The timid, tentative word was out before I could catch it – the reaction was instant.

Auntie stood up, letting Pat fall to the floor like a rag doll. 'Don't you "Auntie" me, lying, thieving little slut that you are' – she snatched the belt from the back of Nunky's chair. 'Admit it. Go on! Say "I am a thief."' No! No! No! The screaming denial fled silently from my unyielding mouth; the word 'thief' inside me was sickening and evil like a snake. In the instant before the dreadful, darkening belting I knew that if I had all the sixpences in the world, not one of them would ever be stolen, nor would I pretend it was, not even for that soothing rocking in the firelit kitchen.

That night, as we knelt to say our prayers, I said one that Auntie never heard:

'Please God, You know I didn't take that sixpence. But Auntie, well, she thinks I did. And if you could just help me this once, I promise that I'll never ask you for anything else and I'll even try to be glad when they dedicate me under that old flag they've got. And Pat, well, I'll tell her and she'll be glad too, even though we don't like it in that little hut. But I expect You know that already, but we do like it in the church, God, and it's not just because of the pretty windows, really it's not. And God, I promise I won't ever take those carrots and things any more, not even if I'm starving I won't. Honest, God, I really do mean it.'

I paused, feeling that I'd given Him quite a lot to think about and I didn't want Him to get tired of listening. But I didn't want Him to think I'd gone away either, so I continued:

'Well, God, I know You're ever so busy, but I was wondering if you could just put a little blister on the foot of the one who did steal that money. I know that a blister couldn't tell Auntie anything, but I've had a blister and they hurt quite a lot, just like being punished does.'

I stopped and waited for a moment then, taking a deep breath, I made my final request:

'Please God, let the night be long.'

Winnie fixed her gaze on my black-stockinged legs. 'So that's wot yer wearin' them 'orrible ole things for, is it?'

I nodded. 'Auntie says they're to cover up the thief-marks. But I didn't take her sixpence and it was the belt that made the marks.'

'Ooh, she din't 'arf get 'it an' all. An' she ain't a thief, she ain't, she ain't, she ain't,' asserted Pat.

'So that's why you ain't bin ter school fer three days, is it.' Winnie wasn't asking a question.

'Yeah, an' she 'it me too, an' me face was all swole up an' she said it was toofache but it wasn't, see, it wasn't and she's 'orrible.' Pat started to cry.

'Oh blimey.' Winnie wrapped a comforting arm around the shaking shoulders.

'We gotta do something!' said Jessica firmly. Joyce nodded.

'Yeah . . .' agreed Winnie. 'Like wot?' She was still hugging Pat.

'Well,' I reasoned, 'perhaps we'd better find out what it is we're going to do something about – I mean, well, what's the matter with Joyce? And you too, Jessica?'

Jessica folded her arms. 'Me first, then. When them ladies come here from London 'cause of the bombs, well, soon as my auntie sees 'em she says to her friends that they was oars. An' – well – jus' lately she's bin askin' all things about my mum and saying how funny it is I haven't got even a little picture of her and all things like that, see. Then I got this ink on me hands through bein' Ink Monitor and it all sort of ends up with 'er shoutin' an' carryin' on an' sayin' as how my mum must be like one of these oars and all things like that. So I gets upset about 'er callin' my mum a stick of wood and I run out an' she run after me and give me a walloping.'

There was a sympathetic pause. We had all lived this sort of story, grown-ups walloping you and you didn't know why.

'Them . . . oars,' said Joyce hesitantly. 'You got it wrong, it's nothink to do wiv boats, it's ladies wot sells their flavours.'

'Oh!' said Winnie.

'Do you mean jellies and things?' I asked.

'No she don't,' muttered Jessica.

'Well, what flavours?' I persisted.

Joyce sniffed loudly. 'Dunno but it's bad things, innit Jessica?' Jessica nodded. Joyce sniffed again. 'It ain't fair, really. My auntie says all them ladies are harlots wot's in the Bible an' I think they were bad because they slept on the temple steps. An' my mum don't even go *near* a temple.'

'Yeah, an' our mum ain't bad she's good, ain't she, 'Ild, an' she went an' picked cherries an' she made us lovely corned beef an' all, so there!' chimed Pat, who seemed to be having her first taste of what Winnie and I called 'High Horse'.

'She sounds proper nice,' soothed Winnie, but there was a sad, wistful sound in her voice.

'What about *you*, then?' asked Jessica.

'Yeah, me an' *all*. An' I ain't got nuffin' else ter say 'cept as 'ow I'm fed up wiv *all* of it, *see!*'

Jessica shrugged off Winnie's edginess. Perhaps she had enough of her own. Winnie read the feeling and glared. Jessica glared back. Were we growing up, I wondered, and was this what growing up was? Feeling everything and everybody getting more and more away from you, and you not knowing why nor how to bring it all back? I sensed that the Gang was already melting away, and I didn't know why. There was Winnie, white-faced and silent; Jessica staring blindly at the mountaintops, a trickle of tears running down her cheeks. I knew she didn't want to go away from us and Winnie and I knew too that she'd never say so. But the silence was getting longer and more uncomfortable. Something had to happen. 'I've made up my mind to run away!' I blurted out.

'What!' they all seemed to say at once. 'What!'

I nodded.

'When?' asked Winnie as if she was talking through a thick fog.

'Next Saturday' – making up my mind quite suddenly.

'Well if you're goin', I'm comin',' declared Winnie.

There was a pause.

'But it's a long *way*. Will you be getting a lift or something?' asked Jessica excitedly.

'No we won't, eh 'Ild?' said Winnie scornfully. 'Ain't you never 'eard of them rich ole men in motorcars wot takes yer away an' strangles yer t'death in a ole sack?'

Jessica nodded anxiously. Joyce looked frightened. 'But my mum says they 'ides in bushes,' she offered, as if hoping the bit about the motorcars wasn't true.

'Mus' be a diff'runt lot,' said Winnie. 'Thing is, 'ow far is it?'

'My uncle says it's two 'undred miles!' said Jessica lightly.

'An' you can walk a mile in fifteen minutes,' declared Connie, who'd just joined the Girl Guides.

'Well, that's . . . um . . . four miles in an hour, then,' offered Joyce.

'Yeah, an' if we hurry up . . .' said Jessica gleefully.

'But that'll take fifty hours!' I said, jerking myself into and out of the sum.

'But 'Ild . . . we don't 'ave ter foller all them *twistin' roads*,' explained Joyce patiently. 'We can cut across fields an' that . . .'

'Why can't we go *now*?' demanded Pat.

'We've got to get food, that's why!' I said crossly.

'Rainin'!' remarked Joyce. The big blobs of raindrops were cold and unfriendly.

'Best get goin' 'ome, then,' declared Winnie.

Home! My eyes felt a bit swimmy and it wasn't the raindrops. But – for now at any rate – the Gang was together again.

The heavy raindrops had thickened into a steady downpour as we let ourselves into the back yard. ''Spect we better wait in the lav,' decided Pat. Auntie had bolted the back door before she'd gone off to Ponty. I placed the bucket beside the coal shed. The clatter of its handle reminded me of its near-empty state. Auntie wouldn't be at all pleased. But then Auntie wouldn't be home for ages, a bit more than two hours. Maybe the rain wouldn't last long and I'd go back to the tip.

The sudden sliding sound of the back-door bolt caused Pat to clutch fearfully at my arm, but when the door opened it was Nunky – Nunky who waved to us to come inside, Nunky who left the kitchen door wide open and quickly disappeared in the direction of the lavatory.

'Are we ever so late, 'Ild?' Pat's uncertainty matched mine as we saw the two steaming buckets, the waiting tub and the crisp white towels. I glanced anxiously at the clock. Five past three. Yet the scene in the kitchen said six o'clock. A sound in the yard caught my attention. From the open doorway I saw Nunky empty the coal bucket. Surely he must know that Auntie hadn't seen it yet? Perhaps I ought to have told him, I thought doubtfully, as he poured the hot water into the waiting tub.

'You can start having your bath.' He didn't look at us as he added the cold water; the wet pit-pat of my sister's fingers was the loudest sound in the room. 'Just carry on as Auntie does' – from the doorway to the dining-room. Then he was gone.

Pat threw me a questioning glance, then without further hesitation she undressed and climbed into the tub. 'You betta wash me 'air first' – her nervousness was obvious as she handed me the wet flannel. I took it reluctantly, wondering why there wasn't a better way to wash hair.

'*I'll* go!' called Nunky's voice suddenly from the next room. Go? Go where? I wondered absently as I set about the business of soaking the meekly bent head.

'There's *daft* you are, girl . . . Fetch me a jug from the larder.' It was Gwyneth. She came into the kitchen and knelt down by the tub. 'Hold this over your eyes.' She handed Pat the squeezed-out flannel. I stood wondering how she intended wetting all that hair. Auntie always needed the flannel. 'You'd best get undressed,' she murmured over her shoulder as she took the jug and dipped it into the water. 'Hold the flannel tight now, Pat,' she instructed. And then she gently poured the contents over the waiting hair. Very soon the strong clean smell of Lifebuoy soap spread itself familiarly about the room, and to my surprise a tearless Pat stepped from the tub looking as if she'd just experienced some sort of miracle.

'They'll be back soon,' said Nunky as he handed Gwyneth a cup of rather strong-looking tea. She nodded and made the funny little sipping sound that I'd hear her make several times whilst she was bathing me. I guessed there must be something wrong, but of course I hadn't dared to ask what.

'Been a funny sort of day . . .' Nunky's voice was saying as he began slicing the bread.

Grown-ups didn't often say things like that. They didn't need to. I'd often thought how odd it was that they always seemed to know just about everything. There didn't ever seem to be a time when they had to ask what they were to do and when they were to do it. It seemed that they could always just turn up in the right place at the right time, already knowing what was required. Like today, for instance. Auntie had gone out shopping to Ponty as usual. She'd bolted the back door and as far as I knew the house was empty. And it hadn't looked like rain when Pat and I went to the tip either. Yet it *had* rained and we'd come home to find not only Nunky unbolting the door but the buckets and the tub already waiting for us to have a bath that we usually didn't have till after tea. So somehow he'd known not only that it was going to rain but also that we'd be coming home, although no one had told us to. Then Gwyneth had arrived and she'd never had anything to do with our bath. Yet she'd just turned up at the right time to do the right thing. Could it really be true, I wondered, that I too was now beginning to move in the mysterious ways of grown-ups? Would I now go around in this world turning up at the right places without ever having to be told; without even *knowing*?

'Stop daydreaming, girl, here comes your Auntie.' Nunky's loud whisper dragged me back to the reality of being told. I managed to smother the feeling of disappointment – after all, I'd now got some idea about being grown-up.

Auntie didn't come into the kitchen right away. Instead she called Nunky into the dining-room. The sound of rustling paper covered most of the low conversation, but I couldn't help hearing about how pleased she was to have been able to get just the right *present*.

'Here, take this,' said Gwyneth, offering me the cup and saucer. I took it over to the sink, and as Gwyneth went into the dining-room I couldn't help noticing that she was limping slightly.

'Is she 'urt?' Pat's whisper was full of concern.

'Really, Gwyneth, you are the limit, couldn't you wait till we came up to Mam's after tea?' Auntie sounded very annoyed as she came into the kitchen. Gwyneth came limping in behind her. The small sip-sip sounds were louder, and I noticed that her face had gone very red. 'Well, sit down. Come on now, get that shoe and stocking off. If you think I've nothing better to do . . .' Gwyneth sank on to the sofa and allowed Auntie's impatient fingers to untie her shoe. 'Great baby! Come on, come on, get that stocking off' – and Nunky, who'd been about to come into the room, was waved impatiently out.

'It's stuck, Bron – it's stuck . . .' moaned Gwyneth as she reluctantly rolled the stocking down towards her foot.

'Rubbish, girl, don't be so cowardly!' said Auntie as she gave the offending part a sharp *tug*.

'Ouch! Ooh, Bron it *hurts*! It hurts, and look – it's bleeding!' Gwyneth sounded like a rather frightened little girl. Over Auntie's shoulder I could see the tears on her face.

'No *wonder*. It's a nasty blister you've got there, and no doubt there's dye in it from your stocking too.' Auntie stood up, sighing with exasperation. 'I'll get the ointment and some lint. But really, Gwyn, your vanity . . .'

The dining-room door slammed behind her, leaving me a clear view of the messy blister and Gwyneth's falling tears. Automatically I turned back to the sink and picked up the cool, damp flannel. Then, unable to speak because of my own choking tears, I laid the cool wetness across Gwyneth's ankle. My prayer had been answered and I felt truly dreadful. The blister I'd asked for had been given. She'd bathed us so gently and taken such care to keep the soapsuds out of our eyes. I felt the tightness forming in my throat. It was as if God was saying:

> You can have what you want,
> But not without knowing,
> Not without sharing.

I struggled again with the tightness, longing for the relief of tears. I'd had my wish – and received the most important lesson in my life.

Chapter 41 ~~~

Pat, for once, wasn't at all upset as we lay together in bed that night. I supposed it was because of the way Gwyneth had washed her hair. Suddenly she spoke: "'Ere, 'Ild, can I tell yer a story 'bout a boy what could fly?'

I rolled over. 'All right, but I think it's one I know,' I said tiredly.

'Yer don't know it 'cause it come out of a book,' she told me flatly.

'What book? We've not got a storybook,' I told her crossly.

'I didn't say it was our book, it was that man's book: you know, that nice man Mr Bryn.'

I was now awake. I couldn't remember him reading a story to us. 'When? What are you talking about?'

Pat sat up a bit. 'It was when all that thunder and lightning 'appened. 'E 'ad two beds in 'is room an' 'e put me in the warm one, see.'

I remembered that night quite clearly. 'Go on,' I told her.

'Well, 'e 'ad this 'lectric torch an' 'e was in the uvver bed, see an' 'e jest read me the story. I didn't mind about the thunder any more.'

I felt a little bit jealous. 'I thought you didn't like him, and what about those shillings?'

Pat leant over me. 'It was 'cause of Mum, see, she'd a bin angry if we took 'em: 'e was a stranger, 'Ild.'

I smiled into the dark as Pat lay down and snuggled close to me. 'I'll tell yer the story termorrer,' she said sleepily. I drifted off to sleep and dreamt of angry bumblebees, but it was not a dream, it was a real sound filling the night: the droning sound of aeroplanes – crumbs, it sounded like hundreds of them! Pat clutched at me just as the siren went. Outside in the night people called to one another. Running feet pounded the pavements. Wardens shouted 'Take cover! Take cover!'

A lady laughed. 'Dew, it's only a practice, man!'

'Blast you, woman, that's Jerry planes up there' – the Warden sounded angry. Other voices took up his words: 'Jerries, real Germans up there in the sky!' More running.

And then the street was silent under the German aeroplanes.

Auntie opened our door. 'Get up. Bring these.' She was gone. Everywhere was dark, but I found the gas masks by the doorway where she'd left them. Crumbs, if the rattles went now . . . which mask was which? Foolishly I scrabbled at the lids; maybe there'd be something inside to tell me; we often put secret things in there. My fingers felt inside first one tin, then the other. No secret things.

'Come on! Come on!' from the blackness below.

'Yes, Auntie, yes, we're coming.' Pat and I felt our way down to where she waited.

'Put them under the stairs, Bron.' Nunky sounded as if he was at the open back door.

Auntie had the cubbyhole door open already, and Pat and I crawled into a deeper darkness. 'Don't move,' said Auntie from outside the cupboard, then she went to wherever Nunky was.

'Give me that tin,' I whispered.

'Wot! Me gas mask?' Pat sounded as if it was the greatest treasure in the world. A panic seized me – it *was* the greatest!

'How do we know it's yours?' I whispered, grabbing blindly for the lidless tin.

'Ooh! *'Ere!* 'Ere *'tis*. Ooh, 'Ild, 'urry *up!* S'posin' it goes *orf!*' My hands now had two masks to feel.

Not the rubber, I told myself. Find the straps, they'll be different lengths. Fingers found webbing in one tin, then the other. I didn't take out the masks. Just let my fingers walk along two lengths of webbing. Which was the shortest? The one on the right. Better do it again to be certain. Of course our names would be written on the webbing, but who could read in the dark? I couldn't, and that was the surest thing I knew right now. My fingers again chose the one on the right. That one had to be Pat's. 'Here, I think it's yours, try it on.'

Pat's hands took the mask. 'Ooh, I'm scared, 'Ild, I don't wanna put it on.'

'You must. Here, let me help.'

'No! I don't like it, I don't like it . . .' She was pushing the mask away; her voice was getting louder and louder. Oh crumbs! I heard Auntie coming back. So did Pat. She was quiet, huddled up against me.

'They're all right.' It was Auntie's voice. The feet went away again.

'Now you keep quiet, or she'll come back again. And we've got to find out which is which, it's important, Pat!' I was urging her to try the mask.

I could feel her shaking. '*Can't*. *You* try 'em on, 'Ild.'

I sat dumb and miserable, staring into the darkness. It wasn't any use me trying them on, they were *both* too big. My straps pulled up double but even so only one mask fitted, and that was Pat's. She mustn't get mine by mistake, it'd be too tight to go over her head, though still too loose for mine.

''Ave yer done it, 'Ild?' Pat's little whisper was hopeful. 'Gi'es it then, 'Ild.' She fumbled with the mask, and suddenly there was a tiny snorting sound.

'That's it, Pat. Quick, get it off. Here's its tin. Now sit with it between your legs and keep your hands on those straps.'

'Is that wot you're doin', 'Ild?'

I moved the tin quietly; put my hands on the straps. 'Yes, Pat. We're all right now.'

★

Nunky brought us some cocoa and stood in the passage holding a dim torch whilst we drank it. Everything was very quiet, and I was sure it must be nearly morning.

'I'm going to bed.' Auntie sounded tired and weary.

Nunky leant in and took our cups. 'Best wait for the All Clear, Bron.' His light swung away, leaving us to the darkness again. Auntie sighed somewhere. Nunky clinked the cups and said, 'Those planes were going to the coast, Bron.' She didn't say anything. 'Bron, they have to get *back*.' He sounded a little angry.

Auntie poked her head into the cupboard. 'Come on, up to bed. Both of you.' She reached out to help us into the passage. Sleepy and stiff, with cramped legs, we followed her sounds, clutching the gas masks.

'In you go.' We crept into bed. Still clutching the tins.

Suddenly I was awake. The room still dark. Gosh, this blinking tin! I'd been lying on it. I put it carefully on the floor and shook my head to clear the buzzing noise. But it wasn't in my head. I lay back on the pillow, ready to sleep again. The buzzing was loud. Closer. And coming closer all the time. Quickly I woke Pat. Reached for my gas mask. We sat huddled together, waiting for someone to call us. The noise was ever so loud. Surely Auntie must hear it. She had. I heard the door open at the end of the passage, Auntie's urgent knocking on Gwyneth's door: 'Gwyn! Quick, something's happening!'

Pat and I scrambled off the bed just as the high piercing screaming sound began. Nunky ran towards us shouting, 'Oh my God, oh my God!' Then we could only hear that screaming whistling sound tearing out of the sky. Hands roughly threw us to the floor. A mattress – ours – landed on top of us, pressing the silent screams of panic into the floor. The booming blast and tearing whistle exploded in a great roaring crash that seemed to go on and on for ever and ever. 'Oh Christ help us! Christ help us!' Nunky was pleading; Auntie was crying for him to stop. Gwyneth lay on the landing, pounding her fists on to the floor.

The noise outside changed. Men shouting; whistles blowing. Nunky raced off downstairs. 'Bloody great bomb, all the help . . .' Feet were pounding and we heard the door slam as Nunky joined them.

'It's those bloody kids! You hear me, it's those bloody kids!' Gwyneth was shrieking. Auntie dragged the mattress off and let it fall to the floor. Gwyneth reeled towards us. 'You don't belong to

273

us and we do get bombed because it's here you did come. I'll . . . I'll . . .' Auntie caught her as she threw herself towards us, they struggled together, Gwyneth shrieking words we couldn't understand. Then suddenly Auntie's hand cracked against the sides of the shrieking face; Gwyneth was struck dumb, a white-nightie'd shape that stood a moment, then folded to the floor sobbing. Pat was sobbing too. And something was hurting all the way across my back.

'Hilda! Is that blackout up?' Auntie was out on the landing waiting. Then she put the light on. 'Now quick, run to the cupboard.' She thrust Pat at Gwyneth. We hurried down the stairs and the light went off. Feeling our way, we found the little cubbyhole shelter and crawled in to wait for the All Clear.

'That bomb. How *near* was it, Bron?' Gwyneth didn't sound like she usually did.

'Near enough,' said Auntie.

'But why? Why *us*?' Gwyneth had tears in her voice. Auntie didn't say anything.

'Bron? Bron? You all OK?' Emlyn or Tommy – I couldn't tell which – was calling.

Auntie opened our little door. Pale light filled the passage. 'Oh, it's you, Emlyn. Yes, it's by here we are.'

He came and crouched to look in. 'You got no windows without cracks at the back, Bron. It's nearly daylight.'

Auntie moved out into the passage. 'The All Clear?' she asked.

Emlyn was walking back into the kitchen. 'Oh, I think they forgot to set it off, there's busy they are down by the church.'

Gwyneth sniffed into hands closed over her face. Auntie was out in the kitchen with Emlyn. I heard her fill the kettle. 'Dew, scared the wits out of most of us, I'd say, Bron. Makes you wonder what it's like in a place like London, where they cop it night after perishing night. And we only got one, mind.'

'EMLYN!' Auntie sounded angry. Gwyneth dropped her hands and stared at me. Her mouth gave a faint smile, but not her eyes. She crawled out of the cupboard backwards, never once looking away from Pat and me. We heard her go upstairs as Auntie called us to come. And we sat on the sofa to sip hot tea and look at the long cracks in the glass panes. Something inside me shivered. Broken glass, broken glass, run, run, run . . . the tea spilled from my cup, staining and burning through my nightie; I watched it, hardly feeling anything, knowing that something was wrong with its colour; the cup shattered on the floor, my fingers were on the door-latch – something spun me round, there was a sound like a sharp slap . . . and another . . . and another . . .

A voice. 'What *in God's name* . . .?' Nunky! I stared at him, feeling as if I'd just awakened from an awful nightmare. 'They must go to bed, Bron. You too. It's shock, see. Shock.'

Auntie nodded slowly. 'She broke a cup. See by there . . .'

'She . . . broke a . . . *cup*?' Nunky's arm was holding me around the shoulders; he was looking down at me as though he couldn't believe something, but it couldn't have been the cup because he'd seen that happen. My face was stinging hot. Pat stared out of tear-stained cheeks; if I turned I'd be able to see Auntie. 'I'm taking them to bed, Bron.' Nunky moved me closer to him and reached out a hand to Pat; Auntie was blotted out of sight. And in the safe quiet of the bedroom tears spilled out of me because there was nothing to hold them in any more.

'Don't cry, bach . . .' Nunky was tucking us in the bed he'd made.

'I'm not crying. Not really. I don't need tears any more.'

He didn't hear me. And I didn't hear myself. But I remember him still being there when the useless tears were all used up and my eyes felt heavy with sleep.

Chapter 42 ~~~

Sewing, I thought lazily, was one of the most silent things a person could do. Slowly my needle tacked binding on to the bright flowered yellow winceyette petticoat. I sighed, partly with relief that the binding was doing what it should around the armhole, and mostly because it was a lovely hot August Saturday and here we were, Pat and I, wasting it. Being made to waste it, sewing winter petticoats on Auntie's front doorstep. No slag heaps this Saturday. Pity, I thought. Odd, too, that I hadn't known how much I'd actually enjoyed going to the tip with my bucket. I glanced at Pat's rather wide French seam: blue this time, not sunshiny yellow. My thoughts idled with my hands – I glanced up at the cloudless sky, saw too the parched-looking mountains dotted with hot, tired, ever-hungry sheep. Now my eyes rested on the slate roofs and lazily smoking chimneys. How quiet everything was! Not a soul to be seen, or even heard. But wait. Yes, there was someone coming up the hill. A lady in a bright-green costume. She was too far away to be properly seen, but she was certainly not of the village: that colour alone told me she must be a stranger.

'You finished?' I glanced at Pat's dirty finger-streaked forehead.

'Nearly.'

My fingers touched the sun-warmed material that lay across my knees; Pat reached out to pick up her fallen reel of cotton . . . 'Ooh, 'Ild! Look, it's a lady an' she's wavin'!' The bright-green arm *was* waving, high in the air. She was much nearer now. We could see round brown glasses and yellow frizzy hair. Who could she be waving at? My gaze left her to examine farther up the road. There was no one waving back – in fact the street was quite deserted. Turning back again, I felt a tremble running all over me. She was someone I knew! But who?

The arm waved harder than ever. 'Coo'ee . . . ! Coo'ee . . .!' The call raced towards us; it sounded strange yet familiar . . . the shape of the lady, too . . . wonderingly I stood up, feeling Pat close beside me.

Words formed inside my head. *Is* it . . . ? Can it *really* be . . . ? I stared harder. A pink chiffon scarf floated in a soft floppy bow under a face that was smiling showing slightly crooked teeth between the bright-red lips.

She called again: "Ilda! Pat!' Then she began to hold open her arms and hurry towards us.

'Mum? Oh, *Mum*!' I cried to the voice, and then we were pressing against the green costume, crying and laughing at the familiar smell and feel of Mum.

'Pleased ter see me, are yer?'

'Come ter take yer 'ome, I 'ave.' The words danced magically around Auntie's kitchen, where Mum had sat herself on the sofa.

'Home!' Both of us seemed to breathe the sacred word rather than say it aloud.

Mum chuckled. "Ome! 'S'wot I said an' it's wot I mean. Now come on, don't be all soppy, get yer clo'es packed; we ain't got all day, yer know.'

Pat and I stopped the growing excited giggly sounds. 'But Mum, what about Roberta – she isn't here and we don't know where she is!'

Mum looked a bit surprised. 'She's been at 'ome for over a year now, works as a waitress she does, thought I told yer in a letter . . .' Her voice trailed off as I shook my head.

'Auntie ain't 'ere, Mum, she's doin' 'er shoppin' an' she won't be back.' Pat sounded worried.

Mum opened her handbag. 'So?' Her hands were opening a posh-looking powder compact; I swallowed hard, wondering what to say.

Pat spoke the next tumbling sentences. '*She* told us not ter move orf the *step*, see, 'cause some kids runned away, an' when she found out we wasn't trusted no more, was we, 'Ild?'

Mum shrugged. 'All kids runs away, done it meself once.' A cloud of scented face-powder flew out of the puff as she slapped it against her face. The compact closed with a snap. Mum stared at us through powder-smeared glasses. 'Jes' go an' get yer things, we're goin' afore she gets back, see. On the four o'clock bus,' she urged, glancing at the mantelpiece clock.

Pat and I ran tiptoe-quiet to the back bedroom where our cases were stacked in a corner. 'Ooh, in't it luvverly! We're *goin'*, 'Ild! Really and truly goin' '*ome*!'

My heart raced with excitement. 'Quick, you take the clothes out of the drawers and I'll pack them.' Hastily we emptied the chest, then took our nighties from under the pillows.

The cases were full. 'Ain't no room for the dolls, 'Ild.' Pat was holding them close to her chest.

'We'll carry them. You got the gas masks yet?'

'Oops, no. I'll gettem now' – Pat nipped back to the end room. I picked up the cases and took them downstairs.

'Our shoes! There isn't room,' I told Mum, who was combing her hair.

'Find a carrier bag or somethink, then,' she said as I went into the larder to do just that. 'There, yer got one. 'Ere . . . *I* 'ad a letter sayin' as you passed fer a Grammar School.'

I nodded. 'Yes, Auntie had one last week. She says I'm not going, though.' My hands were busy with pairs of shoes.

Mum pulled hairs from her comb. A smell of burning filled the room as they sizzled on Auntie's shiny hob. ''S'right. Diff'rent if you was a boy, mind, boys needs it. Still, it shows yer got brains, don't it? I wrote to yer aunties, y'know – Rose an' Lou. Proper shot up the arse fer them, eh? None of *theirs* passed nuthink like that, not even Boysie. 'E's bin killed, yer know – 'bout six weeks ago – shot down in one of them aeroplanes.'

My bag was filled. I stood up. 'You mean Cousin Bill?' I asked, remembering faintly a nice young man who'd pushed our swings in some park or other.

'Yeah, that's the one.'

A sort of panic rushed into me. 'Dad? Is Dad all right?'

Mum shrugged. The handbag was opened again. 'Oh, *'im*. 'E's orlright; on the *Blanche*, 'e was, she copped a torpedo. Yer dad was one of the last ones orf. Almost an' 'ero. 'Cept that – well, 'e was in this 'orspital fer months after.' She seemed about to say more, but quite suddenly she shut up and her face was all stiff as if she didn't like something or somebody. A packet of Woodbines busied her fingers.

'Ooh Mum, Auntie don't allow smokin'' – Pat's eyes were round with awe as Mum struck a match. Smoke from the cigarette came out of her nose; we watched fearfully as it curled upwards and spread itself around the room.

'We're ready, Mum,' I said breathlessly.

'Wot about them fag packets yer wrote t'me on, then?' she asked with a chuckle.

'Oh, they was Uncle Dan's. 'E's gorn to 'eaven, see. But 'e 'ad ter stand outside ter smoke, din't 'e, 'Ild?'

I nodded. 'Mum . . . You really did get those fag packets, then?' My voice held a sort of amazed wonder.

Mum laughed. ''Course I did! Took 'em to work an' showed me mates, we 'ad a good laugh an' all – Christ, the things kids gets up to, says Peg, but your 'Ilda takes the bloomin' biscuit, mate, she takes the biscuit . . .'

Mum was still chuckling. Fag-ash dropped noiselessly on to the floor. I tried to smile; it was hard at first but now Mum was standing up. 'Time we was goin'. 'Ere, yer can't take them dolls, we got enough ter lug around' – the fag-end arched towards the hearth and lay there smoking on the brass fender.

The smile was easier now. I grasped the dolls and did the tiptoe run up to the back bedroom. A moment of sadness touched me as the dolls sat once again side by side on the chest of drawers. But they belonged there – at least, that's where they mostly stayed. I closed the door quietly.

''Urry up, 'Ilda.' Mum was putting Pat's coat on for her down in the passage. Our cases stood at the bottom of the stairs. 'Put this on.' Mum offered my coat, and our best Sunday hats were planted firmly on our heads.

'All ready. 'Ere's yer gas masks' – we hung them obediently round our necks. ''Ilda, you got that there case and the bag to carry.' Mum started towards the front door. 'Come on, Pat.'

Pat, holding Mum's hand, was saying, 'An' are we gonna be in a train *all* night, Mum? Yer really means it?'

The door was open. Mum was taking Pat and her case over the step. My eyes touched the gleaming polished lino. Quickly I darted into the kitchen and hastily swept up the little pile of ash, picked up the cigarette end and poked it well into the fire. Now a quick little rub on the fender. A fender that blurred a little because silly little tears smarted in my eyes. Eyes that took a last photograph of today that had already become a yesterday.

Also of interest

29 INMAN ROAD
Ena Chamberlain

'One needs writers like Ena Chamberlain to reveal how Time smudges and defaces so many of the once-important things, and to show us how powerful they were' – *Ronald Blythe*

This lyrical, poignant autobiography, in the classic tradition of *Cider with Rosie* and *Lark Rise to Candleford*, belongs to the 1920s, to a street in south-west London, to its people – and especially to Ena Chamberlain, the family 'afterthought'. Energetically and vividly she observes and interprets the complex nuances of family relationships and describes the carnival delights of the street – frequently retreating from them to the wonderfully sacrosanct world of her own imagination. *29 Inman Road* is, above all, a celebration of the women who dominate street society; shape it or perish by it. But it is Ena's adored father who is the catalyst for the end of the story – and the end of childhood.

GROWING UP IN LAMBETH
Mary Chamberlain

'This is oral history and social documentary at its best' – *Ann Oakley*

'A portrait of Lambeth written from the heart, a chronicle of generational change' – *Raphael Samuel*

Growing up in Lambeth is about family, neighbourhood and class. Mary Chamberlain's interest stems in part from her family's own roots in this area of South London. She returns to Lambeth, the territory also chosen by Maud Pember Reeves for her classic study of working-class women, *Round About a Pound a Week*, and looks at how women in this area have lived between 1913 and the present. Using a wealth of oral material, the book tells of childhood and adolescence, marriage and motherhood, keeping house, and of the infinitely ingenious ways working-class people have of circumventing and surviving poverty. It also chronicles the changes, looking at new immigrants in the area, and the ways in which traditional means of survival – neighbourliness, street life, extended family ties, the pawnshop – have been eroded at a time of fierce economic hardship. This is a book about opportunities found and made, however great the material deprivation. And above all it is a book about survival.

THE 4-VOLUME AUTOBIOGRAPHY OF KATHLEEN DAYUS

'We must be thankful that Kathleen Dayus has survived to tell her story so movingly and so well' – *Jeremy Seabrook, New Society*

'An evocation of a vanished world as vivid, moving and spiced with humour as any I have read' – *Hazel Leslie, Sunday Telegraph*

'It is a privilege to share her life' – *Good Housekeeping*

Kathleen Dayus has become a legend in her own lifetime. Born into the industrial slums of Birmingham in 1903, she left school at fourteen and started writing at the age of seventy. The indomitable spirit, humour and sheer verve that characterise her life shine out from these marvellous memoirs. Nobody has captured 'her people' with more vitality, wisdom and wit. This extraordinary autobiography, written in the splendid tradition of Helen Forrester's *Tuppence to Cross the Mersey*, is as evocative as any written this century.

HER PEOPLE
Winner of the J.R. Ackerley Prize for Autobiography, 1983

WHERE THERE'S LIFE

ALL MY DAYS

THE BEST OF TIMES